Benjamin Homer Hall, Andrew Dickson White, William A. Carr

A Tribute of Respect by the Citizens of Troy to the Memory of Abraham Lincoln

Benjamin Homer Hall, Andrew Dickson White, William A. Carr

A Tribute of Respect by the Citizens of Troy to the Memory of Abraham Lincoln

ISBN/EAN: 9783337306953

Printed in Europe, USA, Canada, Australia, Japan

Cover: Foto ©ninafisch / pixelio.de

More available books at **www.hansebooks.com**

A

𝔗ribute of 𝔑espect

BY

THE CITIZENS OF TROY,

TO THE

𝔐emory

OF

ABRAHAM LINCOLN.

Compiled by Benj. Homer Hall, 1830-1893

ALBANY, N. Y.:
J. MUNSELL, 78 STATE STREET.
1865.

CONTENTS.

	PAGE.
Introduction,	vii
Friday, April 14th, the day of the assassination,	1
Saturday, April 15th,	1
Assassination of President Lincoln, by George Evans,	2
Proceedings in the Rensselaer County Court,	4
Proceedings in the Police Court,	5
Orders of the National Guard,	6
Scenes in the City,	7
Service at St. John's Church,	9
Address, by Martin I. Townsend,	15
Other Services,	19
The Assassination of the President, by John M. Francis,	20
Our Duty on this day, by B. H. Hall,	22
The National Calamity and Humiliation, by F. B. Hubbell,	24
Abraham Lincoln, by James S. Thorn,	27
Proclamation by the Governor,	28
Recommendation of Bishop Potter,	29
Citizens' Meeting,	30
Sunday, April 16th,	31
"Hung be the Heavens with black," by C. L. MacArthur,	31
Extract from a Sermon, by Rev. Henry C. Potter, D.D.,	32
Sketch of a Sermon, by Rev. S. D. Brown,	36
Sermon, by Rev. Jacob Thomas,	43
Sermon, by Rev. D. S. Gregory,	47
Sermon, by Rev. Edgar Buckingham,	66
Other Services,	78
Monday, April 17th,	87
Announcement by the President,	87
The Assassination of President Lincoln, by A. G. Johnson,	88

The National Bereavement, by W. E. Kisselburgh,........ 90
The Death of President Lincoln, by Mrs. E. Van Sant-
  voord,.. 92
Common Council Proceedings,................................... 93
Address, by Maj. Gen. John E. Wool,........................ 96
Request of the Committe of the Common Council,........ 97
Resolutions of respect, by Jewish Citizens,.................. 98
Tuesday, April 18th,.. 99
Announcement by the Mayor,..................................... 99
Orders to the Tenth Brigade and the Twenty-fourth
  Regiment,.. 100
Proceedings at the Rensselaer Polytechnic Institute,..... 101
Wednesday, April 19th,.. 104
Discourse, by Rev. C. P. Sheldon, D.D.,..................... 104
Sermon, by Rev. J. Wesley Carhart, D.D.,.................. 116
Address, by Rev. D. S. Gregory,............................... 127
Address, by Rev. Duncan Kennedy, D.D.,................... 136
Sermon, by Rev. Joseph A. Prime,............................ 151
Service at the Jewish Synagogue,.............................. 157
Other Services,.. 160
Thursday, April 20th,... 165
Friday, April 21st,... 166
Resolutions of the Board of Supervisors of Rensselaer
  County,... 166
Saturday, April 22d,.. 168
"Sic Semper Tyrannis," by E. H. G. Clark,................. 168
Abraham Lincoln, by Julia A. Burdick,....................... 169
A Dirge, by A. S. Pease,.. 175
Invitation from the Common Council of Albany,........... 177
Order of the National Guard,..................................... 177
Sunday, April 23d,.. 178
In Memoriam A. L., by B. H. Hall,............................. 178
Sermon, by Rev. Marvin R. Vincent,.......................... 181
Substance of a sermon, by Rev. Erastus Wentworth, D.D., 228
Substance of a sermon, by Rev. Edgar Buckingham,...... 229
Meeting of the Concordia Society,............................. 237
Monday, April 24th,.. 238

CONTENTS.

Proclamation by the President,	238
Common Council Proceedings,	240
The Guard of Honor,	241
Tuesday, April 25th,	242
Announcement by the Mayor,	242
Invitation by the Twenty-fourth regiment,	242
Proceedings of the Executive committee of the Troy Young Men's Association,	243
Meeting of Veteran Officers,	244
Officers' Meeting,	245
Wednesday, April 26th,	245
An Account of the Participation of citizens of Troy in the obsequies at Albany,	245
Thursday, April 27th	254
Resolutions of the Troy Young Men's Association,	254
Friday, April 28th,	255
Decline of Amusements, by F. B. Hubbell,	255
Saturday, April 29th,	256
Proclamation by the President,	256
The month of May,	257
"To everything there is a season," by James S. Thorn,	257
A dirge, by Josiah L. Young,	258
Lincoln and Cicero, by B. H. Hall,	260
Letter, and Order of Services, by Bishop Potter,	265
Proclamation by the Mayor,	267
Thursday, June 1st,	268
Discourse, by Rev. Thomas W. Coit, D. D.,	268
Address, by Charlton T. Lewis,	279
Discourse, by Rev. David T. Elliott,	297
Sermon by Rev. Hugh P. McAdam,	318
Other services,	329
Common Council Proceedings,	333

ERRATA.

Page 33, line 14 for *not* read *no*.
" 56, " 22 for *Gods* read *God's*,
" 91, " 3 for *loose* read *loss*.
" 100, " 1 for *Forty* read *Twenty*.
" 153, " 20 for *public* read *republic*.
" 164, " 17 for *volumnious* read *voluminous*.
" 216, " 1 for *of* read *to*.
" 265, " 16 for *Agreeably* read *Agreeable*.

INTRODUCTION.

The tokens of grief and indignation so generally shown, when it was made certain that Abraham Lincoln was dead, gave at once the clearest proof, not only of the deep detestation with which his foul assassination was regarded, but also of the warm esteem in which he, who for four years had guided the affairs of the nation, was held as a ruler and as a man. In many countries an event of this nature, happening at such a juncture of affairs, would have been followed by an uprising of the people, resulting in scenes of indiscriminate and passionate vengeance. Here, however, a different result was witnessed. In a few instances, men of virulent nature and seemingly lost to human sensibility, who had expressed a modified approval of the dreadful deed, received unmistakable warning of the danger of indulging a sentiment so brutal. But the indignation of loyal men found vent, for the most part, in efforts to arrest the murderer and his abettors, whoever they might be, and in demands for their condign punishment.

The spontaneousness and depth of the sorrow evinced on this occasion, bring to remembrance the account given of the occurrences consequent upon the death of Sir Philip Sidney in the year 1586. The grief of the people of England at his loss, say his biographers, was wide-spread and sincere. His body was brought to London and there interred, although the subjects of his late government in the Netherlands begged that it might be suffered to remain among them, and offered, should their request be granted, "to erect for him as fair a monument as any prince had in Christendom, yea, though the same should cost half a ton of gold the building." His funeral was performed with great circumstance and pomp, "the seven United Provinces sending each a representative to testify respect for his memory by their vicarious presence at his obsequies." The universities of Cambridge and Oxford, also, "poured forth three volumes of learned lamentation, on account of the loss of him whom they considered as being their brightest ornament; and indeed so far was the public regret, on this occasion, carried, that, for the first time in the case of a private individual, the whole kingdom went into mourning, and no gentleman of quality, during several months, ventured to appear in a light colored or gaudy dress, either in the resorts of business or of fashion."

Of a similar nature, but wider in extent and more varied in expression, was the mourning for Abraham Lincoln. In truth, history does not present another instance, in which the grief of the civilized world has been unitedly expressed with such real earnestness, at the loss of any man, be he public ruler or private citizen. Throughout the north the manifestations of sorrow were well nigh universal. The funereal tolling of bells; the booming of minute guns; the sable draperies that shrouded the fronts of buildings both public and private, and garbed the interiors of places of public worship and the chambers of legislation and the halls of various organizations; the flags at half mast or furled and festooned with crape; the emblematic decorations expressive of grief; the noble sentences that fell from the lips of the departed, set forth in grand lettering on the extended canvas; the craped arm of private citizen as well as of soldier and government official; the black rose of sorrow or the features of the dead in miniature, worn like a decoration of honor on the garment; the mourning border which edged the sheet of paper on which man wrote to his fellow; the black lines dividing the columns of the daily and weekly journals; the multitudinous representations of those honest features in every home and office and counting-room and shop window; the varied delineations that filled the pictorial papers to repletion; the solemn dirges sung; the prayers uttered, instinct with the earnest inspiration of the soul; the churches thronged with mourning worshippers; the impassioned utterances of those who minister at God's altars; the eyes of the strong man filled with unaccustomed tears; the weeping of women, the clouded faces of little ones, whose being seemed, for a time, overshadowed by a mysterious and sympathetic awe;— these manifestations rendered those dark April days, in this year of victory and sadness, memorable and historic beyond all precedent.

Then came the grand and solemn obsequies. The funeral at Washington inaugurated the imposing ceremonies, and for two weeks, the procession, starting from that city, passed through the land to the wailings of a bereaved and stricken nation. At Baltimore, Harrisburg, Philadelphia, New York, Albany, Buffalo, Cleveland, Columbus, Indianapolis and Chicago the funeral scene was repeated, and thus the honored and beloved dead was borne to his western resting place. Springfield — once the home, now the grave of Abraham Lincoln — where the obsequies begun at Washington were ended, is henceforth sacred among the shrines of the earth, sacred to every lover of labor, common sense, humanity, patriotism and God.

In the pages that follow, an attempt has been made to preserve a record of the manner and the words in which the respect of the citizens of Troy was expressed for the memory of the late President, during the period intermediate the day of the assassination and the day designated as one of humiliation and mourning for the nation. In other cities throughout the land, similar observances obtained, and in many places the manifestations of sorrow were accompanied by displays of solemn grandeur. Not the least remarkable feature of this period, was the unanimity with which the journals of the United States joined in the general tribute of sorrow and respect which was rendered to the memory of the great patriot. The press of the other continent sympathized with these sentiments, and its eulogy and admiration were declared in language as sincere and impassioned as any that was uttered in this land. The intelligence of the death of Mr. Lincoln reached England on the twenty-sixth of April. On the day following, appeared in the editorial columns of the *London Star*, a leading article on his assassination, which is here inserted for the purpose of showing not only the immediate effect produced by the event in England, but also to enable the reader, by comparing this extract with the leaders of our own journals on the same subject, to observe that in the old world and in the new, those who best understood his character were most eulogistic of him as a man, and deplored his death as a loss not only to his country but to the world.

"The appalling tragedy which has just been perpetrated at Washington is absolutely without historical precedent. Not in the records of the fiercest European convulsion, in the darkest hour of partisan hatreds, have we an example of an assassin plot at once so foul and so senseless, so horrible and so successful, as that to which ABRAHAM LINCOLN has already fallen a victim, and from which William H.

Seward can hardly escape. Only in such instances as the murder of William of Orange, of Henri Quatre, or of Capo d'Istria, have we any deed approaching in hideous ferocity to that which has just robbed the United States of one of the greatest of their Presidents. But from the fanatic's hateful point of view there was at least something to be said for men like Balthazar Gerard and Ravaillac. They, at least, might have believed that they saw embodied in their victims the whole living principle and motive power of that religious freedom which they detested. They might have supposed that with the man would die the great hopes and the great cause he inspired and guided. So, too, of Orsini. That unfortunate and guilty being believed, at least, that in Napoleon the Third there stood an embodied and concentrated system. But ABRAHAM LINCOLN was no dictator and no autocrat. He represented simply the resolution and the resources of a great people. The miserable excuse which fanaticism might attempt to plead for other political assassins has no application to the wretch whose felon hand dealt death to the pure and noble magistrate of a free nation. One would gladly, for the poor sake of common humanity, have caught at the idea that the crime was but the work of some maniacal partisan. But the mere nature of the deeds, without any additional evidence whatever, bids defiance to such an idea. While the one murderer was slaying the President of the Republic the other was making his even more dastardly attempt upon the life of the sick and prostrate Secretary. It does not need even the disclosures which have now, too late for any good purpose, reached official quarters to prove that two madmen cannot become simultaneously inspired with the same monstrous project and impelled at the one moment to do their several parts of the one bloody business. The chivalry of the south has had much European compliment of late. It has been discovered to be the fount and origin of all the most noble and knightly qualities which the world heretofore had principally known through the medium of mediæval romance. Let it not be forgotten that southern brains lately planned the conflagration of a peaceful city. It never can be forgotten while history is read that the hands of southern partisans have been reddened by the foulest assassin plot the world has ever known, that they have been treacherously dipped in the blood of one of the best citizens and purest patriots to whom the land of Washington gave birth.

For ABRAHAM LINCOLN one cry of universal regret will be raised all over the civilized earth. We do not believe that even the fiercest partisans of the confederacy in this country will entertain any sentiment at such a time but one of grief and horror. To us ABRAHAM LINCOLN has always seemed the finest character produced by the American war on either side of the struggle. He was great not merely by the force of genius—and only the word genius will describe the power of intellect by which he guided himself and his country through such a crisis—but by the simple, natural strength and grandeur of his character. Talleyrand once said of a great American statesman that without experience he 'divined' his way through any crisis. Mr. LINCOLN thus divined his way through the perilous, exhausting, and unprecedented difficulties which might well have broken the strength and blinded the prescience of the best-trained professional statesman. He seemed to arrive by instinct—by the instinct of a noble, unselfish, and manly nature—at the very ends which the highest of political genius, the longest of political experience, could have done no more than reach. He bore himself fearlessly in danger, calmly in difficulty, modestly in success. The world was at last beginning to know how good, and, in the best sense, how great a man he was. It had long indeed learned that he was as devoid of vanity as of fear, but it had only just come to know what magnanimity and mercy the hour of triumph would prove that he possessed. Reluctant enemies were just beginning to break into eulogy over his wise and noble clemency when the dastard hand of a vile murderer destroyed his noble and valuable life. We in England have something to feel ashamed of when we meditate upon the true greatness of the man so ruthlessly slain. Too many Englishmen lent themselves to the vulgar and ignoble cry which was raised against him. English writers degraded themselves to the level of the coarsest caricaturists when they had to tell of ABRAHAM LINCOLN. They stooped to criticise a foreign patriot as a menial might comment on the bearing of a hero. They sneered at his manners, as if Cromwell was a Chesterfield; they accused him of ugliness, as if Mirabeau was a beauty; they made coarse pleasantry of his figure, as if Peel was a posture-master; they were facetious about his dress, as if Cavour was a D'Orsay; they were indignant about his jokes, as if Palmerston never jested. We do not remember any instance since the wildest days of British fury against the 'Corsican Ogre,' in which a foreign statesman was ever so dealt with in English writings as Mr. LINCOLN. And when we make the comparison we cannot but remember that while Napoleon was our unscrupulous enemy Lincoln was our steady friend. Assailed by the coarsest attacks on this side the ocean, tried by the sorest temptations on that, ABRAHAM LINCOLN calmly and steadfastly maintained a policy of peace with England, and never did a deed, never wrote or spoke a word which was unjust or unfriendly to the British nation. Had such a man died by the hand of disease in the hour of his triumph the world must have mourned for his loss. That he has fallen by the coward hand of a vile assassin exasperates and embitters the grief beyond any power of language to express.

Had Lincoln been a vain man he might almost have ambitioned such a death. The weapon of the murderer has made sure for him an immortal place in history. Disappointment, failure, political change, popular caprice, the efforts of rivals, the malice of enemies, can touch him no more. He lived long enough to accomplish his great patriotic work, and then he became its martyr. It would be idle to speculate as yet upon the effect which his cruel death will produce upon the political fortunes of his country; but the destinies of that country will be cared for. Its hopes are too well sustained to faint and fall even over the grave of so great a patriot and so wise a leader as Abraham Lincoln. There are still clear and vigorous intellects left to conduct what remains of Lincoln's work to a triumphant conclusion. Dramatic justice has, indeed been marvellously wreaked thus far upon the criminal pride of the south. A negro regiment was the first to enter Richmond, and now one of the poor whites, the 'white trash' of a southern state, is called to receive from the south its final submission. We trust and feel assured that even in this hour of just indignation and natural excitement the north may still bear itself with that magnanimous clemency which thus far has illumined its triumph. But it may be that the conquered south has yet to learn that it too must mourn over the bloody grave to which Abraham Lincoln has been consigned by a southern assassin's hand."

On other pages of the same paper, was published the story of the life of Abraham Lincoln, from which, for the purpose of illustrating the fervor with which the cause of the United States was upheld by millions of Englishmen, and the exultation with which they viewed the onward march of freedom and humanity, the following extracts are taken.

"In the moment of victory, Abraham Lincoln has been stricken to death. Not on the battle field, where so many noble patriots have laid down their lives for freedom, not by the unseen shaft of disease before which the greatest and noblest must sooner or later fall — but brutally murdered by an assassin of the slave power while he sat beside his wife enjoying a much needed relaxation from the heavy cares of state. Noble, generous, forgiving, his only thoughts since the capture of Richmond have been of mercy. At a meeting of the cabinet on the morning of his death he spoke very kindly of Lee, and others of the confederates, and while his thoughts were thus all of forgiveness, the miscreant stole behind him and shot him through the brain. Unconscious from the moment he received the fatal wound, the great and noble-hearted patriot breathed his last on the following morning. Nothing else was needed to sanctify the name and memory of Abraham Lincoln to the people of the United States, and to all lovers of freedom throughout the world, than this his martyr-death. Raised from the ranks of the common people to take upon himself the responsibility of the most gigantic struggle the world has ever witnessed between the forces of freedom and slavery, he guided the destinies of his country with unwavering hand through all the terrors and dangers of the conflict, and placed her so high and safe among the nations of the world that the dastards of despotism dare no longer question the strength and majesty of freedom. With a firm faith in his God, his country, and his principles of freedom for all men, whatever their color and condition, he has stood unmoved amid the shock of armies and the clamors of faction; he quailed not when defeat in the field seemed to herald the triumph of the foe; he boasted not of victory, nor sought to arrogate to himself the honors of the great deeds which have resounded through the world; but, gentle and modest as he was great and good, he took the chaplet from his own brow to place it on the lowly graves of the soldiers whose blood has been so liberally poured forth to consecrate the soil of America for freedom. He dies and makes no sign, but the impress of his noble character and aims will be borne by his country while time endures. He dies, but his country lives; freedom has triumphed; the broken chains at the feet of the slaves are the mute witnesses of his victory. It was on the evening of the fourteenth of April, the day which saw the federal flag raised once more on Fort Sumter amid the hoarse reverberation of cannon and the cheers of liberated slaves, that the President received his death blow. The wretched conspirators who sought to destroy their country that slavery might triumph over its ruins panted for Lincoln's life since the day he was first elected to guide the destinies of the republic. When in the act of passing from his home in Illinois to assume the reins of office he was apprised by General Scott that the barbarians of slavery had resolved to assassinate him. The plan was to raise a riot in Baltimore as he passed through that city on his way to Washington, and in the midst of the tumult Mr. Lincoln was to be slain. The messenger who brought the news of the conspiracy to Mr. Lincoln at Harrisburg was Frederick W. Seward, son of the statesman who now lies low beside his chief, stricken down by another desperate miscreant on the same day as the President. Mr. Lincoln, with his usual prudence, at once stopped in his triumphal progress towards the capital, and, disguised as a countryman, passed safely through Baltimore by the night train, and arrived at the White House in Washington. The speech which he made to his neighbors of Springfield when he set out on his perilous mission has a mournful interest in view of his sudden and awful death. At the railway depot on Monday, the eleventh of February, 1860, a large concourse of his fellow citizens had assembled to bid him farewell. 'My friends,' he said, 'no one not in my position can appreciate the sadness I feel at this parting. To this people I owe all that I am. Here I have lived more than a quarter of a century; here my children were born, and here one of them lies buried. I know not how soon I shall see you again. A duty devolves upon me which is, perhaps, greater than that which has devolved upon any other man since the days of Washington. He never would have succeeded except for the aid of Divine Providence, upon which he at all times relied. I feel that I cannot succeed without the same Divine aid which sustained him, and on the same Almighty Being I place my reliance for support, and I hope you, my friends, will all pray that I may receive that Divine assistance without which I cannot succeed, but with which success is certain. Again, I bid you all an affectionate farewell.'

The touching address was given with deep emotion, and many of the auditors replied to his request for their prayers by exclaiming, 'We will pray for you.' Thus this devout, simple-hearted, and courageous man went forth to his high task, not leaning on his own strength, but humbly trusting in the power of an Almighty arm. Those gentle utterances are but the key to all the speeches and proclamations which he has made during his troubled career. No one ever heard him utter a bitter word against the rebels, but many have confessed that they felt rebuked in his presence, his manner was so calm, his thoughts and words were so magnanimous, his great heart was so full of gentleness and compassion. And yet it is this

man who has been held up to the southern people by
the lying politicians and most mischievous journalists
of the south as a kind of human demon who delighted
in blood, as a man regardless of law and justice, who
when he spoke of God or humanity spake but in
mockery of the sacred name and the sacred rights of
the people. The southern heart has been fired, as
the phrase went, by the most furious appeals to the
passions of an ignorant people against a ruler who
never would have touched a single southern right or
harmed a real southern man had these truculent
politicians not crowned their frenzy by rebellion.
Even in the midst of the late most sanguinary outburst of ferocity he has mitigated the woes of war,
and so tempered justice by mercy that not a single
traitor has perished on the scaffold. We would that
we could add that the passions of the southern demagogues were sought to be assauged by the universal
efforts of the press and the politicians of those countries where the American struggle excited an overwhelming interest. But history will proclaim to the
eternal humiliation of our country how an influential
section of the English press outbade the journalists of
the south in their slander and invective against the
great man who has been so cruelly slain — how his
every action was twisted and tortured into a wrong,
his every noble aspiration spoken of as a desire for
blood, his personal appearance caricatured, his lowly
origin made the theme for scorn, by men as base-born

as he but without the nobleness of soul which made Lincoln a prince among princes—how even that proclamation which conferred liberty upon four millions of down-trodden slaves was reviled as a base effort to incite the negroes to servile war. The men who penned those revolting slanders were probably alike ignorant and reckless of their effect, but it cannot but be a painful reflection to Englishmen that the deluded southern rebels were encouraged in their efforts to destroy a free nation for the purpose of building a slave empire on the ruins by the writings and speeches of men who could boast of free England as their country. Their virulent abuse in all probability never reached him whom it was designed to wound, and even if the miserable writers had been factious Americans instead of degenerate Englishmen, Lincoln would have had nothing but a smile for their malignant efforts. Nor had these unworthy effusions any effect upon the great body of the people of England. They saw at once the sterling integrity and appreciated the high purpose of the American ruler; they took the universal testimony of the people of the country over which he ruled in preference to the partisan abuse of the pro-slavery organs, so that long before the emancipation proclamation was issued the efforts and intentions of Abraham Lincoln were thoroughly understood by the Commons of Great Britain. When, however, the moment had arrived for Lincoln calling a race to freedom, and the news was received in this country that, so far as the fiat of the President of the United States in the execution of his constitutional authority during a state of war could strike the fetters from the slave and purge the commonwealth from its foul stain, the order had gone forth and the slaves had a legal title to their freedom, nothing could thereafter shake the faith of the people in the liberator. Many touching proofs of the sincerity of these convictions were afforded during the struggle. In every public meeting of our countrymen when the name of President Lincoln was mentioned it was received with a burst of ringing cheers. Perhaps the most notable occasion was when Henry Ward Beecher addressed the inhabitants of London in Exeter Hall. It was at a time when the pro-slavery press was most rampant, when for days they had been heaping upon the head of Mr. Ward Beecher, one of the pioneer abolitionists of the north, and upon Mr. Lincoln, as the leader of the abolitionist party, all the vials of their abuse, and when, if ever, it might have been supposed that the cause of right must be overborne by the power of slander and misrepresentation. No sooner, however, was the name of Lincoln mentioned by Mr. Beecher in the course of his speech than enthusiastic cheers, which seemed as if they would never stop, burst forth from the vast assemblage. It was the same everywhere throughout the country, and the American people now amongst us, stunned and overwhelmed as they are by the news, may believe that their feeling of an irreparable loss is shared in by the vast masses of the English people. For, in truth, a man like Abraham Lincoln is claimed by humanity as her own. He was in name and in heart an American citizen, and his great work had been appointed for him in that new continent where two great battles have already been won for human freedom; but he soon showed by his actions and the magnanimity of his character that he belonged to that illustrious band whose work is for the human race, and whose name and fame shall never die out amongst men. In his hands was placed a most sacred trust. In the United States the right of the majority to govern, and perfect freedom to all to take part in the business of government, were the basis of the constitution. It had never been questioned until the southern leaders, defeated at the ballot-box, sought to achieve by the sword what they failed to achieve at the polling-booth. The question was the extension or the non-extension of slavery, and the ultimate issue was the triumph or failure of free institutions. We need not recall how triumphantly the enemies of freedom pointed their finger in scorn at what they called the failure of the experiment of free institutions. The very uprising of the southern slave power was held to be the end of the republic. They never dreamed that the obscure man of the people, who had been raised to the highest post of honor which it was possible for a citizen to fill, would grasp the helm with so vigorous a grasp, and so pilot the ship of state among the fearful breakers as to bring her safe to port with colors flying and not a spar lost. Alas! that the firm hand should now be nerveless, the bold heart cold and lifeless, and that the cup of joy should be so rudely dashed from the lips of the great people whom he had so faithfully served in the crisis of their destiny!

The assassination seems unquestionably to have been the result of a conspiracy to which various southern sympathizers were parties. The villain whose hand struck down President Lincoln is stated to be a person named J. Wilkes Booth, a brother of Edwin Booth, the actor, and in his trunk was found a letter which showed that the horrid deed was to have been perpetrated on the fourth of March, when Mr. Lincoln's second term of office began. It has, therefore, been no sudden inspiration of frenzy caused by the fall of Richmond, but the deliberate calculation of cold blooded miscreants. The intention was not consummated sooner because some expected instructions, or aid, or encouragement, had not been received from Richmond. We cannot believe that the designs of the conspirators were known to and approved by the heads of the southern government, but it is not at all impossible that some leading secessionists may have aided in the conspiracy and encouraged its execution. It was known that the earlier attempt when Mr. Lincoln was about to take office was known to and approved by many persons of influence and standing, and more than one influential fanatic in the course of the war has openly offered rewards for the heads of northern abolitionists. The murder was at length effected in the most cruel and barbarous manner. Seated in the theatre at Washington, beside his wife and another lady, and attended by only one officer, a stranger suddenly made his appearance at the door of the box, and stated that he had despatches from General Grant. That general had been advertised to be present on the same evening, but he and his wife had gone to Burlington on a visit. The simple state of the republican President permitted the stranger easily to get access to his victim, who it would seem never turned his head — his thoughts probably far away on those fields of battle where so many have died that the republic might live. The assassin instantly raised his pistol and shot the President in the back of the head, the bullet lodging in the brain. We have as yet no details of the scene of consternation in the theatre, the anguish of Mrs. Lincoln, and the despair of the people when they saw one so beloved so basely smitten; but there needs no description. It is easy to imagine it all — all except the unutterable anguish of the woman who has been the support and solace of the President during many weary months of anxiety and suffering. To his wife Mr. Lincoln was tenderly attached. His first action after receiving the notice of his election by the Chicago convention of 1860 as the candidate of the republican party was to leave his political friends with whom he had been waiting for the news, and proceed home saying, 'There's a little woman down at our house would like to hear this. I will go and tell her.' The barbarians were not content with this one noble victim. About the same time another, and even more callous, southern fiend proceeded to the residence of Mr. Seward, and, under pretence of carrying medicine to the sick chamber, managed to get access to the chamber where the secretary of state lay suffering from his recent accident. Mr. Frederick W. Seward, the son of the secretary, attempted to prevent him, but was cruelly wounded. A male attendant was stabbed through the lungs, and then the miscreant sprang forward to the bed and stabbed with many wounds the statesman who lay helpless. When the cries of the nurse and of a young daughter who was by her father's bedside brought Major Seward, another son, to his father's apartment, the assassin likewise fell upon him and severely wounded him. Most foul deed that ever pen recorded or demon perpetrated! A sick man lying helpless on his couch of pain thus barbarously assailed, a son eager to save a father's life thus foully wounded! It illustrates in a yet more awful manner the innate barbarism of that system of society based on slavery which can breed criminals of so deep a dye. The official report of Mr. Stantont which will be found elsewhere, expressly states tha' these deeds of horror were the result of a conspiracy among the rebels, and the greatness of the enormities must now prove to the world that the attempt to set fire to New York, and to destroy in one horrible holocaust the women and children, the aged and infirm, of a populous city was no hallucination of the federal government, but a grim reality of desperadoes — the spawn of the slave power. These are specimens of that chivalry of the south over which some English men and women have been heretofore shedding maudlin tears. It is a chivalry which can murder a gentle and noble man in presence of his wife; which can stab a father with furious blows on his sick bed in presence of a little daughter who ministers to his wants, and which can ruthlessly sacrifice two sons as they strive to save a father's life.

* * * * * * * *

The election of Mr. Lincoln was hailed with delight by the people of the northern states, little dreaming that their right to elect him would have to be sustained in so fearful a manner, and when the time came for him to proceed to Washington to execute the functions of President the whole country watched his progress with intense satisfaction. As he passed eastwards he had to make speeches at almost every town of any note, and many of the expressions which then fell from his lips were sufficiently remarkable. When passing through Indiana he thus spoke of state rights. 'By the way, in what consists the special sacredness of a state? If a state and a county in a given case should be equal in extent of territory and equal in number of inhabitants, in what as a matter of principle, is the state better than the county? On what principle may a state, being not more than one-fiftieth part of the nation in soil and population, break up the nation, and then coerce a proportionably larger subdivision of itself in the most arbitrary manner? What mysterious right to play tyrant is conferred on a district of country with its people by merely calling it a state?' In New Jersey he made use of a characteristic expression, which has been frequently quoted since. 'I shall do all that may be in my power to promote a peaceful settlement of all our difficulties. The man does not live who is more devoted to peace than I am, none who will do more to preserve it; but it may be necessay to put the foot down firmly.' How firmly, the south, the north, we and all men now know. When raising a flag in Philadelphia, he asked whether the Union could be saved upon the Declaration of Independence, and in answering his own question uttered words which sound prophetically after the occurrence which has so troubled the country—'If this country cannot be saved without giving up that principle I was about to say I would rather be assassinated on this spot than surrender it'—and his last words on the occasion were —'I have said nothing but what I am willing to live by, and, if it be the pleasure of Almighty God, die by.' He has stood by these principles during his life, and he had completed the most triumphant defence of these principles when called on to die; but dying he bequeathes a new life to the nation, and being dead he yet speaketh.

Mr. Lincoln's policy was to woo the south to submission to the constitutionally expressed will of the people by every argument which would be supposed to have weight with American citizens. His inaugural address was a pleading with them to give up their mad design to break up the nation, and it was thus he conjured them to think well upon the fatal step they were about to take: 'I am loth to close. We are not enemies, but friends. We must not be enemies. Though passion may have strained it must not break our bonds of affection. The mystic cords of memory, stretching from every battle-field and patriot grave to every living heart and hearth stone all over this broad land, will yet swell the chorus of the Union, when again touched, as they surely will be, by the better angels of our nature.' His appeal was vain. The men to whom it was addressed for a long series of years had been educating themselves into the monstrous delusion that slavery was a Divine institution; that it was the natural basis for society; that a slave empire could be established so powerful, that abolitionism would for ever be abashed, and southern interests reign supreme. The politicians clamored for war, the editors wrote up war, the clergy preached up a war for slavery, until the poor deluded common people rushed blindly into the conflict. The north had no choice; Mr. Lincoln as the President had no choice but to enforce the laws, and to use whatever powers the constitution gave him for the suppression of the rebellion. This is not the place to recount the varied fortunes of the field. In the west the national arms were almost uniformly successful, in the east the forces of the Union failed to capture Richmond until weary years of effort had been wasted and several successive generals tried and removed. But the elasticity of free institutions permitted of these changes of commanders, and the patriotism of the people supported the President in whatever appointments he deemed best for the furtherance of the cause until by his happy selection of Grant, who had proved victorious in the west, and Grant's no less admirable appointments of Sherman, Sheridan, Thomas and others, the power of the south has been completely crushed. President Lincoln at first incurred much odium among many sincere friends of the slave in this country, and was taunted by the supporters of the slave confederacy because he did not from the outset inaugurate an anti-slavery war. But his true position began to be appreciated. Some of the border slave states remained loyal, and he could not at once attack slavery without encroaching upon the rights of these loyal people to regulate their own affairs. The northern democrats, moreover, polled more than one million of votes, while the purely abolitionist element among his own supporters was comparatively small. Had he at once raised an anti-slavery banner in all likelihood he would have retarded in place of advancing the cause. He repressed all attempts prematurely to proclaim emancipation until perfectly satisfied in his own mind that he had the constitutional power during a state of war to do so, and that the proclamation would tend to lessen the power of the rebels and more speedily bring peace to his torn and bleeding country. The policy has been the saving of the Union. The slaves crowded the federal lines in order to gain their freedom, and eagerly availed themselves of the privilege to enlist under the federal banners to aid in the freedom of their friends and brethren of the negro race. The emancipation proclamation of Abraham Lincoln was a grand and sublime act; and when, in announcing his policy to Congress, he declared that they who were at the head of affairs in those times could not escape history, he truly shadowed forth that all who had in any way contributed to that crowning act of justice would occupy in history a most conspicuous and enviable place. The cause of the Union has prospered from the day the proclamation was issued until at length the greatest army of the rebels has surrendered to the great soldier whom President Lincoln's sagacity selected as the fit man to lead the armies of the republic.

The personal appearance of Mr. Lincoln has often been described. He was six feet four in height, and of that thin, wiry build which is somewhat characteristic of Americans. But all observers unite in describing his countenance as singularly pleasing, and the eye mild and gentle. One English observer, not particularly prepossessed in his favour, describes his countenance as peculiarly soft, with an almost feminine expression of melancholy. While all observers unite in thus describing the late President, those who knew him more intimately are equally of one opinion as to his disposition being as kind, courteous, and gentle as his mild expression denoted. He was never heard to say a bitter word against the rebels, but invariably in his public proclamations and by his acts he sought to win them back to that fealty without undue shedding of blood. But with all this gentleness he was inexorably firm. Men of all parties have gone to him to attempt to move him from some of his positions; but while listening courteously to their statements he never failed to indicate that what he had himself resolved, after careful consideration, he should abide by until he saw that it was unsuited to the circumstances of his country. He had an overflowing and ready humor. This trait in his character has given many shafts to the venomous slanderers of the great man who has been so suddenly removed from his proud position; but it is scarcely necessary to say that all the *bon-mots* attributed to the President are not genuine. One slander which has been often repeated by his enemies it may be as well to contradict here once for all. It has been asserted and re-asserted, and now apparently deemed to be beyond the reach of cavil, that Mr. Lincoln, when riding over the field of Gettysburg, called for a comic song to drive away serious thoughts. The statement is a gratuitous and baseless calumny, invented by those who would as readily destroy a reputation as the southern assassins would wreak their vengeance upon a helpless victim. These have, indeed, accomplished the death of a noble-hearted patriot; but while they have killed the body, they cannot touch his deathless fame, they cannot mar his glorious work, they cannot rob him of his immortal reward."

In full accord with the sentiments of the English press as set forth in these extracts, was the expression of the feelings of Englishmen in the various meetings of sympathy held in London and at other places. At the meeting held in St. James's Hall in London, under the auspices of the Emancipation society, on the evening of Saturday, the twenty-ninth day of April, at which William Evans, Esq., the president of that society, was chairman, the platform was filled with members of parliament and the leaders of the popular party in the metropolis; the hall was crowded with people who were unanimously in sympathy with the speakers and the object of the meeting; while the sombre drapery of the hall, surmounted by the American flag, was a mute expression of that deep grief for America's loss which filled every heart. The speeches were no mere formal expresions of horror of the crime, or regret for the death of a chief magistrate of great eminence and worth. These sentiments were indeed uppermost in the minds of all; but those who met on that occasion were thoroughly at one with the people of the north in their great task of subduing the slaveholders' rebellion, and building up the Union on the more sure and enduring basis of freedom.

From the speeches delivered on that occasion, the speech of Mr. W. E. Forster, member of parliament for Bradford has been selected as an example of the spirit that pervaded the meeting, and as an evidence of the similarity of the effect produced by the sad event, on the people and the representatives of the people, both in England and the United States Mr. Forster spoke as follows:

"The resolution which has been entrusted to me, and which I now move, is as follows:

'Resolved,— That this meeting desires to give utterance to the feelings of grief and horror with which it has heard of the assassination of President Lincoln, and the murderous attack upon Mr. Seward, and to convey to Mrs. Lincoln and to the United States government and people an expression of its profound sympathy and heartfelt condolence.' In moving this resolution I wish to say but a few words. There are many speakers here this evening, and you will agree with me that this is a time at which many should have an opportunity of trying to express their feelings, and I am sure that all who speak will agree with me in saying that we can find no words that really can express what we feel. This is a time when that tie of blood which binds Englishmen to Americans, and of which we so often talk, is indeed truly felt. A thrill of grief, horror, and indignation has swept throughout the length and breadth of Europe, as this terrible news has been conveyed to the nations, and it possesses the heart of almost every Englishman as though some terrible calamity had befallen himself. It is to the credit of our country, and it would indeed be to our shame, were it otherwise, that such is the case. With very few exceptions, rich and poor, friends of the north, and friends of the south, all are anxious to show that they forget all differences with our American kinsmen in social or political arrangements, all disagreements with them in matters of policy, in overwhelming sympathy with them in this their most sore trial. But while America has thus especial claims upon the sympathy of England it certainly does preëminently become that society, of which you, sir, are the chairman, and all of us, who, though not members of that society, have advocated its principles, that there should be a restoration of the Union with emancipation for its condition — to take the lead in expressing its indignation at the assassination which has taken place. The freedom from the bond of slavery will be a blessing to this country and to the world, and we hasten to come forward to express our sympathy when the man who has done so much to obtain that result is thus struck down. He was the man to whom of all men it would seem that God had entrusted the duty of restoring the Union, and of freeing it from slavery, and he has been struck down just at that time when he had reason to hope that that task, to accomplish which he had been toiling with such devotion and such single-minded earnestness, had been accomplished. That the commission of such a crime as this should have been permitted, and permitted at such a time, may well seem to be a mystery, but

> 'God moves in a mysterious way
> His wonders to perform;
> He plants his footsteps in the sea,
> And rides upon the storm.'

And are not the whole of us beginning to see that in this civil war which has raged throughout America, and in this fearful revolution through which this people are passing, God has been working, and his work is still to purge that country and that people from the sin of slavery? But this murdered patriot had read the lesson and had learned it. The handwriting upon the wall was guiding him. From those words of solemn beauty which he was led to utter at his recent inauguration, though even then the knife of the assassin was hanging over his head, he saw, it is plain, that God had willed that this offence should cease, and that there should be woe upon all those, whether in the north or in the south, through whom this offence had come, and if we can thoroughly prophesy any one result that will follow from this foul crime, it is this, that the offence will all the more speedily cease, and that slavery will be a thing of the past. Like you, sir, I do not charge this crime upon the leaders of the south. It would be unpardonable of any Englishman to add fuel to that fire of anger and to that burning of heart from which every American must pray he may be preserved, by saying or insinuating that any of these leaders either instigated this crime or were acquainted with it, but I do trace it to the influence of that system of slavery which those leaders have rebelled and have fought to preserve. Doubtless this assassin and his miserable accomplices were men of morbid nature and anomalous monsters, but it needed the influence of such a social system as this — that system which gratified every bad passion and reeked it upon the weak and powerless, and which burnt black men alive, and murdered white men because they were abolitionists — I say it needed the influence of a system like this to train such a miserable man as this Booth to become a parricide. Any man who has studied the experience of the last few years must feel that there is no peace and safety to that country until the system of slavery is totally abolished, and if he required further proof that there can be no terms possible between the Union and slavery, this must convince him. I have only one word more to add, and that is, that we must not allow the ship that leaves our shores to-night to take merely the message of our sympathy with the widow and the orphan, and with that country which has truly lost its father. I am sure this meeting will not be content with merely expressing its sympathy with our kinsmen in their present calamity, but that we shall express also our faith in their future and our confident belief that we have so learned the lesson of our common history that even at this hour of their need they will show what strength a free Christian people have to bear up against the blow than which no greater one has fallen upon a commonwealth. They will show how they can bear up against it without their power being paralysed and without any diminution of their self-reliance and self-restraint, and may we not also express our hopeful trust that those rulers to whom God has now entrusted their fate will be so imbued with the spirit of the patriot statesman they have just lost, and so imbued with the spirit of mingled firmness and moderation which has been exercised with integrity and judgment under circumstances than which none were ever more trying, that they will carry out the good work he began, and they will honor the name of Abraham Lincoln, which will be preëminent in all future history, and I hope they will continue his work of restoring peace to their country, and ensure freedom to all who dwell in it, undisturbed even by that temptation of vengeance to which I believe they will not yield, but which must beset them with a strength proportionate to the unparalleled atrocity of the crime which has provided it."

In view of sentiments such as have been above cited, and by comparing them with the utterances of the pulpit, of the press, and of popular assemblies in this country, we can readily perceive the similarity in the manifestations of humanity everywhere, and that there are chords in the nature of man which wherever and whenever struck by certain influences, will vibrate in unison.

In after years, when the memory of Abraham Lincoln shall remain as the most glorious recollection of the times which are now passing, and when his name shall have become inseparably linked in the minds of men with all that is grand in design and godlike in achievement, it may afford some slight gratification to our descendants to know that we, their ancestors, offered our modest but heartfelt tribute of praise to his patriotism, his integrity, his magnanimity, and his enduring worth.

B. H. H.

Troy, November 14th, 1865.

LINCOLN MEMORIAL.

FRIDAY, APRIL 14TH, 1865.

At a very late hour, persons connected with the telegraph and newspaper offices of the city, were the recipients of intelligence that an attempt had been made at Washington, early in the evening, to assassinate several of the officers of the government, and that Abraham Lincoln and William H. Seward had received injuries, which it was feared would prove fatal. Later messages contradicted these statements, and at midnight the few to whom the conflicting telegrams were known, could but surmise as to the real import of the news received.

SATURDAY, APRIL 15TH, 1865.

Early in the morning, the details of the fearful tragedy enacted at Washington the evening previous, were received by telegraph, and before daybreak the worst fears suggested by the first contradictory reports were realized with an intensity of horror unparalleled.

The very minute account of the terrible transaction, given in the morning papers, left only the faintest hope of the recovery of the President and Secretary of State. As to the former, even this hope was dispelled, when a few hours later the news came that Abraham Lincoln had died at twenty-two minutes after seven o'clock.

Assassination of President Lincoln and Secretary Seward.

BY GEORGE EVANS.

The telegraphic wires convey to us this morning, from Washington, the startling and terrible announcement of the assassination of President Lincoln and Secretary Seward.

In the case of the President, it appears that he, with Mrs. Lincoln, last evening, attended Ford's Theatre, and while seated in his private box, and during a pause in the play, a man entered the box and shot him through the head, the weapon used being a common single-barreled revolver. As soon as the fact was discovered, the wildest excitement prevailed, and amid the tumult the brutal assassin escaped. The details are given in full in our telegraphic columns.

Gen. Grant, who it was expected would accompany the President to the theatre, left Washington during the evening for New Jersey.

In the case of Secretary Seward, the assassin went to his residence, and claiming to be a messenger from the Secretary's physician, with medicine, demanded admission to Mr. Seward's chamber. Being refused, he used violence towards those who presented themselves, and forced his way into the Secretary's room. Mr. Seward was lying in bed, and the cowardly murderer inflicted several severe, and, it is feared, fatal wounds upon his neck and body.

This intelligence will cast a deep gloom over the country. The hearts of the loyal people of the north were centred in their President. His honesty and sagacity have made him the idol of the nation, and just when victory has perched upon our banners, and the storm of war is about subsiding, and just when the intricate and difficult questions relating to the reorganization of government in the rebellious states called for his calm judgment and wise forethought, just at this time to lose his services to the country is a calamity which will be deeply felt. In this fiendish act the worst fears of many friends all over the country, who have watched his movements with intense anxiety, are fully realized. We have frequently heard the fear expressed that something of this kind might happen to him. Now the blow has fallen, and the nation is called to mourn.

We give the latest intelligence received down to four o'clock this morning. Should we get any further information by six o'clock, we will give it to our readers in a second edition. — *Troy Daily Whig.*

Proceedings in the Rensselaer County Court and Court of Sessions.

At the opening of the county court and court of sessions at the Court House this morning, Judge Robertson presiding, Martin I. Townsend, Esq., in a few brief and feeling remarks, called the attention of the court to the fearful intelligence, that during the last night, Abraham Lincoln, President of the United States, had been murdered by the hand of an assassin. On his motion, seconded by District Attorney Colby, it was ordered that in consideration of the profound respect which this court entertained for Abraham Lincoln, the late President of the United States, both as an officer and as a man, this court do now adjourn. On motion of Mr. Edwin Brownell, the clerk of the court, it was ordered that the Court House be appropriately draped in mourning. His Honor Judge Robertson then spoke as follows:

The news of the morning, which has been just announced, is sad indeed. It will deeply grieve every loyal heart in the land. It is painful beyond expression to contemplate the head of this great nation, stricken down in an instant by the hand of an assassin.

For four long years Abraham Lincoln has labored earnestly, prayerfully, as few men can labor, to carry this nation through a conflict such as the world has never before seen. For four long years he has endured the bitterest scorn and hate of the enemies of his country; has had heaped upon him all the obloquy the heart of traitor could conceive or the tongue of traitor utter; yet has he kept on in the path of duty, turning neither to the right hand nor to the left, never hesitating, never doubting, never uttering a word of bitterness or complaint, but devoting all the energies of both body and mind to the salvation of his country.

The whole people had learned to love him and to trust him — to have faith in his statesmanship as well as in his purity.

Thus laboring and thus beloved, he lived to see the great rebellion crushed, the enemies of his country vanquished. In the hour of his country's triumph he is taken from us by the hand of a wretch whose memory will be execrated by the virtuous of all nations to the end of time. Why he was thus taken we cannot divine. It is enough for us to know that it must have been for some wise purpose. The nation will mourn, yet bow in submission.

It is fitting that every mark of respect should be paid to the memory of the departed.

I order the proceedings of the court at this time to be published, and that the clerk enter them in full on the minutes. The court will now adjourn.

Proceedings in the Police Court.

At the opening of the court, Thomas Neary, Esq., the police justice, announced the death of the President of the United States by the hand of an assassin. He stated that in view of the general gloom that pervaded the community by reason of this sad event, it was proper there should be a suspension of business on this occasion. He then adjourned the court until the Monday next following.

Orders of the National Guard.

By general order No. 7, previously issued, a parade of the 24th regiment New York State National Guard had been arranged to take place on the 17th instant. The parade was postponed, and a funeral salute was directed by the following orders:

Head Qrs. 24th Regt., N. Y. S. N. G.,
Troy, April 15th, 1865.
General Order No. 8.

General order No. 7, dated at these head-quarters, April 14th, is hereby revoked. By order.

I. McConihe Jr., Col. Com'g.
G. G. Moore, Adj't.

Head Qrs. 24th Regt., N. Y. S. N. G.,
Troy, April 15th, 1865.
Special Order No. 10.

In compliance with paragraph 299, general regulations, it is hereby ordered that a gun shall be fired at every half hour, beginning at sunrise and ending at sunset to-morrow, the 16th day of April, the same being the day following the reception of the official intelligence of the death of the President of the United States. Captain John M. Landon, commanding Company A, is charged with the execution of the above order. It is also ordered that the colors shall be displayed at half mast on the several armories of this command at sunrise to-morrow, the 16th day of April, and remain at half mast until sunset. By order.

      I. McConihe Jr., Col. Com'g.
G. G. Moore, Adj't.

The effect produced by the sad event was such as had seldom been witnessed in this city. A settled gloom rested on every face, and not only women but men — strong men — were seen to weep in the streets. At an early hour, moved thereto by a common impulse, business was suspended. Shops, counting rooms, offices, warehouses and places of amusement were closed, a few shops only remaining open, and those not so much for purposes of traffic, as affording centres for the discussion of the news and the exchange of words of grief, fear or revenge. Crowds thronged about the bulletin-boards which had so lately heralded our final victories, but which now promulgated this saddest of stories. At the newspaper offices incessant inquiries were made for fuller intelligence, and this intelligence when printed was presented by the daily journals in columns encased in mourning lines and borders. Flags which had for years past floated in token of victories achieved, and which of late had been flung out with the greatest manifestations of joy and triumph, were now raised at half staff and festooned with crape. Public buildings were draped with the emblems of mourning, and on the front of private dwellings from the poorest tenement to the stateliest residence, was to be seen some token of the general sorrow.

All classes of citizens gave themselves up to the indulgence of an all-pervading and unaffected grief. Men who until now had been silent and apparently unconcerned spectators of the events of the last four years, or who had openly opposed the course of the President in our national troubles, were foremost in lamenting his death and deploring this culmination of our national woe. No chance word which hinted, even remotely, approbation of the foul deed, was allowed to be uttered with impunity, and a few instances of ill-timed levity or partizan bitterness met with rebukes so stern and decisive that a repetition of the offence was not attempted. From the steeples of the city at intervals, during the day, the bells tolled out their mournful music, and kept time in solemn tone to the sad symphony of every heart.

About eleven o'clock in the morning His Honor Uri Gilbert, the mayor of the city, sent private messages to the clergy, recommending that the various churches be opened for a service of prayer and humiliation, in view of the national bereavement, at five o'clock in the afternoon. This recommendation also appeared in the early editions of the afternoon journals. In compliance with the suggestion thus made, religious services were held in many of the churches at the hour designated. These services were necessarily extemporaneous, and an account of a few only has been preserved.

SERVICE AT ST. JOHN'S CHURCH.

REV. HENRY C. POTTER, D.D., RECTOR,

No service having then been appointed by the Bishop of the Diocese, and the occasion being so utterly exceptional and unprecedented, the following order of service, adapted in part from the English prayer book, was used at St. John's (Protestant Episcopal) Church.

HYMN 80.

Almighty Lord, before thy throne
    Thy mourning people bend:
'Tis on thy pardoning grace alone,
    Our prostrate hopes depend.

Dark judgments, from thy heavy hand,
    Thy dreadful power display;
Yet mercy spares our guilty land,
    And still we live to pray.

O turn us, turn us, mighty Lord,
    Convert us by thy grace;
Then shall our hearts obey thy word,
    And see again thy face.

Then, should oppressing foes invade,
    We will not sink in fear;
Secure of all-sufficient aid,
    When God, our God, is near.

Minister.— The Lord be with you.

Answer.— And with thy spirit.

Minister.— Let us pray.

O Most mighty God, terrible in thy judgments and wonderful in thy doings toward the children of men, who in thy heavy displeasure hast suffered the life of our Chief Magistrate to be taken away by the hands of cruel and bloody men; we thy sinful creatures, here assembled before thee, do humbly confess that they were the crying sins of this nation which have brought down this heavy judgment upon us. But, O gracious God, when thou makest inquisition for blood, lay not the guilt of this innocent blood (the shedding whereof nothing but the blood of thy Son can expiate), lay it not to our charge, we beseech thee, nor let it be required of us or our posterity. Be merciful, O Lord, be merciful unto thy people whom thou hast redeemed, and be not angry with us forever; but pardon us for thy mercies sake, through the merits of thy Son Jesus Christ our Lord. *Amen.*

O Almighty Lord God, who by thy wisdom not only guidest and orderest all things most suitably to thine own justice; but also performest thy pleasure in such a manner, that we cannot but acknowledge thee to be righteous in all thy ways and holy in all thy works: We thy sinful people do here fall down before thee, confessing thy judgments were right in permitting cruel men, sons of Belial, to imbrue their hands in the blood of thy servant the President of the United States, we having drawn down the same by the long provocation of our sin and weakness. For which we do therefore, here humble ourselves before thee; beseeching thee to deliver this nation from blood-guiltiness, and to turn from us and our posterity all those judgments which we by our folly have worthily deserved. Grant this for the all-sufficient merits of thy Son, our Saviour Jesus Christ. Amen.

Blessed God, just and powerful, who didst permit thy servant, our honored Chief Magistrate, to be given up to the violent outrages of unscrupulous and wicked men, to be mocked and scoffed at, and maligned, and at the last murdered by them: though we cannot reflect upon so foul an act but with horror and astonishment; yet do we most gratefully commemorate the many excellencies which shone forth in the character of thy servant, whom thou wast pleased to endue with an eminent measure of exemplary patience, meekness and charity, before the face of all his enemies. And, albeit thou didst suffer them to proceed to such an height of violence as to kill him, yet hast thou in great mercy preserved his successor in office, and by thy wonderful providence hast continued to us the triumphs of the cause of these United States of America, and the blessed tokens of speedy and lasting peace. For these, thy great mercies, we glorify thy name, through Jesus Christ our blessed Saviour. *Amen.*

Almighty and everlasting God, whose righteousness is like the strong mountains, and thy judgments like the great deep; and who by that barbarous murder committed yesterday upon the sacred person of the President of the United States, hast taught us that neither the greatest of rulers nor the best of men are more secure from violence than from natural death, teach us also hereby, so to number our days that we may apply our hearts unto wisdom. And grant that neither the splendour of anything that is great, nor the conceit of anything that is good in us, may withdraw our eyes from looking upon ourselves, as sinful dust and ashes; but that according to the example of this blessed Martyr, we may press forward in the cause of truth and freedom and righteousness, in faith and patience, humility and meekness, mortification and self-denial, charity and constant perseverance unto the end. And all this for thy Son our Lord Jesus Christ's sake, to whom, with thee and the Holy Ghost, be all honour and glory, world without end. *Amen.*

The Lesson.

St. Matthew, xxi. 33-42.

There was a certain householder, which planted a vineyard, and hedged it round about, and digged a winepress in it, and built a tower, and let it out to husbandmen, and went into a far country : and when the time of the fruit drew near, he sent his servants to the husbandmen, that they might receive the fruits of it. And the husbandmen took his servants, and beat one, and killed another, and stoned another. Again, he sent other servants more than the first: and they did unto them likewise. But last of all he sent unto them his son, saying, They will reverence my son. But when the husbandmen saw the son, they said among themselves, This is the heir; come, let us kill him, and let us seize on his inheritance. And they caught him, and cast him out of the vineyard, and slew him. When the lord therefore of the vineyard cometh, what will he do unto those husbandmen? They say unto him, He will miserably destroy those wicked men, and will let out his vineyard unto other husbandmen, which shall render him the fruits in their seasons. Jesus saith unto them, Did ye never read in the Scriptures, The stone which the builders rejected, the same is become the head of the corner: this is the Lord's doing, and it is marvellous in our eyes?

Hymn 12.

God moves in a mysterious way
   His wonders to perform;
He plants his footsteps in the sea,
   And rides upon the storm.

Deep in unfathomable mines,
   With never-failing skill,
He treasures up his bright designs,
   And works his gracious will.

Ye fearful saints, fresh courage take;
   The clouds ye so much dread
Are big with mercy, and shall break
   In blessings on your head.

Judge not the Lord by feeble sense,
   But trust him for his grace:
Behind a frowning providence
   He hides a smiling face.

His purposes will ripen fast,
   Unfolding every hour:
The bud may have a bitter taste,
   But sweet will be the flower.

Blind unbelief is sure to err,
   And scan his work in vain:
God is his own interpreter,
   And he will make it plain.

Prayers.

Prayer for persons under affliction and appropriate Collects.

Service at the First Presbyterian Church.
Rev. Marvin R. Vincent, Pastor.

A large audience assembled to participate in the service. Prayers were offered and hymns sung expressive of the all-pervading sorrow. Short addresses were made by the pastor and by members of the congregation. The principal address was the following:

ADDRESS.
BY MARTIN I. TOWNSEND, ESQ.

We are come together to-day, to consider one of the saddest events that ever befell a nation. Our Chief Magistrate, whom we loved as a father rather than reverenced as a ruler, has fallen by the hand of an assassin, and the nation is in tears. Yet I stand not here to mourn for Abraham Lincoln. He has been fortunate in a degree rarely attained by mortals. He has been spared to fill his full measure of usefulness, as well as his full measure of fame. He has seen his imperilled country come triumphant out of one of the most deadly struggles in which a nation was ever engaged. He has seen the embattled hosts which were set in hostile array against her, melt away before the serried ranks of his country's armies, and their vaunted leaders prisoners of war. In a word, he had seen that cause of which he had been called to be the leader —the cause of his country, the cause of humanity— crowned by the blessing of God, and had come to know that his toils and anxieties during four long and dreadful years of darkness and of conflict, were not in vain, but had preserved the liberties of his country, had secured to her a glorious and happy future, and had enrolled his name high upon the record of the benefactors of mankind. Mr. Lincoln was more fortunate in his death than in his life. He died in an instant, without sorrow or pain. He died in the maturity of his powers, and in the fullness of his fame, before a single mistake had fixed the slightest blot or blemish upon the fair shield of his wisdom and patriotism. He died at a moment when every people that loves our country was joining in the grand chorus of praise, rising to Heaven throughout our own broad land.

It is for our country that I weep. It is for humanity that I blush, when I think that any creature who has enjoyed the blessings of American liberty, and worn the human form, could be found base enough to imbrue his hands in the blood of one so loving and so beloved, in the blood of one whose heart beat so warmly for his fellow men. But this dispensation was doubtless designed to teach the American people a great and solemn lesson. We have been at school for the last four years. We have been studying as a lesson, the brutalizing influence of slavery, not upon oppressed black men, but upon the white—the governing race. We have seen what miseries have been heaped upon our poor, helpless, imprisoned, and suffering sons and brothers at the Libby prison, at Salisbury, and that living Hades, the pens of Andersonville; and we have seen now, that the same fiendish spirit, born of slavery, can raise its dastard and assassin hand, and strike down our best beloved and most honored. The man who doubts to-day the wicked and debasing influence of slavery upon the white population of this country, has been blind to the events of the last four years, and would not believe, though "one rose from the dead." Indeed, the period in which we live is big with lessons of solemn instruction. Although we have all admitted, in a general way, that God cares for the lowly and the humble as well as for men of high degree, we have lived to a great extent in a condition of practical doubt upon the subject. But to-day we can see that not a tear has fallen from the eye of a bereaved or suffering slave mother, through the length and breadth of all our land, that God has not treasured up for judgment. And the lesson we are to learn from it is, that if any nation wishes to prosper, even for the world that now is, that nation must free itself from oppression, though practised upon the least of God's little ones.

There is another lesson which we have been set to learn in these times. It is the lesson of God's sovereignty. I do not mean a sovereignty which excludes all agency of man. But I mean that God overrules the counsels and actions of men in such a manner, as to work out the greatest good for that race for whom the world was created and the Saviour died. What poor, short-sighted mortal was able to foresee that the first gun fired upon Fort Sumter sounded the knell of slavery? Who of us, on that gloomy day, when good men mourned over the sad defeat of the Union forces at Bull Run, could see any silver lining upon the dark cloud that enveloped this smitten land? Yet how clearly now can we see God's hand in that dispensation. How clearly now can we see that God had a great work to do; that he meant that the shackles of millions of slaves should be broken, that they should be broken by the strong hands and stalwart arms of the toiling freemen of the North, and that he suffered defeat to overtake our armies, that the loyal of the whole land should come forth from their farms and their workshops, and devote themselves soul and body to the accomplishment of his sacred work. And we have reason to be thankful this day, that we have been spared to see this work accomplished. Our armies are everywhere triumphant; our nation is everywhere honored; our land is purged of the dreadful plague-spot of slavery; and although God has smitten us in the person of our beloved President, we feel, as we never felt before, that he loves our land and our people, and means his chastisements only for our good. Let it be ours to profit by the solemn lessons which he is teaching us in these days.

Other Services.

The service in the Second Street Presbyterian Church, consisted of appropriate music, prayer and an address by the pastor, the Rev. Duncan Kennedy, D.D. The scene was one of deep interest, and the heavy and beautiful drapery of the building, served, if possible, to increase the solemnity. The address was, for the most part, an expression of deep sympathy in the universal sorrow. The speaker directed attention to the mystery that enshrouded the dread event, and enforced the duty of Christian submission to the inscrutable dispensation, and of unfailing trust in the superintending providence of God.

At St. Mary's (Roman Catholic) church, the service, under the direction of the pastor, the Rev. Peter Havermans, was solemn and impressive. The psalm *Miserere* was intoned from the altar and was taken up by the choir. The music was grand and effective. Suitable prayers were also read at the altar, and such remarks were made by the pastor as the occasion called for.

Services of a similar character were held in the North Baptist church, Rev. C. P. Sheldon, D.D., pastor; in the South Troy Methodist Episcopal church, Rev. D. T. Elliott, pastor; in the Second Presbyterian church, Rev. D. S. Gregory, D.D., pastor, and in other churches in the city, of which no account is preserved.

The Assassination of the President.

BY JOHN M. FRANCIS.

We have no heart to dwell upon the details of the awful calamity. The wail of a great people ascends to heaven; the vengeance of a just God, swift as lightning-darts and scathing as thunder-bolts, will be visited upon the guilty, their murderous associates and fiendish abettors.

Sad, sad beyond the power of language to express, is the loss of our true-hearted, our pure-minded, our trusted and loving President. He was gentle as a woman, yet firm as a Jackson. He loved his country with the pure devotion of a child for its mother. But he had the strength of giant manhood and the sagacity of astute statesmanship to defend the Union he had sworn to support. He was merciful; he was kind. Never was heart more susceptible to pity than Abraham Lincoln's. He was ready to forgive the worst where pardon promised reformation, and where there was reasonable hope that the interests of the country would not be jeopardized by such forgiveness. Even to the hour he was killed by the assassin's fire, Abraham Lincoln was laboring with all the zeal of his nature, with all the abilities of a mind that grasped as if by intuition the salient points of great questions, to compose our national difficulties, to pacify the country, to reëstablish Peace upon the basis of everlasting Justice,— at the same time giving amnesty and offering blessings to those who had sought to destroy the

Union, to strike down civilization, and to ruin a just and loyal people.

> " His life was gentle, and the elements .
> So mix'd in him, that nature might stand up
> And say to all the world, *This was a man!*"

We cannot analyze the character of our deceased President here and now. In his hands the future of our country was secure. The people trusted him and looked up to him as children to a kind, loving, watchful and noble hearted parent. The blow that struck him down has fired the souls of thousands who before were ready to forgive the rebel leaders, and offer to them the terms of conciliation and clemency. Henceforth, those words are blotted from the lexicon of the American people, and nothing short of the condign punishment of the guilty wretches who plunged this nation in fratricidal war, and who have prosecuted their murderous enterprise with the ferocity of barbarians, will satisfy the demands of the republic.

The nation mourns; the people are bowed down with sorrow,—but every loyal heart, trustful even in its awful affliction, feels that the republic shall live.

Abraham Lincoln is dead, but his works shall live after him and during all coming time. And his memory shall be enshrined with Washington's— "*First in the hearts of his countrymen.*"

It is a solemn hour. We feel that the republic has lost its truest friend, its great protector, its trusted saviour. But thank God, Abraham Lincoln lived to save his country. Thank God, he saw the finishing blows dealt to the gigantic rebellion. His policy was vindicated; the cause nearest his heart had triumphed. Men die, but principles never perish.—*Troy Daily Times.*

OUR DUTY ON THIS DAY.
BY B. H. HALL.

In contemplating the horrible crime that has done to death the head of this nation, in the most cowardly manner known to human demonism, we should still think like men, and not allow our better judgment to be paralyzed by devices of vengeance. We can not believe that the act of the assassin of President Lincoln can awaken much sympathy in the hearts of any except the most virulent and abandoned traitors, and we hazard the conjecture that when the circumstances of the act become fully known, but very few will be found implicated in it. Let us not, then, talk about visiting vengeance on a whole people, many of whom are now subdued, for *this* crime of a few.

God is our witness, that none feel more deeply than we, the terrible significance of this dastardly crime. On the day when a large portion of Christendom was commemorating in litanies and tears the atrocious death of the Saviour of men, Abraham Lincoln, the type of human rights and progress, fell by the hands of a man imbued with the same spirit that crucified that Saviour. On the day in which the flag of our country was again raised over the walls of a nation's redeemed fortress, the guiding spirit that had brought about that redemption passed out of its murdered body. Indiscriminate vengeance is neither lawful, Christian nor human. The mysteries of Providence are beyond our ken, but for all this our hearts should be strong, not troubled; our faith uplifting, not drooping. Let the ministers of God, as they this day lead their people in acts of solemn devotion, remind them that vengeance belongs to Him and the laws of the country. What may be in store for this distracted and bleeding land is locked in the bosom of Omniscience. Of one thing, however, we are assured, and that is, that he who has led us on in triumph through four years of struggle, will not now desert us. As for the southern people, the hand that held out to them the chalice of tenderest mercy is extended in death, and they as well as we have lost *the best earthly friend.* Let us pause, ere we draw rash conclusions, and then perhaps sounds from above may reach us, and a vision be granted of things beyond the terrible present.

> "At last I heard a voice upon the slope
> Cry to the summit: Is there any hope?
> To which an answer pealed from that high land,
> But in a tongue no man could understand;
> And on the glimmering limit, far withdrawn,
> God made Himself an awful rose of dawn."

Troy Daily Times.

The National Calamity and Humiliation.

BY F. B. HUBBELL.

All public interest to-day mournfully centres upon the tragic death of the President of the United States by the hands of an assassin! What words to write! What a sentence to burst upon the public ear, so recently filled with rejoicings of the populace, whose heart beat quicker because the nation was emerging from scenes of blood and carnage to enjoy once more the blessings of an honored and bravely won peace, and because the flag of the union was once more to float over an undivided country!

President Lincoln expired at twenty minutes past seven o'clock this morning, April 15, 1865. He died in the service of a grateful country, while yet his brow was freshly crowned with the highest honors the republic could bestow. His name is given immortality, and to-day is enshrined in the hearts of millions who in his life dissented from his policy and denied him their suffrages.

Under such a calamity, words are feeble, and seem idle. The suddenness of the shock well nigh palsies the powers of speech and thought. Men, friends, pass each other on the street, without the usual recognition, because the mind is too busy with itself, and silence is the natural language of sorrow.

Until this deplorable event, for weeks the prospects

of the country had been gradually brightening. Foremost in the heaven-blessed work of peace and conciliation, had been President Lincoln. Already had the fruits of his policy, during his brief visit to Richmond, began to reveal themselves in the important appeal made to the Virginia legislature by the leading men of that state. Disregarding all appeals to return to Washington, heeding not for a moment suggestions of personal danger, he remained in the late rebel capital, simply because he believed his presence and influence there could aid an honorable and speedy close of the war: and every day's developments plainly demonstrated that he judged rightly. Upon no class in the country does this calamity fall with more crushing weight than upon the union men of the south, who had justly and naturally come to look to President Lincoln as the pilot who was to bring the nation safely through all dangers.

This hope is now gone, and clouds loom up in the future. "New masters, new laws." The President had adopted a policy which was becoming well understood, and which was rapidly receiving the unanimous favor of the best minds of men of all parties north and south. The hopes built upon this happily changing feature in our affairs disappears. What was reasonable certainty now becomes the greatest uncertainty. The rolling, boisterous sea is before us, and the ship is in the hands of untried mariners.

From the time it was known Mr. Lincoln was

elected for the second term, party opposition to him, or his administration, was modified to a degree never known on the accession of a president to office. The terrible crisis the country had passed through had softened asperities, and men began to consider their duties in the higher relations to country—to saving the republic from utter ruin. Day by day this modified sentiment was growing stronger. While some of the President's early and hitherto most steadfast friends felt impelled to differ with his views and withhold approval of some of his acts, the party which had opposed the President gave unerring signs of a disposition cordially to sustain him.

Humanly speaking, we believe the lives of Abraham Lincoln and William H. Seward were of more value to this country, in the crisis we are passing through, than the lives of any two men in the world. Their experience during the past four years, their familiarity with all questions—domestic and foreign—the anxious desire of both to see the great internal controversy closed, their ability to rise above small to grasp and make secure great interests, and the fact that both had the confidence of the country, and that to both was assigned the helm for four years to come, made them the nation's hope, as far as men confide in men. But God is over all. The devisings of mortals are nothing. For some inscrutably wise purpose, the Almighty afflicts this people.—*Troy Daily Press.*

Abraham Lincoln.

BY JAMES S. THORN.

There are little knots on the corners to-day,
   And with bated breath they utter
Not alone a dirge o'er th' inanimate clay,
   But avenging whispers mutter.

There are aching hearts in the households to-night;
   There are eyes that are red with weeping;
And tender hearts, oh not bursting quite,
   In the gall of despair are steeping.

They are sobbing to-day on the old camp-ground,
   And spirits undaunted by foeman,
That trembled not when the battery frowned,
   Are blanched as the cheek of woman.

Comes a nation's wail o'er her prostrate son,
   For her joy has been changed to sorrow:
She fears there's the dusk of doubt begun,
   And alas! who can tell the morrow?

So pure and so wise, aye, so grandly good,
   Sic semper tyrannis belies him:
Greatest of living men he stood;
   Dying, the world shall prize him.

Though the head lies low, yet the body lives:
   There are heart-strings that death cannot sever:
HE taketh away, but yet HE gives,
   And the Union shall last forever.

We are tasting to-day of the bitter cup:
   Oh lesson, we heed thy warning.
We know but ONE who can lift us up:
   'Tis night, it will yet be morning.

>   The dead of to-day will grow divine
>   Like the martyrs of ancient story,
>   And with Washington's, Lincoln's name shall shine
>   On the scroll of our country's glory.
>   *Troy Daily Times.*

Saturday, April 15th, 1865.

Later in the day appeared the proclamation of Reuben E. Fenton, governor of the state, and the recommendation of Horatio Potter, bishop of the diocese of New York. They are here inserted because they form a part of the history of the occasion, and served to give direction to some of the religious services of the subsequent days.

Proclamation by the Governor.

The fearful tragedy at Washington has converted an occasion of rejoicing over national victory into one of national mourning. It is fitting, therefore, that the 20th of April, heretofore set apart as a day of thanksgiving, should now be dedicated to services appropriate to a season of national bereavement.

Bowing reverently to the providence of God, let us assemble in our places of worship on that day, to acknowledge our dependence on him who has brought sudden darkness on the land in the very hour of its restoration to union, peace and liberty.

In witness whereof, I have hereunto set my hand and affixed the privy seal of the state, at the city of

Albany, this fifteenth day of April, in the year of our Lord one thousand eight hundred and sixty-five.

By the Governor: R. E. FENTON.
GEO. S. HASTINGS, Private Secretary.

RECOMMENDATION OF BISHOP POTTER.

NEW YORK, April 15th, 1865.

To the Clergy and Laity of the Diocese of New York—
DEAR BROTHERS: With agony which I have no language to express, I appeal to you to offer up your prayers for this bereaved and mourning nation. The beloved and revered Chief Magistrate of the United States is no more. The malignant passions which have just proved impotent to destroy the government, have successfully done the assassin's work upon the life of its honored head. A glorious career of service and devotion is crowned with a martyr's death. I request most respectfully that to-morrow, and for the next two weeks, the prayer for a person under affliction be used for the country with these slight changes: Instead of "the sorrows of thy servant," read "the sorrows of thy servants, the people of this nation;" and instead of "him" and "his," read "us" and "ours." I also appoint the prayer in time of war and tumults to be read. I would also recommend that after the solemnities of the Easter Sunday shall have been concluded, the churches of the diocese be clothed in mourning. Praying God to give you his blessing, and to sanctify this sore bereavement to

our beloved country, I remain your affectionate brother in Christ.

HORATIO POTTER, Bishop of New York.

CITIZENS' MEETING.

At a large meeting of citizens, held at St. Nicholas Hall, on Saturday evening, April 15th, to give expression to public feeling on the recent murder of Abraham Lincoln, President of the United States, Charles Eddy presided, and Charles E. Davenport was Secretary. On motion, a committee of five — William Hagan, J. M. Hawley, N. Davenport, Alderman Cox and W. N. Barringer — were appointed to draft and report resolutions. The meeting was addressed by S. R. Clexton, D. A. Wells, P. H. Baerman, W. N. Barringer and Rev. Mr. R. R. Meredith. The committee reported the following resolutions, which were adopted:

Whereas, We have heard with profound sorrow in this hour of our country's peril, of the death of the chief magistrate of the nation, Abraham Lincoln, by the hand of an assassin, therefore

Resolved, That, although we feel deeply on this subject, yet, believing in an overruling Providence, we strive calmly to submit, with the thought that our lamented President may have finished the work given him to do, and that God will raise up a man to complete the work so nearly accomplished of reuniting our country in bonds of perpetual union.

Resolved, That we hope all loyal citizens will pay a proper respect to the day set apart by the Governor of this State for religious services appropriate to this sad national calamity.

Resolved, That we have full confidence in the patriotism and will of Andrew Johnson to finish the work of restoration so ably commenced by the late President.

Resolved, That this hall be draped in mourning for the residue of the year in testimony of respect for the memory of the able and patriotic statesman, Abraham Lincoln, late President of the United States.

CHARLES EDDY, Chairman.
CHARLES E. DAVENPORT, Secretary.

SUNDAY, APRIL 16TH, 1865.

"HUNG BE THE HEAVENS WITH BLACK."

BY C. L. MAC ARTHUR.

We stand appalled before the awful tragedy which has been precipitated upon the American people. Words are tame to express the agonies of the national heart. The tongue is dumb, and paralyzed in the effort to speak the great feelings of the hour. The President of the United States, in the calm moment of repose, surrounded by his family and trusted friends, in the midst of an assemblage of thousands where were gathered the talent and beauty of the Federal Capital, is suddenly shot by an assassin! Can any thing in the possible range of human events be more agonizing, tragic and appalling? In atrocity, yes. The great and gifted Secretary of State, lying on his sick bed, wan and emaciated, with a broken arm and a fractured jaw, with the balance vibrating doubtfully between life and death, is approached in the dead hour of night by an assassin, and the dagger is mercilessly thrust at the throat and the heart of the victim! That such fiendish acts could be perpetrated by any one bearing "the human form divine," make us shudder to belong to the same race. The heart sickens at the recital of these facts, and the pen unwillingly records them. We present elsewhere the fullest details of this awful tragedy which have reached us. We refrain from further comment.—*Troy News.*

EXTRACT FROM A SERMON PREACHED AT ST. JOHN'S (EPISCOPAL) CHURCH ON THE MORNING OF EASTER SUNDAY.

BY REV. HENRY C. POTTER, D.D.

* * * * * * * * * * It is in view, supremely, of our bereavements, that the great fact of which this Easter Morning is at once the seal and proclamation — the fact I mean of the resurrection — is so precious. Death loses, indeed, but little of its mystery, but it is robbed forever of its terror. Our friends are borne away out of our sight but we know that they have not perished. All that was most central to their character and personality shall, one day, live again. The mortal eyes with which so lovingly they looked upon us may, verily, have been closed, but the radiant tenderness that shone in them, has, believe me, an enduring existence. The lips that smiled encouragement upon our weariness, and uttered their word of reassurance in our ear may, truly, have been sealed in death forever; but both smile and speech, through Christ, shall live again, in an existence as real, as tender, and ineffably more glorious than before. The hand that once held ours and pledged its constant friendship in its loving grasp, may long ago have relaxed its steadfast hold and chilled and stiffened in the grave, but the constancy and fidelity which it silently uttered, have no more perished than the being and character of him, of whom they were the expression. I know not *what* that body shall be, but I do know that God will give to every ransomed soul a body, "as it hath pleased Him." Death is not longer a master but a servant—no longer a victor over human hopes, but a gleaner of human treasures into the everlasting garner of the Lord! In that store-house all the sweetness and beauty and nobility of the past, as of the present and the future, shall be gathered. The virtue of martyrs; the sweet innocence of childhood; the glories of patriotism, uplifting itself above the level of our common life, like yonder mountains; the fragrance of self-sacrifice and faith and love — all these shall somehow be embodied in that resurrection unto life, which the Master's victory on this Easter Morning purchased for his people forever!

And this, as it is our supreme and only consolation in all our private sorrows, so it must be in view of that tragedy of horror, before which, this morning, a nation stands aghast. Ah! how darkened is our Easter-feast to-day. The sun rises, as of old, to usher in the morning when the Lord of life and glory rent assunder the bars of the grave and brought life and immortality to light; but the shadow of an overwhelming grief is upon us, and we cannot raise ourselves to the gladness of the occasion. The Easter fact *is* here. God forbid, that now, of all times, we should for a moment forget it! But the trappings of our common woe mingle with our Easter blossoms, and our songs are mixed with tears. "The malignant passions which have just proved impotent to destroy the government, have successfully done the assassin's work upon the life of its honored head." A glorious career of service and devotion, rendered, much of it, amid the scorn and obloquy of foreign and domestic traitors; a career often impeded by the timid and time-serving unfaithfulness of professed friends, is crowned with a martyr's death. The barbarism of slavery, incarnated, first, in the brutal bully of the senate chamber, then in a monstrous and fiendish rebellion, with all its violation of the most sacred oaths, and its ingenious and demoniacal cruelty to prisoners, and now most fitly impersonated in the garb and weapon of the assassin, has struck its last blow at our beloved and revered chief magistrate. But, ah! thank God, how impotent a blow! How little of our great ruler has perished! A devout though self-distrustful follower of his Master; spending the earliest moments of the day amid all the pressure of his high responsibility, (as those who then sought him learned), in communion with the source of all wisdom ; bearing his gentle testimony, as I heard not long ago, from one to whom he said it, that he loved and leaned on Him who is the strength and righteousness of them that trust him ; brought to the Master, as have been so many, by that which took from him the darling of his eyes — how surely may we believe that the best and highest part of him is forever immortal, and, that just as his memory will live among us, and grow brighter and more radiant as the ages roll along, so is he himself even now, alive from the dead, ere long to take on that spiritual body which God giveth to them that have pleased him !

And, therefore, let not the notes of our mourning stifle those of our gratitude and hope — gratitude and hope for him whom we have lost, and praise and thanksgiving to the Master, who, in this, as in all our sorrows, gives us, on this Easter morning, the clear and unclouded assurance of the life which is to come ! For that life, feeling more keenly than ever, this morning, how fleeting are all the goodly shows of this, let us earnestly look and long, until, with us, too, as with patriots and saints and martyrs who have gone before us, this mortal shall put on immortality and death be swallowed up in victory !

SKETCH OF A SERMON PREACHED IN THE STATE STREET METHODIST EPISCOPAL CHURCH, ON SUNDAY MORNING:

BY REV. S. D. BROWN.

Trust ye in the Lord forever; for in the Lord Jehovah is everlasting strength.—ISAIAH, xxvi, 4.

The nation is in mourning. Its head has been stricken and now lies low in death, and the chief of its councillors stands ready to depart. No language can describe the shock, as yestermorn the disastrous tidings reached us. For the moment, it seemed as if the very foundations had given way, and even hope was lost.

The President of our republic is dead, the victim of a base assassin's power. Seldom, in the history of modern times, has the head of a great nation been assassinated. In Rome, in the days of her corruption and decline, assassination of rulers was common; but in later years it has seldom occurred. *Our* nation is now among those whose chief has fallen by the blow of the murderer.

We have but partially recovered from the shock. It is not yet time fully to gather up the lessons of the hour, much less to eulogize the departed. Yet it seems fitting, that allusion should be made to this sad event. It is the voice of God, and the pulpit should to-day, make an application to the hearts of the people.

I have had no time for preparation. Busily engaged during the day, I had but a few moments late at night, to throw my thoughts into any systematic form, and can give you only those thoughts which, amid busy cares, have been passing through my mind.

It seems mysterious that God should have permitted this dire tragedy. Other diabolical plans have been formed, but they have been signally foiled by an unseen hand. God could have prevented *this* also, but he has allowed it to be successful, why? It reveals the vanity of all confidence in man, the instability of all of earth.

During the last four years, there have been seasons of doubt and perplexity. We had passed through these and were now confident—confident in *him*. When, a few months since, he was reëlected, men felt that all would be well, that *he* would lead the nation to victory and peace. He was inaugurated with greater solemnity than any who preceded him. Scarcely a month passes and the hope of the nation is dead.

This calamity comes amid victory. The shouts of a jubilant people have died away in a piercing wail. The past few months have been months of continued triumph. Never did so many events happen in the history of any people in a single month, as have in ours, during the last four weeks, culminating in the fall of the rebel capital, the surrender of their proudest chief and grandest army.

How quickly has this change come! At the opening of the week the national heart was buoyant. Bells were ringing, flags flying, drums beating, and people shouting, from Maine to the Rocky mountains. Yet ere the week closed, the nation is bowed with this great sorrow.

And it is what we least expected. Defeat to our arms we thought possible, for it is the fortune of war, but none anticipated or even thought of such an event as this.

It has occurred not only in the midst of general rejoicings, but on the evening of that day, when the flag of our country was again thrown to the breeze, from the ruins of Sumter. The anniversary of the opening of the war was celebrated amid omens of returning peace. How impressively does it then teach the vanity of human hopes. But it is also designed and calculated to lead us nearer to God, to prompt to higher trust in him. "Trust ye in the Lord." This has been the great lesson of this war. We entered it with confidence in the resources and prowess of the nation, but in the first great struggle were defeated. How the national heart sunk as the tidings of that disaster flew along the wires. Then men began to look to a higher power for aid, and earnestly pray.

The men in whom we have most trusted have failed. There is not a man in a prominent position in the army to-day, who was so at the opening of the war. Some have fallen, others have retired. The victory has been achieved by men who had no previous military fame to excite confidence. Defeat has come when we were most confident, victory when we were depressed and looked to God.

The clouds of war were now passing. We felt that we had the right man to reconstruct this nation, and confided in his wisdom. But at the moment when we need statesmanship rather than military genius, he has fallen. Perhaps we were trusting too much in him. Has not the nation felt the need of reliance upon God as never before? Such at least have been my feelings. Never in my history did I feel as now, that there is none other in whom man may trust.

God has a purpose in permitting this great evil. Our late President had nobly acted his part and carried us successfully through the struggle. And his name shall be honored by the latest generations of men. But may not another instrument, a man of different character be needed at the present moment?

It is a singular fact, that the two most favorable to leniency to the rebels have been stricken. Other members of the government were embraced in the fiendish plan, but as to them, it failed. May it not be, that God is teaching that those guilty of the great crime of treason shall receive condign punishment? We consign to death the man who murders one; they have murdered thousands. They have labored to overthrow a government instituted by God and which was the hope of humanity. God designs they shall be punished, not for the purpose of retaliation, but to deter others; not to gratify feelings of revenge, but to save posterity. Clemency and magnanimity are virtues in some circumstances, in others they are but weakness. Clemency to the guilty is cruelty to the innocent, and sad will it be for the nation, if our treatment of the leading traitors proclaims that treason is not esteemed a crime.

This event will exert another important influence. In this war we have demonstrated, to the confusion of European statesmen, that a government may be free and liberal in its character, and yet possess strength to maintain itself. And now, we are proving that this strength is not in its elected head, but in the body of its people. The President dies but the people live, and hence the power abides. Abraham Lincoln expires, and in a few hours, his successor is quietly inducted, and to-day the government is moving on as if nothing had occurred. There will be no shock, the armies will not be turned from their course, financial and commercial interests will not be disturbed, and even governmental securities will scarcely be affected.

But especially are we admonished to trust in the Lord. We are prone to rely upon the human instrument. We relied on Lincoln and God took him. We have been distrustful of his successor. Then should we look beyond him to God.

In the Lord Jehovah is everlasting strength. He can carry out his own purposes. This event, calamitous as it is, can be overruled for the nation's good. The history of the world evinces this. When Christ was crucified, his enemies felt they had fully triumphed. The disciples were in despair. That Saturday he lay in the grave was to them much like the yesterday to us. But that event, apparently so calamitous, became the corner stone of the Christian system. When James was slain, Stephen stoned, Peter and John thrown into prison, and the disciples driven from Jerusalem, all appeared dark and gloomy: but a new impetus was given to the work.

A few years since, *our* church sent its first missionary to Liberia. The church was enthusiastic. A few months passed and tidings came that our devoted missionary was sleeping in the sands of the African coast. Depression followed and we felt that the African mission was buried in the grave of Cox. But his dying cry "Let a thousand fall rather than Africa be given up," roused the church, and the mission lives and prospers. "God buries his workmen but carries on his work."

The early part of the struggle for freedom in Holland was mostly sustained by the personal efforts and influence of William, Prince of Orange. Others faltered and failed; he stood firm. Others despaired; he was confident, and by his zeal and perseverance he conducted the nation through long years of conflict, until the hope of Holland's freedom became bright and cheering. Yet, when the dagger of the assassin struck his heart, as it has now reached the heart of our President, it seemed the knell of every hope. The feeling of Holland has been paralleled only by ours. But God raised up other agents to complete the work he had so nobly prosecuted, and, although he lived not to see it, Holland was free.

So will it be in *our* case. The Lord Jehovah liveth and will provide other agents in the place of him who has fallen. The officers of our army failed, but God raised up Grant and Sherman and Sheridan. He can as easily provide *statesmen*.

Then let us trust in the Lord, for in him is *everlasting* strength. Enemies may strike down princes, but cannot palsy the arm Divine. The late President shall not see it, but God will carry the nation through.

"All things work together for good to them who love God, to them who are the called according to his purpose." Hath not God chosen this nation, and will he desert it now? Is it not a Christian country, doing more for men than any other on the earth, and will he suffer it to be destroyed? Never! But this our fair republic, under the protection of Heaven, shall long remain, a blessing to mankind and a model for the world.*

* The sermon of which the above is a sketch, was in the main extemporaneous. In a note to the editor, the writer says :— "Many

Sermon Preached in the African Methodist Episcopal Zion Church.

BY REV. JACOB THOMAS.

Know ye not that there is a prince and a great man fallen this day in Israel? — 2 SAMUEL, iii, 38.

My friends, we meet at this hour with sad hearts. We have been stricken. The blow has fallen heavily upon us, and a nation mourns to day. Truly a prince and a great man in Israel has fallen. We cannot but weep bitter tears that so great and good a man as Abraham Lincoln, has been cut down in the midst of his usefulness by a death so cruel. At the moment he was about to realize the great results of his four years labor, just as victory had perched upon our banners, he fell a martyr to freedom. We shall never look upon his like again.

A few days ago joy and gladness filled every heart. All who were loyal to the government rejoiced and gave thanks to Almighty God because of the victory won, the downfall of the rebel capital. This intelligence was too glorious to be unalloyed. Ere our joy had subsided, sorrow overtook us. News reached us from Washington of the bloody deed perpetrated there. We would not believe it. It could not be

of the thoughts were suggested by the excitement of the hour, and cannot now be recalled. I have, therefore, simply copied the brief supplying such additions and explanations only, as were necessary to make it intelligible."

possible that a creature in the form of man could be found so God-forsaken, as to take the life of the man who had malice for none but charity for all! The hours between the first rumor and the confirmation of the report, were hours of dreadful suspense. But the truth came at last. There was no longer room for doubt. It was too true, that on last Friday evening, whilst enjoying at a place of amusement a few moments of relaxation from toil, accompanied by his wife and a few friends, unconscious of danger near, he was brutally murdered—shot down by the cowardly hand of an assassin. Palsied be the tongue, withered be the arm of the guilty, execrable wretch who committed this, the blackest of all crimes. Yes, our dear President is no more. The beloved of his country, the father and friend of the oppressed, the champion of universal freedom, has fallen a victim to southern malice and revenge. Kind heaven weeps to-day over the bloody spectacle.

We, as a people, feel more than all others that we are bereaved. We had learned to love Mr. Lincoln as we have never loved man before. We idolized his very name. We looked up to him as our saviour, our deliverer. His name was familiar with our children, and our prayers ascended to God in his behalf. He had taught us to love him. The interest he manifested in behalf of the oppressed, the weak and those who had none to help them, had won for him a large place in our heart. It was something so new to us to see such sentiments manifested by the chief magistrate of the United States that we could not help but love him. Is it to be wondered at that we mourn to-day? Nay, we have seen old gray-headed men and young maidens weep because of this affliction. Had disease attacked him and he had passed away according to the natural course of nature, we could have consoled ourselves with the thought that it was God's will it should be so. But falling as he did by the hand of the wicked, we derive our consolation only from the assurance that by his uprightness, his honesty and his principles of Christianity, he is now enjoying that rest that remains for the just.

Our text is a fitting one for the occasion. A great man has fallen. From whatever stand-point we view Mr. Lincoln, we find in him the marks of true greatness. A few years ago this plain, homely lawyer was scarcely known outside of his own state. But how soon did he become the point of attraction. Not only was he the centre of observation in this country, but the civilized world was watching him. He far exceeded the expectations of all men. He became as the ark of safety to his country, the praise and glory of his fellow men. To us as a despised people, he was a second Moses — a second Daniel in wisdom. From a humble position in life he reached the very summit of honor, occupied the highest seat that it was in the power of the American people to give him, and filled that seat as no man ever filled it before him. The mind that conceived and drew up the Proclamation of Emancipation was a great mind. The results of this grand deed are patent to all. He was a philanthropist in the most extensive sense of the word — benevolent, kind, and ever ready to make others happy. One of the most prominent features in the character of our departed friend was his merciful disposition even towards his foes. He was strictly honest; this is admitted by his worst enemies. "Honest Abe," he was familiarly called by all classes. He was honest with his people, honest to himself, honest to his God. This is what God requires of all men, to be honest in heart. The exterior of this great man may have been plain, homely and awkward, but the interior was beautifully finished and furnished with Christian graces. It was his reliance upon God that carried him safely through the storm of four years duration. It was this that has made him blessed in the favor of God, forever.

Yes, Abraham Lincoln is no more, and we mingle our tears with those of the mourning widow and bereaved friend. We feel that in his loss our punishment is more that we can bear, yet in God is our consolation. Let us hope for the best. An all-wise God has permitted this great grief to come upon us. Let us look to him for deliverance in the time of our distress. We are humbled, we are mortified, we are brought very low. Our trust must be in God. Whilst we mourn, he whose death we deplore, is enjoying the reward of his labor, happy with his God, mingling with those kindred spirits who went before him. The two truest and greatest men that ever lived on earth, John Brown and Abraham Lincoln, have met in glory, and they cease not to give praise and honor to him that liveth forever and ever. The memory of Abraham Lincoln will ever be dear to us. It is engraved upon our hearts. It can never be effaced. He has been our true friend and we never can forget him. We feel as though God had raised him up for a special purpose, and that having accomplished the labor assigned him, he has gone to his rest. May God protect us and keep us from farther evils.

SERMON PREACHED IN THE SECOND PRESBYTERIAN CHURCH, ON SUNDAY MORNING.

BY REV. D. S. GREGORY.

The Lord God Omnipotent reigneth. — REVELATION, xix, 6.

One thought to-day fills every heart. God has sent us a subject for our solemn consideration. To-day there is a nation mourning. I have seen the strong man pass along these streets of the city weeping like a child. The transition from the highest joy to the profoundest sorrow has been so sudden, so instantaneous, that it has left a nation with a broken heart and closed mouth. It seems almost better to be silent to-day in these sanctuaries and let God speak. He has never spoken so before to any people. In the capital of this nation there lies dead this morning one who but yesterday was the honored and beloved ruler of this land. But it is not simply that a president is dead. Other and honored presidents of this republic have been called from the places of state to the great account and no such mourning been witnessed as fills the land to-day. One has fallen now, who more than any other, was identified with this grand struggle in which we have been engaged for these four years, — one who was strangely designated by God to take the lead among us, and who had honestly and nobly and unselfishly done his work, and quietly found his place in the nation's heart. This man has been removed in a moment by an assassin's hand, and his chief counsellor lies unconscious, a victim to the same fiendish spirit, which hoped in that one hour to reach also the life of the leader of our hosts.

It was a blow aimed at the nation and which sought in an hour to destroy the work of these years, and to stay the onward march of truth and justice. Ah, vain thought! There is one upon the throne who rules all things and who cannot be reached by the murderous bullet or the assassin's dagger! "*The Lord God Omnipotent reigneth,*" and truth and justice shall prevail! What other refuge have we to-day? What other consolation in this our national bereavement? It is a dark day, but "the Lord God Omnipotent reigneth." Let us dwell upon the thought, that our faith in God's truth, in God's justice, and in God's love may not be shaken by this our national calamity.

1st. Our faith in this Great Ruler and His government assures us, that not one word of His truth uttered among this people can fall to the ground.

The great King who is above all presidents, has all along the history of this nation, been uttering among us and through us to the world with peculiar clearness, His proclamation of truth and universal freedom. Our pilgrim forefathers built upon *God's word of freedom* at the first, and our fathers on that memorable day of 1776 made this same word of freedom the basis of their "Declaration," and, again, in later years made it the foundation of the national constitution. They proclaimed freedom for man *in the name of God*, but they were merely instruments in His hands whose word they proclaimed. It was but His repeated proclamation of His word of emancipation to man. Whatever else awaits us we know that He who has made these utterances is omnipotent. Yes, there is omnipotence in every word of God uttered among men.

The *efficiency*, the *omnipotence*, the *almightiness of God's word*, are expressions that sound strangely to us perhaps, for with us words are but the breath shaped and made articulate, and then, to all appearance, dying away on the air. There is nothing which seems at first thought more fleeting and powerless than our words. And even when we rise above this first thought and consider man's words of eloquence, sent, with aid of logic and rhetoric, out of the depths of one human soul aroused to the highest pitch of feeling and enthusiasm, into another such soul, to rouse and kindle it and stir it to its profoundest depths,— there is nothing like omnipotence about it all. There is nothing in its power but the working of plain, rational, moral and æsthetic principles. It is truth instructing, motive swaying, beauty delighting, and emotion exciting. And so far as we see the outward workings of God's words, there seems to be nothing more in them than in these words of power which man utters. We know that the most eloquent words of the orator in legislative halls, or in the forum, or on the rostrum, fail to attain in most cases, even with the use of all these means, what he who utters them desires. To look at the matter outwardly it seems as if these words of God fail in the same way and are almost equally powerless. But notwithstanding all this seeming, God's written revelation brings before us the *omnipotence of God's word* of promise and grace. It presents it as differing from all human words in this, that it infallibly and unerringly works what God sends it to accomplish. Every word of God is the *expression of a Divine force* in man or in the universe. Whatever its mission it knows no failure. God is with it.

The prophet Isaiah illustrates this infallible efficiency of God's word in its relation to the church and to man *by one of the great processes of nature.* He represents the rain and the snow as descending from heaven, doing their work and returning again to the heavens only when it is finished, and God declares that His word goes thus out of His mouth and returns only when it has done that for which it was sent. To the careless observer the rain and the snow might seem to fall upon the earth and to sink into its bosom and perish. It is not so. Every drop, every little crystal has its circuit by which it returns to the heavens as inevitably as the earth returns to its place in its orbit at its appointed season. In running its round each accomplishes its own work. No atom returns to its place without having completed that to which it was appointed. It returns not to heaven till it "has watered the earth, and made it bear and put forth, and has given seed to the sower and bread to the eater."

To the human eye the rain-drop and the snow-crystal fall carelessly upon mountain or valley, but that is not the end of their work. One drop on the mountain sinks into the pores in the granite or limestone. God meets it as His messenger with the frost, and thus breaks off an atom of the rock here and there. Another drop falls upon these little atoms and gathers them up in its bosom. God meets it as His messenger with the might of gravitation and bears the water and the lime-rock down the mountain into the valley to unite with the drops that have fallen there, in enriching and moistening the valley soil. There in the lowlands they hold dissolved the rich treasures of the earth which are needed to make seed for the sower and bread for the eater. God meets one of these drops as His messenger with the forces of capillary attraction and vegetable life in the roots of the wheat, and the drop with its freight is drawn up into the plant and in due time sent out into the grains, and when it has deposited all its load, it passes out at the pores of the plant and up again into the heavens to do a like work when God shall send it forth once more as the rain-drop or the snow-crystal. It has at last left the wheat ready for the harvest, and returned to the place whence it came, but it has finished its work first. No atom of it all is lost. We cannot trace it all, but it all does its work, and its return to its place is inevitable, because God's word of omnipotence has sent it and His hand of omnipotence directed it. Just so *the word of God uttered among men* has its inevitable circuit, and never fails to do its appointed work before it returns to Him whose mouth first spoke it. That word shall accomplish its mission just as certainly as the rain-drop. The King upon the throne of the universe directs all the wisdom and power of His government to this end. While the Lord God Omnipotent reigns His word must be a power in the world.

With men there is always a distinction between *speaking* and *doing*. The greatest talkers are often the most insignificant and worthless workers. The man who is full of plans, and who is always proclaiming them and preparing grand machinery with which to execute them, is often in effect the veriest idler, doing nothing, or at best doing nothing as it should be done. It sometimes seems as if there were very little connection between man's words and his deeds. But there is nothing of this with God. With Him speaking and doing are one. Whatever He speaks He speaks in omnipotence. With Him to promise is to perform. The work of creation is the omnipotent working of God's word. So of the works of providence and redemption. The word of creation and the work of creation, the word of providence and the work of providence, the word of redemption and the work of redemption, are not to be set apart as our human words and works.

Take an example. This vast *creation is but an embodiment of God's word.* The apostle Peter in the 3d chapter of his 2d epistle, teaches that " *by the word of God* the heavens were of old, and the earth standing out of the water and in the water." "He spake and it was done. He commanded and it stood fast." It carries us back in imagination into that limitless past. There was a day when the earth had no existence, when the sun and the planets had as yet no being. There was a day when no comet winged its way with lightning speed around yonder sun, because comet and sun as yet were not. There was a time—I will not call it a *day*, for there were no days then—when not even one lonely star shot its rays across immensity. Empty space — mighty infinitude of empty space! Had there been a creature to send out a greeting into that mighty deep, no echo would have come back from that infinite waste, but that one of "God! God! God!" God everywhere and God alone!

The momentous hour appointed in the counsels of eternity came and God's *word of creation* was spoken. It said to the worlds "Be" and they were. From non-existence and nothingness came every atom of the universe into being, and, as He uttered yet again word upon word, beauty and order took their place everywhere. The earth and the moon whirled round their centre, and with all the planets and comets round. the sun, their hundreds and thousands of millions of miles. And our sun with its train, with the myriad suns of our star-system with their trains, circled round Alcyone in their orbits of millions of millions of miles. And star-mass after star-mass infinite in number, scattered throughout the universe to the immeasurable distances of its remotest bounds, commenced around the great centre of all motion those movements only to be measured by the endless cycles of eternity. It was the simple *word of God* that gave them all being, and sent them on their awful way, clothing them with beauty and peopling them with living and intelligent things. Look out upon it all! Gird up your imagination for a flight from sun to sun, and star to star, and system to system, and star-mass to star-mass, until you are overwhelmed with a sense of your nothingness and its infinitude. Remember then that all this is only *God's word* — one utterance of His lips! "He commanded and it stood fast."

Now God's *word of freedom* proclaimed to man is not, as we too often think, so much empty breath. It is the same omnipotent word that works at one time instantaneously, as in creation, and then again slowly and through the ages, as in providence. God reigns, an absolute sovereign, and every one of His utterances is the expression of a Divine force in His vast realm, and whether working without time or with time, works its results infallibly and with almighty power. It cannot fail, because it is the word of omnipotence and omnipotence cannot fail. The gospel proclamation of freedom to man is working out His purpose among men just as certainly and just as irresistibly as the rain-drop fulfils its mission, or as electricity, or gravitation, or any one of these great forces of nature, its mission.

It seems a sad day for us who have been watching through these years the progress of God's truth among this people. The powers of darkness against which His word has been making its way so steadily and so grandly for these generations, until the nation's proclamation had come to be at one with God's proclamation, seem to have roused themselves and gathered up their energies for one last fiendish effort to stay that resistless march of truth over the nations and through the ages. Vain, wholly vain! Whatever betide, God's word has gone forth to the nation, and that cannot fail. See what it has already done for human freedom. One man has stood forth before the world as the representative of these great Divine principles. To-day he is gone, and you may sweep away all such men, and the grand principles will still remain the same.

Through whatever throes the nation may pass, though the land from east to west, and from north to south be again drenched in blood, and all our great ones be called to sleep with him who has already gone to his last sleep, God's word of freedom will still be doing its almighty work in its myriad ways, and, when these human eyes are blinded with tears, even when lost to human sight and almost to human faith, it will still be working irresistibly as ever toward the ushering in of the day of His glory. "The Lord God omnipotent reigneth." Not one word of His shall fall to the ground. This nation shall be regenerated; man, made in Gods image, shall be freed from his bondage and lifted up from his debasement; and we shall be crowned with God's richest blessings. The day hastens on apace when we shall proclaim to the world that the time of freedom and blessing is come, and when the voice of all nations shall respond with a shout of joy and exultation "Alleluia, The Lord God omnipotent reigneth."

2d. Our faith in this Great Ruler and His government assures us, of the triumph of His justice.

Justice is one of the grandest principles in God's government. He is Himself just, always just, and in all His ways there is never the slightest departure from justice. There is no yielding of justice even to love. The one principle which runs through His mighty realm of the universe is "An eye for an eye and a tooth for a tooth." There is never any departure from it there. He embodied this stern idea of justice in that Jewish constitution, which in its fundamental principles is the model for all time, "An eye for an eye and a tooth for a tooth." He has not departed one hairbreadth from it even in the work of redemption. When Christ was sent forth to die for lost sinners, love did not put justice away but found in the Incarnate Son a satisfaction to justice, so that in Jesus, God is both "merciful and just to forgive us our sins," is "just, and yet the justifier of the ungodly." Everywhere His justice reigns. It may seem at times as if there were no just Ruler in the world, none to uphold eternal justice. Things may seem to go all wrong, but it is not so, can not be so while God reigns. With the *individual* the account may not be strictly balanced here, for there is for him a resurrection from the dead, a judgment beyond the grave, a final and eternal adjustment of the great account. Not so with the *nation*. Its account will be settled here. There is no resurrection of the dead nation. When it goes down in the tide of time it is gone forever—body and soul. Its name may still remain. Historians and orators may speak and poets sing its praises, and the mighty wave of influence which sums up the power of all its living thoughts, and words, and deeds, shall doubtless roll out into the utmost bounds of space and down toward the remotest shores of the ocean of eternity, but the *nation*, the body politic itself, sleeps a sleep that knows no waking. The judgment trump will not disturb it. It shall summon no ghost of departed empire or state to appear before the great judge. Cæsars and Napoleons will be there, but only as men; their thrones and sceptres shall have perished. Kings and presidents will be there, but only as men; their glory and their power shall have faded. They shall be there with the sins of the emperor and king and president on their heads, but with nothing but their manhood before God. Not the highest and mightiest of them all, shall bear up with him the lost and dead state restored to life.

This earth itself is the scene of *national judgment:* the scene of national reward as well as of national retribution. God appears in history judging the nations and dispensing strict justice among them. "Behold He cometh to judge the earth." "He shall judge the earth with righteousness." As He executed judgment upon Moab and Ammon and Edom and Philistia, cutting off man and beast, visiting their coasts with desolation, that they might not be remembered among the nations, so has He been executing judgment upon the nations in all time, blotting one by one out of existence as their measure was filled.

That day when the trump of God shall sound and the archangel's voice rend the heavens and shake the earth with his "Come up to judgment," will be a day of awful grandeur to one who from afar off can behold the rolling up of these heavens and the melting of this solid globe, and see the whirling dust of the myriads of the dead small and great, as it is gathered from earth and ocean and hurried up—up by the arm of Omnipotence, while still fashioning into bone and sinew and nerve and flesh, to where the thrones of judgment are set. But had I the imagination, I could portray a scene of like, if not equal grandeur as it passes day by day before that eye of Omniscience which takes in all things in one vision, on this great theatre of the world in the judgment of the nations. There is that same Eternal Judge, that same eternal law of righteousness. The trumpet, which summons to that judgment, is the gathered thunder of the providences which have startled the nations in all time, and that judgment is the history of this world for all those ages which are but as one instant to God. Wrecks of nations, instead of the dust of men, are hurried up to that throne to be consumed from before His presence or hurried away into oblivion.

In the light of this thought, the events in the career of a nation, acquire a new significance as well as a new importance. The hand of the Great Ruler is there dispensing judgment, and we know that nothing shall go counter to the eternal principles of His justice. However dark it may seem, the "Lord God omnipotent reigns." A God of justice is on the throne. For four years we have been looking on, to see the treachery of men in rebellion against a righteous and good government. The wicked have seemed at times to prevail, though scoffing at humanity and scorning the truth and mocking God. This splendid heritage here, whose foundations our fathers laid in God's own truth, whose fair fields and towering bulwarks they watered and cemented with their blood, and which gave such grand promise for the future to our children and to all this great, lost, wailing humanity, whose cry comes up from the bondage of all lands,— this princely heritage we have seen desolated, that law which is of God we have seen defiled, these altars we have seen desecrated, these million watching, aching eyes we have seen filled with tears, and these myriad broken hearts with anguish. God has been looking upon the treachery of treacherous ones, and the all-just One has seemed standing by silently, with His robe of omnipotence put off, while the wicked has devoured the man that is more righteous than he, and while His people have been crying in agony day and night "How long? Hath God forgotten?"

And now again, just as the light seemed breaking and Jehovah taking His place of justice once more, the land has to day been shrouded in deeper darkness by this most horrible murder of modern times, which has taken from us our beloved and honored Chief Magistrate. Again and more bitterly are we disposed to cry "How long? Hath God forgotten?" He has seemed so slow in the fulfilment of His promises and in the execution of His threatenings. His justice and his omnipotence have seemed so to stand aside while the wicked have wrought their pleasure in the nation. But the Eternal God of justice is on his throne yet, and I hear a voice saying "Take courage. Do things seem to you to go all wrong? Does it seem to you at times that wickedness prospers and prevails? Does God seem to hide His face when you cry, while the old landmarks are removed, and the old and strong foundations are broken up? Is He, the great judge of all the earth, slow in visiting transgression? Take courage. God is on the throne. He only seems to you to wait. Even this seeming delay is full of the mercy of God." "What if some did not believe? shall that make the faith of God of none effect?" Nay, rather, every threatened judgment of God shall meet with perfect and complete fulfilment in due season, in that hour which God sees best for us and best for the world and best for his own great glory.

> "His purposes will ripen fast,
> Unfolding every hour."

Remember that while here the faith and patience of the steadfast in this nation are being tried, and yonder the wicked are treasuring up wrath against the day of wrath, the Lord God omnipotent is above all, working out His own mighty purposes of salvation in His own wise and infinitely grand and sublime way, and believe that He in His justice is "not slack as some men count slackness." Oh, in that great final day it will appear that God was not too slow for the rebellious, not too slow for the treacherous and the scoffer, aye, and above all, not too slow for the good and the glory of His own beloved! Eternal justice shall everywhere prevail, for the "Lord God Omnipotent reigneth," and works as truly in the darkness as in the light.

3d. Our faith in this great Ruler and His government assures us, that it shall be well with those who have God's truth and justice on their side. God's *love* shall prevail no less than His justice.

In the darkness do we know that it will be well with us? Yes, O yes!

> "I cannot always trace the way
> Where thou, Almighty One, dost move;
> But I can always, always say,
> That God is love, that God is love."

Can it be so to day, as this stricken nation weeps? Is it for the *best?* Is it in love to those who hold by God's truth and justice? It almost seems to us in our blindness as if it could not be! We are overwhelmed when we think of the awful event! Taken when we least thought of it and in so horrible a way!

Well may the nation mourn! The man is gone, who, acknowledged or unacknowledged, has been the great earthly leader in this mighty life and death struggle of the nation, the man whom God seemed so strangely to designate for the place,—gone just after the voice of the people had given their approval to his general course in the past by calling him to the presidency for a second term,—gone when, by his honesty and integrity, he had won the hearts of the men, who most differed with him,—gone in the hour of triumph, when the symbol of national authority had just been restored again to wave forever over the chief stronghold of a godless rebellion, and the mightiest army of that rebellion had just been ground to powder by Almighty justice,—gone in the hour when the blood and tears and groans of these millions had knit the nation's heart to his as to none before but the sainted Washington,—gone in the hour of his greatest magnanimity, when his mighty heart had been opened to receive even traitors back to fellowship,—gone just four years from the first attack upon the nation's life at Sumter, and on the very day that the emblem of authority, justice and liberty had been restored again to wave forever over that same Sumter,—and gone too by foul conspiracy which struck at the heart of the nation by murder in cold blood, the very fitting embodiment of the spirit of secession, the *spirit of murder*,— gone by a crime such as heaven has not looked upon in these modern ages since the crucifixion! What wonder that the nation mourns! Can such a thing be well? Can there be love or mercy in such a thing? "No, no, it cannot be"— our hearts would say. But when we look at God's ways with us, and remember that God reigns, we must say by faith "Yes, it is *well.*" "It is *best*. God has done it."

We can look back over these four years now and see how God has led us. It has not been in our ways. If we could have made the history, there would have been no Bull Run, and therefore, no Donelson and Vicksburg and Chattanooga and Atlanta, no peninsular campaign, no Antietam, no Gettysburg, no Wilderness, no Petersburg and Richmond, none of this blood and tears and wailing, and no human proclamation of freedom to man. But God has made it otherwise. If man could have had his way we should to-day, by the reach of this plot, which has taken our Chief Magistrate, have been left rulerless, leaderless, statesmanless. God reigns, and the very day that has taken so much has proved to us by saving so much, that, while God's truth prevails and God's justice triumphs, it shall all be well with us if we hold fast our faith in Him. Let us bow in His presence then to-day, and, while we acknowledge His right to reign, confess by faith that He does all things well.

But as the nation mourns, let it ask anxiously, "Why has God done it?" It would be vain to try to shut our eyes to the fact that we are a different people to-day from what we were on the morning of yesterday. The almost slumbering sense of justice has been aroused, and one mighty yearning for vengeance has gone up to heaven from a sorely tried, long forbearing and much forgiving nation. The thought of the Christian heart of this land and its stern determination is that there shall henceforth be no more talk of that *weak* mercy which would call upon our rulers to override all the principles of eternal justice to save the lives of men who are a million times murderers. I do but read the thoughts of men everywhere when I say it.

But let the nation, while it stands by God's justice, beware of passion to-day, and, while this sad event is fixing in the depths of the heart, the truth, that by the principles of God's word, the forgiveness, by the national authorities, of those political leaders whose hands are so dyed in blood, would be a crime against the present and the future — against the living and the dead — against humanity and against God, — let every thing like personal enmity and vindictiveness be put away, while we go forward to the right in God's name. And if these tears do but nerve the nation *to mingle a wise justice with a wise love* it shall be found at the great day of final reckoning that they have not been in vain. But oh, above all, whatever befall, let us believe that "the Lord God Omnipotent reigneth!"

SERMON PREACHED IN THE UNITARIAN CHURCH.

BY REV. E. BUCKINGHAM.

The preacher is incapable of adequate speech, in the midst of the feelings with which the community is oppressed. He can do no more on such an occasion, than make the attempt to interpret our own thoughts to us, or rather to interpret to us the thoughts with which God is visiting us. Many common expressions of truth at once present themselves to our minds, as that "good is to come out of evil," that "God's providence is over all," that "our country is safe with God," that "we bow with submission before him." Such sentiments are almost universal. Public proclamations and common conversations, the newspapers and the churches speak them; they are in the hearts of the people.

Yet they do not forbid the heaviness of the heart. They cannot prevent our amazement and terror, our wondering of mind and wandering of thought, our sense of bereavement and affliction. Our suffering is not national only, but personal as well. We shudder at the crime, its treachery and its violence; the hatred and malice of it; the contempt for the country and of its millions shown in it; the contempt for the voices of the wise and of the multitudes. We shudder at the dreadful impiety of it. The scene and circumstance add to the acuteness of the pain with which we are overwhelmed. In the midst of his family, in innocent festivities which he had attended only from kindly motives, out of regard for the wishes of his neighbors and fellow-citizens, in a moment, the President was taken out of life. No farewell was allowed to wife and children; no farewell to his countrymen; no opportunity was given for a last expression of his wishes and his love. It would have been awful had he been a hereditary ruler, imposed on the people,—if he had been a man of unhappy character, from whom the people were alienated. But he had the confidence of the nation; probably no ruler in the world ever enjoyed the confidence of his people in so great a degree. We trusted in his integrity, his calmness, his wisdom, his kindness.

He was one of us; we all felt that he belonged to us. It was not that he was born in a condition of life from which the great majority derive their origin, or that he had tried poverty and labor with the humblest, and so might be disposed to understand the lot of the people, and know how to sympathize with them. It was his nature to be one with humanity, and the elevation of his office, the immensity of his responsibilities, and the laboriousness of his cares never at all diminished in his heart the sense of being one with the people. Their sorrows and their joys, their dangers and their security he felt as his own. He was to them as a member of their families and as an individual friend.

Few persons in the world, comparatively, have ever shown in an equal degree this sense of the common humanity. Robert Burns, the poet of the poor, who sung their humble griefs, their humble virtues or happiness; John Wesley, the preacher of the poor, who went to find them and sought them out, and bore the gospel of salvation to them, were men of like disposition. And when we have called to mind a few such, as literature, religion, or statesmanship recount them to us, we find no more who can be said to resemble our President, till we reach the apostles, in their large and tender hearts, or ask if such sense of human sympathy was not the peculiar element in the loveliness of Jesus Christ. Where, in history beside, do we find among the great and exalted such simplicity, such naturalness, such fullness and tenderness of heart, as in the sublime speech of Mr. Lincoln at Gettysburg? his personal letter to the centenarian voter at Sturbridge? the letters which he wrote from his high position to the humble bereaved, whose afflictions were brought to his notice? and in his manners and expressions to the wounded, sick and suffering, when he chanced to meet them, or walked through the hospital to give his personal thanks and the thanks of the nation to them for the patriotism and fidelity which they had exhibited?

We couple his name with that of Washington. None greater than Washington, it is the national belief, has appeared in the course of history; and the careful thinkers and patriot minds of other nations unite with us in our estimate. But exalted as was the personal character of Washington, we feel that our nation has been immeasurably blessed in the grandeur of two men, who stand equally among the greatest and best of the world. It is singular how deeply into society, the love for Mr. Lincoln penetrates. His name was dear in the family circle. Little children knew and loved it. A whole race of our fellow-men, under the Providence of God, owned him as their benefactor and father. He gave them life. He changed them to men. He gave them wives and husbands, parents and children. He gave them liberty to say "father" and "mother." He consecrated marriage to them, and permitted them to speak of home. He gave them prospects and hopes, and the enjoyment of blessed liberty. I do not ask, whether another in similar circumstances might not have done the same, or have done it at an earlier day, or in some more striking manner. Mr. Lincoln did it not as a statesman only, but as a man. He did it with his heart.

I shall not ask what his place was among the historical statesmen of the world, nor whether he was a great man, beyond his goodness, nor in what intellectual abilities or force of character especially he was great. Partly because the age is not ready for the discussion, as we must remove to some distance in order to estimate magnitude; nor is it necessary in our admiration, love and sorrow, to attempt the measure of his power. And partly, also, because only the great can comprehend the great. A clown cannot comprehend a Newton. Pontius Pilate could not comprehend Jesus Christ. History, alone, in the course of ages, can find authority to give the verdict of greatness.

Mr. Lincoln had borne his honors modestly and simply. He had not used them for his avarice or his ambition. He made no personal enemies in the bestowal of office, in the irritation of those to whom office was denied, through their conviction that it was bestowed for the furtherance of sinister ends of his own. He fell under no suspicion of using his high position for selfish objects; his office through him incurred no such contempt. He governed, or rather, with singular truth it may be said, he served, not according to his own wisdom, but according to the wishes of the people, whose servant he was, as he carefully made himself acquainted with them. We never felt that he was imposing on us. He was not using, contrarily to our will, the power we had intrusted to him. We found in him no special theories or abstractions, in pride of which he was pursuing his own way. He followed out no cold and heartless logic, to which the people must succumb. He indulged in no conceits. He indulged in no self-will. For such reasons, we confided in him and loved him.

And in estimating the will of the people, that he might guide his action in accordance with it, it is remarkable how he did not consider alone, as public sentiment, the expressions of men in public station, nor influential newspapers, nor resolutions of conventions only. He saw a public mind, a popular will beyond all these. Nor was it alone the momentary expressions of public will, that he considered as public sentiment, from whatever sources they might be found to originate. He seems sometimes to have seen into men's sentiments more deeply than they saw themselves. He seems, with more than usual depth of insight, to have looked into human hearts in order to find therein the will of God. In man, he reverenced the voice of God; and, in his knowledge of God, he sought more clearly to read the thought of human nature, the general conscience, the universal and the final will.

In our overwhelming sadness, we say, "it is the worst news since the war begun." In a sense it is so. It appears to our hearts as in many ways the most horrible. Yet we trust it is not so bad for the nation, as great defeats in war would have been. It cannot be thought to be so bad, as treason of parties and states; nor so injurious as the foreign sympathy which has been so largely given to the cause of the rebellion; nor as the intervention of foreign powers and their recognition of the Confederate States would have been. The nation lives. The common idea that nations depend on individuals, and that their places, when vacated, cannot be supplied, history does not sustain. Among the modern discoveries of science, none is more remarkable, and perhaps none better established than this, that the course of nations has its order and its law, and that God is working out, through all apparently accidental changes, still, his vast designs. The death of Julius Cæsar is a scarcely noticeable event in the course which the Roman people and empire were pursuing. It wrought no greater freedom to the aristocracy or the populace; it excited no further war; the national prosperity was not destroyed by it. When Marat died under the dagger of Charlotte Corday, the French Revolution became none the less sanguinary and horrible. Charles the first died his violent death, but tyranny did not die with him. Louis the sixteenth was also put to a violent end, but royalty lived in the hearts or the genius of the French people, and after a brief period again revived. Henry the fourth died by the hand of an assassin, but the Roman and the Protestant faith alike survived. Many more rulers and prime ministers have died by assassination. But nations are not subject to the dagger of an assassin, and the life of a nation is not concentrated into the life of an individual. The vitality of a nation, we have learned, is in the hearts of the people; in their private morals, in their schools for popular education, in their domestic virtues, in the religion which they believe in, in the liberty they love. The progress of our own nation has not been retarded in its essential elements, by the conspiracy that aimed originally at its life, and the war by which it has striven to maintain its existence; no more can it be, by the individual hand that again sought its destruction by taking away the life of its chosen, its trusted and beloved ruler.

The lives of great men work more after death than during life. "Being dead, he yet speaketh" is true of all. The shadows of great men reach far down the ages; or rather, the light with which they shine, and the inspiration which their genius and virtues transmit, are found increasing often as the ages pass. The moral character, the elemental ideas of Cæsar, Alexander and Napoleon, are a living power in the world at the present day. Jesus was more felt at Jerusalem, and through the world, when the disciples and the people could no longer look upon his outward form, and fear and malice had succeeded in silencing his outward utterance. Whether it be through 'natural' causes, so understood, or 'supernatural' means, men live in their influence after death with more efficiency for the world, than during the continuance of their mortal life. The great and good are never nearer in spiritual power, than when they seem finally to have gone away from us. They impress the world more deeply by their wisdom; their counsels are better heeded; their virtues are more admired and more carefully and successfully imitated. The spirit that God has once sent into the world, he seems never to take away from it. The mortal dies and is seen no more; the family and the world are never, in the workings of Divine providence, bereaved of the good God has once bestowed upon them. It multiplies with every year; succeeding ages only find it greater still.

And while we are now overcome with the most poignant grief in the sudden loss which we have sustained, it seems to be the general conviction, that Mr. Lincoln's work on earth was done. The war, immense as it was, is finished. The nation is essentially at peace. If we undertake to review the greatness of the work he has accomplished, we cannot measure it. We can only compare it with great religious movements, with the Reformation, or with the establishment of Christianity itself. This new organization of liberty deserves to be set side by side with no less important events in the progress of humanity. Which is greater, the present, or the first American Revolution, some might hesitate to decide. By the proclamation of freedom, Mr. Lincoln opened one half of our land to the people, to liberal institutions, to the new civilization, and to the possibilities of advancing religion, as well as gave liberty to slaves.

His work can never be undone. The nation is safe. Possibly it is safer than in the continuance of his life. He was merciful, and the people treasure up no revenge. He was gentle; he was lenient; was he weak in tenderness? was he too accessible to personal sympathies? was personal friendship, or the power of distinguished names too great in influence over him?

Possibly, the interests of the nation may be safer in the hands of a less forgiving man. Possibly we need the sternness of another mind, which will less readily believe in the possibility of conciliating the perjured and malignant, a man who will entertain a juster fear of the demoniacal spirit which the rebel leaders have shown, and will decide, and help us to decide, that, while we would not hurt a hair of the head of one of them, we yet can never allow them to live in the same land with us, nor, while necessarily remaining, even step on to its soil except under military guard. We have now seen the spirit of the slaveholder in this last outbreak of malignity and wickedness; it is well for us to know the infinitely broad distinction between liberty and slavery, and provide for an eternal separation between them.

Had I chosen a text, as the introduction of my discourse, I should have reminded you how, like Moses, our president has seen the promised land, and overlooked it far and wide, the inheritance of the people, and has not himself been permitted to enter into enjoyment of it. I should have told you how, like the aged Simeon, he might say, Lord, now lettest thou thy servant depart in peace, for mine eyes have seen thy salvation"—or how, also, like the dying Stephen, he would have said, "Lord, lay not this sin to their charge." But texts of written record are unnecessary: Providence speaks directly to our hearts.

And let us not suffer this season of our deep and

agonized feeling to pass without impressing upon our hearts its appropriate lessons, and taking to ourselves most earnest resolutions: The great necessity is, that we should consecrate ourselves with more thoroughness to humanity. The grief of the hour is wide-extended; millions feel it. We feel more deeply than ever, how much our own personal interests are complicated with those of all the world beside. In the face of every man we see a brother. The tears which others shed, are for our loss as well as theirs. And the affliction which has now come upon us all alike, inspires us to feel more truly the private sorrows of those, who, in the events of the war, have consecrated to their country in death the beloved members of their own households. It teaches us more clearly the liability of man to suffer; and calls us to survey with more lively sympathy the sorrows of the race. And long as the dispensation of sorrow shall be an ordinance of God's wise and merciful government, so long must our hearts take to themselves the lesson of sympathy with man.

Especially, in this connection, must we impress our hearts with a sense of justice to the colored race. For their sakes, on account of the position which we, as a nation, have assumed and held in regard to them, we have passed through the terrors of our long-continued war, as we passed for the same reason through long-continued anxieties and miseries that preceded it. We have suffered, terribly suffered, for the course which we have pursued. Do we now intend justice? Do we longer think to save and advance our national welfare by despising and oppressing, or by neglecting the colored race? Have we still no faith in justice? shall we still think, by some indirections, to save ourselves, while we hide from the commandments of God? Have not the judgments of the Almighty been severe, and plain? Let us do our duties; let us with all our hearts and with all faithfulness give liberty and equality to the oppressed, and not tempt judgments more bitter, more dreadful than those which we sustain.

Let us purify our politics. We cannot but call to mind, in the hour of national anguish, how much of baseness and iniquity have characterised the intrigues of politicians; on what worldliness, what earthly expediency, what distrust and denial of everlasting principles of right great parties have based themselves, in their attempts to attain the government of the nation. We do no good with base men. We have no need of them. They mean no good to us. We follow them but to destruction. We corrupt the vital sources of morality in our own hearts, and the sources of national life, while we yield to their influence and follow the guidance of their principles.

Lastly. Now, in the hour, when wickedness has wrought so signal a triumph, has laid the hope of the nation low, and filled the eyes and hearts of all with tears and anguish,—let us consider the final truth,—

that all sin is of the same character. Whatsoever its manifestations, howsoever dreadful its violence or light its appearance, in elementary principle it is all the same. To justify a degree of it in our own hearts, is to justify the worst degree of it in another's. To demand impunity for any sin of our own, whatsoever the apparent reason for indulgence of it, is to give leave for others to riot in demoniacal wickedness. We see in this last enormity of maliciousness, which has laid low a great beloved man, the horrible character, not alone of one man's wickedness, but of sin itself. In every good man's life, in the life and temper of Jesus Christ, we see the beauty and loveliness of that principle which is the opposite of sin. Which do we choose? Whose side, in the universe, do we assume? Now, while our hearts are tenderly affected, deeply impressed, let us renew our vows of consecration to the spirit of holiness and good; let us choose the right, the absolute, eternal right; let us labor with the good and God, for its progress and prevalence over all the world.*

Other Services.

Extemporaneous addresses or remarks having reference to the sad event, were made from almost every other pulpit in the city. Full reports of these have not been preserved, but an abstract of some of them follows.

* This sermon was preached from a brief, and has been written out since it was delivered.

At the First Baptist Church, the pastor, the Rev. Dr. George C. Baldwin read the eighty-ninth psalm, and selected for his text the first fifteen verses of the psalm, in one of which occurs the words, "The north and the south thou hast created them." He spoke of the present affliction as viewed by the light of holy writ and especially of the psalm he had read, wherein the Almighty is praised as the keeper of His covenants with His people, and lauded for the manifestations of His wonderful power. He pictured the effects of rebellion and slavery, paid a faithful tribute to the memory of the late President, and exhorted all, especially the young, to imitate his example in their character and life. Here, as in other churches, the scene was impressive, and sobs of emotion were often audible among the congregation.

The pastor of the North Baptist Church, the Rev. Dr. C. P. Sheldon, read for the morning lesson, a portion of the third chapter of the second book of Samuel, in which the death of Abner is narrated, and in which David laments the loss of his friend in these words, "Thy hands were not bound, nor thy feet put into fetters: as a man falleth before wicked men, so fellest thou." The speaker referred to some of the proofs of the barbarism of slavery, noting especially the assault on Sumner, the firing on the troops of Massachusetts in Baltimore, and finally the tragedy just enacted. He expressed his thankfulness for the constitutional provision determining at once his successor in case of a President's death, and declared his joy that the nation still lives. The sermon of the evening related to the successful progress of the war and the recent victories of the union armies, and in these favors the preacher bade his people recognize the work wrought by the hand of God for this nation.

Respecting the service at Christ Church, the rector, the Rev. J. N. Mulford, in a note says:

"As we met on last Easter Sunday for morning prayer, our hearts were sad with the nation's great affliction.

"Around that day associations of former years cast a feeling of holy joy, and the recollection of the great fact in Christian history which we were called to celebrate would have made it a day of gladness. But every heart was sick and suffering with a wound yet fresh and bleeding. Our great and good President lay dead — slain by the hand of an assassin. Though sad, we did not forget that light from the tomb of Christ shed cheerful rays even into the darkness caused by this event: for there is no page of human sorrow that is not brightened by the power of His resurrection. Therefore, we joined heartily in the services of the day, and sang our Easter chants with thankful, though subdued and chastened feeling.

"In the extempore address, I remember having remarked that this terrible shock which caused our nation to pause in the midst of its triumphal march, would do good if it drew us out of our self confidence to put our trust more in God; that we were thinking too much of our own strength and wisdom in the toil and success of war; that while we could not see the meaning of this dark providence we were compelled to stand still and have faith in God; that two things were as clear as ever, viz:—God was still the ruler of nations—And our faith in Him should be as strong as when we were in the flush of prosperity; that while standing now in the dawn of peace by the body of our fallen leader, we appreciated as not even in the perplexities of war, the splendour of that calm judgment and determined will, that, under God, led us safely through the manifold dangers of the great rebellion; and that to-day, in the sudden and terrible death of President Lincoln, the people were crushed with a sense of sorrow and helplessness, as if the angel that cursed Egypt had slain the first born of every family in this land."

The Easter sermon of the Rev. Dr. J. I. Tucker, at the Church of the Holy Cross, was interspersed with allusions to the calamity the nation had sustained. He enforced the duty of a stronger exercise of religious principle, to enable all men and especially Christian men, to rise above the gloom of the occasion.

At the State Street Methodist Episcopal Church, Rev. Dr. E. Wentworth stated, that he had felt impelled, under an overwhelming sense of the awfulness of the occasion, to lay aside his previously prepared discourse, and devote his thoughts to the one great idea that absorbed the attention of the people—the sudden and tragical death of their Chief Magistrate. He selected as his text the eighth verse of the seventh chapter of Micah:—"*Rejoice not against me, O mine enemy: when I fall, I shall arise; when I sit in darkness, the Lord shall be a light unto me.*"

He commented upon the facts that it was natural to rejoice in the calamities of an enemy and that foreign nations had rejoiced in our calamities, and expressed the belief that men would be found who would even rejoice in this last calamity that carries us back to the crimes of the dark ages. He noticed our successive falls as a nation, and our subsequent recoveries. "Truth and righteousness," said the speaker, "are often crushed, but they rise again. Abraham Lincoln falls, but in falling is exalted to the honors of martyrdom. No name in American history, not even Washington's, will occupy a more conspicuous place than that of Abraham Lincoln. His work is done. Others will finish what he had so nobly commenced and brought so nearly to a glorious termination. We sit in darkness to day, but God is our light. He teaches us in this event, that he will not allow us to trust in an arm of flesh." The speaker in concluding, recited the forty-sixth psalm, beginning "*God is our refuge and strength, a very present help in trouble.*" In the evening he delivered the same sermon in the North Second Street Methodist Episcopal Church.

The Rev. R. R. Meredith, pastor of the North Troy

Methodist Episcopal Church, preached to a crowded audience in the evening, selecting as the basis of his sermon the fifty-third verse of the twenty-second chapter of St. Luke's gospel: "*But this is your hour, and the power of darkness.*" He set before his auditors their duty in this crisis of the nation, and drew inferences from the occurences of the time both appropriate and impressive.

The Rev. Marvin R. Vincent, at the First Presbyterian Church, introduced in a previously prepared sermon on the "Perversion of human judgment," some appropriate allusions to the mournful occasion, citing the foul murder of the President as the crowning illustration of his theme. Looking beyond the mere tool who fired the weapon, to the spirit that prompted the deed, he attributed the deed entirely to slavery.

At the Park Presbyterian Church, the Rev. Alexander Dickson preached in the morning from the twelfth verse of the fourteenth chapter of the gospel of St. Matthew, "*And his disciples came, and took up the body, and buried it, and went and told Jesus.*" In the evening, his discourse was based on these words, "*For he doth not afflict willingly nor grieve the children of men,*" recorded in the thirty-third verse of the third chapter of Lamentations.

In the Roman Catholic churches of the city, the impression produced by the addresses of the respective clergymen, served to temper the jubilant character of the Easter exercises.

At St. Mary's Church a very large congregation assembled at high mass. After the singing of the gospel, the pastor, the Rev. Peter Havermans, ascended the pulpit, and addressed the audience at considerable length and with much earnestness, respecting the public calamity that had befallen the country. He stated that he could not imagine any event that was more to be regretted at this time, than the death of President Lincoln, and that he looked upon his assassination, as one of the greatest crimes that could be committed; that he had no words at his command adequately to give expression to his feelings. "Every one" said the speaker, "is horror-stricken at the tragic deed which has taken place at the capital of the nation. The wickedness of the act is heightened by every aggravating circumstance that can surround crime. The murder was committed on Good Friday, at a public entertainment, given partly as a compliment to the unsuspecting victim, at the moment that the rebellion had been crushed, and at a time when the magnanimity and goodness of the President had begun to be seen and was foreshadowing, as far as the public interest would permit, a lenient disposition toward his rebellious brethren of the south.

"The President's popularity had become so great during the critical time in which he had so wisely and humanely carried on the war, that he had been almost unanimously reelected, and had now succeeded in bringing the war to a close, in a way that challenged the admiration of the world, and promised to this country a future and a destiny exalted and enduring. He had consequently gained the confidence of all parties. His political enemies had become his friends and admirers, and the powers of Europe that had been jealous of us and had indirectly, at least, given ' aid and comfort' to the south, had found, contrary to their expectations, that the American people were able to manage their own affairs, settle their own troubles, and maintain their own government.

"At this moment it is, that a foul plot is formed by cowardly assassins, to blight, if it were possible, the fair hopes of the people, cripple and upset the government, and destroy the very life and existence of the nation, by murdering the President, Vice President and Secretary of state.

"The conspirators hoped, at the very least, to clog the wheels of government and thus produce anarchy and confusion, and to take revenge for the failure of the rebellion not only by the destruction of the heads of the several departments of state to whom the business of the nation is confided, but by inciting internal commotions throughout the entire community. This fiendish plot has succeeded only in part, and the fearful result is the monstrous crime which has astounded us. If then it was ever necessary, it is now, that we should send up our supplications to heaven, and pray for the dear country in which our lot is cast."

In the course of his address, the speaker alluded to

the significant facts that the union army entered Richmond on Palm Sunday, and that the President was assassinated on Good Friday, and concluded by announcing a service in the church, at the hour of the President's funeral, on the Wednesday following.

The Rev. James Keveny, the pastor of St. Peter's Church, during the services of the day, spoke with deep feeling concerning the sad event, and denounced the perpetrators and abettors of the horrid crime in language both stern and affecting.

At St. Joseph's Church, the pastor, the Rev. Aug. J. Thebaud, said in substance, that not only had a great crime been committed but an awful calamity also, had befallen the country, in the cruel and cold-blooded murder of the Chief Magistrate of the American nation. Until the sad news of the President's death was announced, the hearts of all had been filled with joyous expectations of returning peace, but by the intelligence of the lamentable event, the people's fondest hopes were blasted, and God alone could foresee the consequences of the foul deed which deprived the country of its worthy head. He earnestly exhorted the people to pray God to avert from the nation the misfortunes that appeared to threaten it, and to turn everything to its safety and to the people's welfare.

In the discourse of the Rev. James M. Pullman, pastor of the Universalist Church, the speaker paid a touching tribute to the character of the late President, and educed such solemn lessons from his cruel death, as were consonant with the occasion.

Many of the churches were draped with emblems of mourning. In some, these manifestations of grief were confined to the pulpit, but in others, sable trappings and appropriate mourning devices appeared at all prominent points. The booming of cannon from the hill east of the city at half-hour intervals, suggested a striking yet mournful contrast to the solemn stillness that pervaded the streets. The black drapery, waving on the fronts of public buildings and shops and dwellings, together with the partially clouded sky, added to the gloom of the day.

MONDAY, APRIL 17TH, 1865.

As soon as the time for the obsequies of the late President, at Washington, had been determined, Andrew Johnson, the President of the United States, directed the publication of the following

ANNOUNCEMENT.

To the People of the United States:

The undersigned is directed to announce, that the funeral ceremonies of the lamented Chief Magistrate will take place at the Executive Mansion, in this city, at twelve o'clock, noon, on Wednesday, the nineteenth instant.

The various religious denominations throughout the country are invited to meet in their respective places of worship at that hour, for the purpose of solemnizing the occasion with appropriate ceremonies.

(Signed)

W. HUNTER,
Acting Secretary of State.

Department of State, Washington, April 17th, 1865.

THE ASSASSINATION OF PRESIDENT LINCOLN.

BY A. G. JOHNSON.

A great calamity has befallen the nation. The death of Mr. Lincoln will drape the land in mourning, will fill all the people with profound sorrow, and cause everywhere fearful forebodings for the future. Mr. Lincoln had taken strong hold of the affections of the people. No man since Washington, had inspired them with such a feeling of attachment and confidence. It was not the feeling of awe and veneration with which Washington was regarded. It was not the fierce and passionate admiration that Jackson inspired. It was love and respect rather than awe and admiration. He had none of the shining qualities of a popular leader. He was neither handsome in person, nor graceful in manners, nor brilliant in conversation, nor eloquent in speech. But his temper was amiable, his manners were genial and gracious, his talk was pleasant and sensible, and his speeches were unequalled for clearness of statement and logical argument. He was slow in forming opinions, and arriving at conclusions, but sound in judgment, and firm in execution. He was a safe counsellor, a sure guide, a trusty and prudent ruler. What labors he has had to perform! What difficulties to meet and overcome! What cares and perplexities have surrounded him on every side! And how bravely, cheerfully and hopefully he has borne himself through all his labors and trials!

His election was made the pretence and occasion of a rebellion threatening to destroy the life of the nation. He has struggled to quell that rebellion and save his country, and in the hour of his triumph and the nation's salvation, he is stricken by the pistol shot of an assassin. It is sad to reflect that the blow should have been struck, and the time should have been chosen for it, when the peculiar qualities of character for which he was distinguished, were most needed. The people of the north would have heeded his advice, and followed his counsels. The people of the south would have been won by his justice and mercy. Of all men in public life, he was the least under the influence of bad passions. He would not be moved by fear, love, hate or revenge, to swerve from the path of duty. In this time of transition from war to peace, from slavery to freedom, from rebellion to submission, the country had everything to hope from his moderation, his wisdom, his mild and merciful disposition, his conciliatory spirit, his forbearing temper, his readiness to forgive. It did seem as if the country needed just such a man, with gentleness so mingled with firmness, with shrewdness so blended with simplicity, with justice so tempered by mercy, and with a goodness of heart, never ruffled by opposition, never soured by disappointment, and never embittered by hate. He was ever ready to love those that hated him, and to do good to those that despitefully entreated him.

The good man is dead, but the country he has saved will be the monument of his fame. The people will embalm his memory in their hearts. The President is dead, but the nation lives.— *Troy Daily Whig.*

The National Bereavement.

BY W. E. KISSELBURGH.

The horror with which the intelligence of the assassination of the President was received, and the anguish caused by his death throughout the North, are in no wise abated by the few hours which have elapsed since the unwelcome tidings brought their grief to every household. But time enables us more calmly to review the situation, and the effect upon the nation's destiny. Greatly as we mourn our late beloved President, ripe as he was in the experience of the past, and successfully as he has conduct d the nation through four years of dark and desperate peril,— and the last man in the land, as it would appear, we could afford to loose,— we begin to feel that God's good Providence has directed the blow, and that he who doeth all things well, had some.great and beneficial purpose to subserve in the agonizing bereavement which has fallen upon His people. None of us now doubt that Abraham Lincoln was God's chosen instrument to lead the nation through the tribulation of the past. So should we feel that having fulfilled the mission he was sent to perform—living long enough to see the bow of hope span the national horizon, and long enough to disarm malice and hate and envy in the minds and breasts of all — he has been called away to an infinitely better reward and a higher sphere of glory. The maligned, the ridiculed, the insulted man — hated as no man ever was hated — died beloved as no man since Washington ever was loved.

We must take courage from the light of the past. The hand that struck us down will raise us up again. We must gather nearer to the altar of our country than ever before, and more firmly basing the principles of our government upon the everlasting truths of Justice and Liberty, make it what Abraham Lincoln sought to make it, the purest, freest, best on earth. As he fell a martyr to liberty, we must — not in a spirit of blood-thirstiness or revenge — demand an atonement at the hands of those men who struck him down and who have labored to strike down the government of the country. We must not forget that treason has done this work, and in dealing with it, no false considerations for the wounded honor, the fictitious pride of the leaders of the rebellion, must deter us from following the principles of everlasting justice.— *Troy Daily Times.*

The Death of President Lincoln.

BY MRS. E. VAN SANTVOORD.

A Nation's mighty heart
   Throbs with a voiceless woe;
The skies in pity weep,
   The winds are sobbing low.
The gentle stars have veiled their light,
And deep'ning gloom enshrouds the night.

The patriot heart is stilled —
   Stilled by a murderer's hand!
Strong men are bowed in grief,
   And mourning fills the land.
And countless eyes are dimmed with tears,
Sad hearts oppressed with anxious fears.

A few brief days agone
   Bells rang with merry peal;
And brightening omens told
   Our country's future weal;
Flags floated on the sun-lit air,
The night was o'er of our despair.

How changed the joyous scene !
·Now draped in midnight gloom
The stars and stripes *he* loved:—
Oh, plant them o'er his tomb;
Thus may the sacred emblem keep
Sweet vigil o'er his peaceful sleep.

That warm and kindly heart,
It knew no bitter thought;
With hopeful faith and love,
Its deeds of mercy wrought;
It ne'er betrayed our fervent trust.
Our Country guards the hallowed dust!

Troy Daily Times.

April 15, 1865.

COMMON COUNCIL PROCEEDINGS.

SPECIAL MEETING.

Monday Evening, April 17, 1865.

Members Present—Hon. URI GILBERT, Mayor; Hon. JOHN MORAN, Recorder, and Aldermen COX, FALES, FITZGERALD, FLEMING, HAY, HISLOP, HARRITY, KEMP, MCMANUS, MURPHY, MORRIS, NORTON, PRENTICE, SMART, STANTON, STARBUCK, SEARS, STANNARD.

On motion of Alderman Kemp, the customary routine of business was dispensed with. His Honor the Mayor stated the object of the meeting as follows:

"The sudden and awful death of the President of the United States, by the hand of a midnight assassin, has cast a gloom over the nation, clothed every house in mourning, and filled the hearts of the people with grief which words cannot adequately describe. That we may in our corporate capacity, and in behalf of the citizens of Troy, give such public expression to the deep feeling of sadness called forth by this mournful event, which has come upon us at a time when all hearts were rejoicing at the success of our arms, and the prospect of a speedy peace to the nation, we have assembled here this evening to take such action as becomes a bereaved people under such a sad calamity. Gentlemen, the matter is in your hands, and I am confident whatever you propose will be worthy the city and befitting the occasion."

Alderman Kemp offered the following resolutions:

At a time when the heavy hand of national sorrow has been laid upon us like a weary burthen, and the mourning that is in our streets reflects the gloom visible in every countenance, the Common Council of the city of Troy deem it meet and proper to give a public expression and an enduring record of the grief so universally felt by the community. Leaving it to the historian to record the tragic events; to men of sacred calling to draw lessons of wisdom; to the stricken family to bow down, and the entire people to mourn, we desire to join in the general wail that is rising from every city and hamlet in the land; therefore,

Resolved, That while we would not be unmoved at the murder of a citizen, however humble, we doubly shudder at the assassination of the head of the nation;

and the cruel death of Abraham Lincoln, President of the United States, will be remembered, through all recorded time, as one of the most fearful events in the world's annals.

Resolved, That whatever differences of sentiment may have been entertained between a portion of the people of the United States and the lamented dead, they are all buried at the grave ; and in the great departed we see a man of spotless purity of character, of unchallenged honesty of purpose, of signal originality of mind, a man moulded, as it appeared, to play the mighty part that he performed so grandly, a man who carried the nation through the four years' fiery storm of war, and fell when the haven of peace was in sight.

Resolved, That such a calamity as this proves more fully the strength of our institutions, and illustrates the wisdom of the form of government adopted by our fathers — institutions that survive the culmination of any conspiracy, however foul and successful — a government binding the hearts of the people in links that are the more firmly riveted by every attempt to burst them asunder. To a nation thus sustained by its own innate strength, renewed allegiance is due after a calamity such as this.

Resolved, That the citizens of Troy be requested to participate in such exercises as may be appointed for Wednesday next, when the funeral of the late President is to take place, by closing their places of business, attending at the regular houses of worship, and in such other manner as shall seem most appropriate to prove the general grief. And that a committee of five, of which his Honor the Mayor shall be chairman, be appointed to arrange such public exercises as they shall deem best, and to suggest such other solemnities as shall cause the day to be fittingly observed in Troy.

The resolutions were adopted, and the Mayor appointed as the remainder of the committee, Recorder Moran and Aldermen Kemp, Starbuck and Norton.

On motion of Alderman Norton, Major-General John E. Wool was invited to address the Board, and did so in words suited to the solemn occasion.

Then, on motion, the Board adjourned.

JAMES S. THORN, Clerk.

GEN. WOOL'S remarks were as follows:

"The intelligence of the death of the honored President of the United States is so unexpected, and the manner of that death so astounding and atrocious, as almost to paralyze thought and speech. Men meet on the streets with downcast look and saddened face and pass without a word. The emblems of mourning that are exhibited everywhere throughout the city, the flag of our country furled and draped in black, the suspension of business—these bespeak more emphatically the feelings of the people than words.

"The virtues and excellencies, the patriotism and conscientiousness, the honesty and ability of Abraham Lincoln are known to you all, and will be remembered so long as this nation shall last or man shall recognize the higher qualities of his race. Mr. Lincoln's most fitting eulogy finds expression in the great love of the people of this nation.

"It is proper that honor should be done to his memory in this as well as in every city of the land, and not only in them, but in every town and village and hamlet of the Union. The acting secretary of state has invited the various religious denominations throughout the country, to meet within their respective places of worship at the time of the obsequies of the President at Washington, for the purpose of solemnizing the occasion with appropriate ceremonies. In response to this announcement, I notice that the Governor of Illinois, in the spirit of your proceedings this evening, has called upon the people of that state, the home of her martyred son, to respect the invitation sent out from Washington. An observance of the day of the funeral such as is thus suggested meets my hearty approval. Let there be no military display or out door pageant, but let the total suspension of business and the solemn services of the church, be our expression of sorrow and mourning on the sad occasion."

After the adjournment of the Board, the committee drew up the following request which was sent in the form of a note, to the pastors of all the churches in the city.

REQUEST OF THE COMMITTEE.

Pursuant to resolution adopted at a special meeting of the Common Council of the city of Troy, the undersigned, a committee appointed for that purpose, respectfully request that the clergymen of the city coöperate in their respective churches and places of worship on Wednesday next, the 19th inst., at 12 o'clock, noon, in the observance of such religious services as may be suitable to solemnize and commemorate the obsequies of Abraham Lincoln, late President of the United States.

Dated Troy, April 17th, 1865.

URI GILBERT,
JOHN MORAN,
WILLIAM KEMP,   } Committee.
THOMAS NORTON,
GEO. H. STARBUCK,

RESOLUTIONS OF RESPECT.

At a meeting of the Jewish citizens of this city, held at their Hall, April 17th, 1865, the following preamble and resolutions were passed:

Whereas, His Excellency Abraham Lincoln, the President of the United States, died on the morning of the 15th of April, from wounds received at the hands of an assassin; therefore,

Resolved, That in the death of our beloved President, our whole country has lost its best and dearest friend; that his life is the brightest page of our nation's sorrows; that we prayerfully ask Him who ruleth all the people of the earth in His providence, to work out His purpose in this appalling calamity that has gone so near to the hearts of the American people, and to decree and hasten that end which our lamented President so nearly consummated, and to which he died a martyr, namely, religious liberty, and the restoration and perpetuation of the American union.

It was further resolved, that the Anshe Chesed congregation of this city, in Wotkyns's block, be open for religious service on Wednesday, April 19th, 1865, from 10 A. M. till 12 o'clock M.

A. KSINSKY, President.
B. LICHTENSTEINE, Secretary.

TUESDAY, APRIL 18TH, 1865.

ANNOUNCEMENT BY THE MAYOR.

To the Citizens of Troy:

In accordance with the resolutions adopted by the common council of the city of Troy, requesting an observance of the day appointed for the funeral of the late President of the United States, it is especially urged that a solemn and suitable commemoration of the occasion be had in Troy; that the bells be tolled from half past eleven o'clock A. M., until twelve M.; that services be held in all the city churches for one hour, commencing at noon; and that all business be suspended for the remainder of the day. It is also suggested that the flags be placed at half-mast, and emblems of mourning be affixed to public and private buildings. URI GILBERT, Mayor.

Troy, April 18th, 1865.

Orders to the Tenth Brigade and the Forty Fourth Regiment.

Head Qrs., 10th Brig., 3d Div., N. Y. N. G., }
Troy, *April* 18*th*, 1865.   }

General Order No. 5.

The undersigned has this day received official information from the war department, and also from Maj. Gen. John Tayler Cooper, commanding Third division, N. Y. N. G., announcing the death of the illustrious Abraham Lincoln, late President of the United States, that he died at twenty-two minutes after seven o'clock on the morning of Saturday, the 15th day of April, 1865, of a mortal wound inflicted upon him by an assassin. With profound sorrow we mourn his death as a national calamity: and as a mark of respect to the Chief Magistrate of the nation, and Commander-in-Chief of its armies, I do hereby order and direct the commanding officer of the several regiments comprising the Tenth brigade N. Y. N. G., the day following the reception of this order, to cause the regimental color to be displayed at half-staff, and also on the day of the funeral, on their respective arsenals and armories, and that said arsenals and armories will be appropriately draped in mourning for thirty days. And I do further order that all regiments provided with artillery and ammunition cause a gun to be fired every half hour between sunrise and sunset. And I do further order and direct that all officers of the Tenth brigade while on duty, will wear the badge of mourning on their left arm and swords, and on the colors and arms of the commands and regiments, for the period of six months.

DARIUS ALLEN,
BRIG. GEN., Comd'g Tenth Brig., N. G.
ASA W. WICKES, Aid de Camp.

HEAD QRS., 24TH REGT., N. Y. S. N. G., }
Troy, N. Y., April 18th, 1865. }

GENERAL ORDER No. 10.

Brigade order No. 5, dated Headquarters 10th Brigade, 3d Division, N. Y. N. G., Troy, April 18, 1865, is hereby promulgated. The commandants of the several armories of this command will cause their armories to be draped in mourning, in compliance with brigade orders, and the colors to be displayed at half-staff to morrow, the 19th day of April.

Capt. Landon, commanding A company, will tomorrow, April 19th, that being the day appointed for the funeral solemnities of the late President of the United States, cause half hourly guns to be fired, beginning at sunrise and ending at sunset. By order.

I. McCONIHE Jr., Col. Com.
G. G. MOORE, Adj.

PROCEEDINGS AT THE RENSSELAER POLYTECHNIC INSTITUTE.

A full meeting of the faculty and students of the institute with a representation of its board of trustees, the director Professor Drowne in the chair, was held in the Institute Hall,—appropriately draped for the occasion—on Tuesday afternoon, April 18th, at 5 o'clock, to give a united expression of the feelings of all present in reference to the calamity sustained by the nation, in the loss, by mad assassination, of its devoted and accepted Chief Magistrate. At the close of some appropriate introductory remarks, by the director, Judge Gould of the board of trustees was introduced and made an earnest and impressive address; after which the following resolutions, prepared by a committee of the faculty, were read by its secretary.

Whereas, He, whose ways are not as our ways, has, in His divine wisdom, mysteriously mingled glory and gloom in the cups of present national experience, by suffering our devoted and beloved President, Abraham Lincoln, to fall a victim to him that lieth in wait for blood, while crowning victories were cheering all patriot hearts.

Resolved, That we mourn the loss of a tried, trusted, and loved civil leader; a leader, calm, safe, wise, kind and good; that we peculiarly sympathize with his stricken family; and that we would unite with all our bereaved countrymen in expressing mutual sympathies, and offering common prayers, in view of this, the nation's loss and sorrow.

Resolved, That we continue to put steadfast trust in the God of our Fathers, in whom it is better to trust than to put confidence in man; and that we render unabated gratitude, praise and thanksgiving to our

God for His blessing thus far upon the holy work of national restoration, and for His continued merciful preservation to us of so many yet remaining able civil and military leaders.

Resolved, That, so far as in us lies, we will unite with willing fellow-countrymen everywhere in working to "strengthen the things which remain" by giving hearty support to all upon whom, under Divine direction, rests the work of guiding the nation in this trying hour.

Resolved, That, in honor of the memory of the late President, we will wear the usual badge of mourning for thirty days; and will attend such public exercises as may be appointed by the authorities on the day of his funeral.

Resolved, That these resolutions be published in the papers of the city of Troy.

S. EDWARD WARREN,
H. B. NASON,   } Committee.
P. H. BAERMANN.

After motion, seconded in behalf of all the students, to adopt the above resolutions, they were supported by Professor Warren in a few remarks, and by Professor Baermann in a stirring address, and were then unanimously adopted, when the director, after brief closing remarks, declared the exercises of the hour to be closed.

WEDNESDAY, APRIL 19TH, 1865.

DISCOURSE DELIVERED AT THE NORTH BAPTIST CHURCH.

BY REV. C. P. SHELDON, D.D.

Know ye not that there is a prince and a great man fallen this day in Israel?— 2 SAMUEL, iii, 38.

These words were uttered in reference to one of the most renowned princes and ablest military commanders of the early kingdom of Israel. He was most foully and brutally assassinated by a hostile rival. The words are in a higher and better sense appropriate and true of the personage, whose cruel and bloody assassination has suddenly plunged our nation into grief and mourning. Such sorrow, in some of the elements which enter into it, the nation has never felt in the loss of any public officer or man. It never mourned as it now mourns. The great and the good have at other times passed away. Presidents have before this died, even while occupying the chair of office and with its great responsibilities resting upon them; but never in times of national peril, and by the hand of human violence. The great and good WASHINGTON, the successful leader of our armies through the struggle of the Revolution, and the wise and honored first President of the Republic, died unexpectedly and suddenly; but by natural disease, and in the quietness of his peaceful home, surrounded by his family and friends. His public mission had been fulfilled, the duties of office had been laid aside, and in a simple and unostentatious manner he was filling the position of a citizen, "first in the hearts of his countrymen," the most loved and revered of all. His death overwhelmed the nation in profoundest grief, but it came in the usual order of Divine providence. The country was at peace, the government was stable, and every department of it was in healthful and successful operation.

The excellent and patriotic HARRISON was called away soon after he assumed the duties of the Presidential office; but his death was also in a time of profoundest peace, and when order and law reigned supreme throughout the land. He had served his country well in other public stations, and at an age considerably advanced, and with physical health not a little enfeebled, he entered upon the duties of his high place. But the burden was too heavy: nature was overtaxed and gave way. The nation mourned this first loss of its executive head, and as for a good man and a true patriot. But there was nothing in the event to shock particularly the national sensibilities.

Similarly did the sturdy and honest TAYLOR pass from the executive chair to the grave. Called unexpectedly by a people who had admired his heroic valor in leading armies and winning battles, and who had unbounded trust in his sterling integrity to assume the cares and responsibilities of the chief magistracy, and to meet the excitements incident to such a position, the change from the simple manner of life which had characterized him in the camp and his own quiet home, proved too great even for him, and he passed away in the first months of his presidential career. The nation was sadly disappointed, and again deeply wounded; but the event was not out of the·ordinary course of nature, and was submitted to as such. The country had just passed victoriously through a brief foreign war, was reposing in a secured peace, and pursuing its path of unbounded prosperity.

How different in all the elements and circumstances attending it, the event, that has now startled and shocked the nation, and plunged it in deepest gloom and profoundest sorrow! We were suffering from the most causeless, atrocious, and gigantic rebellion, that had ever been sprung upon a people, and were in the midst of the collisions, struggles and desolations of a vast civil war. After four weary years of campaigns, battles, and victories mingled with reverses, we had reached a point, where the successful and speedy issue of the struggle was manifest. The power of the rebellion was completely broken, its strongholds were in our possession, its resources of men and material were exhausted, its capital had fallen, its pretended government was a fugitive, its principal army broken and defeated had surrendered, its leading generals were prisoners in our hands, and the dawnings of approaching peace were illuminating the land. The nation was hopeful, confident and rejoicing. Its Executive Chief was calm and vigorous, firm and strong in body and mind. Around him was a united and able cabinet, and in him centred the hope, confidence and affections of the people, as they had not at any previous period of his difficult yet successful administration. All hearts turned to him, much in feeling and manner, as in the nation's infancy they had turned to the illustrious and noble WASHINGTON.

In an hour of relaxation from official care and labor, surrounded by members of his family and personal friends, in a place of peaceful amusement, unarmed, unguarded, unsuspecting, a brutal assassin, the agent of a band of conspirators, and the impersonation of the demoniacal spirit and damnable hate which had so animated the rebellion, stole upon him, and with a suddenness that prevented the intervention of any averting human hand, by one fatal shot laid him low in death, and then brandishing a dagger and crying "*sic semper tyrannis*," amid the awful shock and terrible confusion, fled from the scene. It was a fearful tragedy, darker, fouler, more hellish than any which had before occurred in human history. And it seems to have been one of a series of acts, which were intended to strike down the several chief officers of the government, one other of whom, at about the same hour and by another hand, was well nigh butchered to death, upon a sick bed and in his own peaceful home.

The nation was struck dumb at the suddenness and indescribable atrocity of the deed. Its great heart almost ceased to beat, and it bowed itself in tears and an agony of sorrow, and cried unto God for help. And now it rises up with the stern demand for vengeance upon the perpetrators, instigators, and abettors of the horrid crime. Had ABRAHAM LINCOLN died in the ordinary course of disease, or even, as the commander in chief of our military forces, fallen upon the field of battle, great and terrible as the nation would have felt the calamity to be, it would have calmly and submissively bowed to the appointment of Providence, and under its great loss, patiently pursued the path divinely marked out for it. It seeks, it strives, and we believe it will be helped to do so now. But oh, it is so hard. So deep is the darkness that enshrouds the event, it has in it such elements of human agency and demoniacal passion and hate, that it becomes the sorest trial ever laid upon the nation's faith and trust. But still we must, we will bow and trust. We will see in it the hand of God, and hear in it the voice of God. We will sadly bear away and lay in the grave the mutilated and lifeless form of our great and good President. We will commit to Him "who ruleth over all" and to future developments, the explanation of this great sorrow, too dark for us now to understand and comprehend, and then, leaning upon His arm and seeking His guidance, we will with one mind, one heart, and one purpose, arise to give the finishing blow to this unholy rebellion, to consolidate our government and country in peace, and to pursue the path of national prosperity and greatness.

Let us now for a moment consider the questions, what have we lost? who was ABRAHAM LINCOLN? Born in Kentucky in 1809, a poor boy, destitute of the ordinary means of education and culture, by honest industry and indomitable energy, he at length placed himself in the front rank of one of the most honored and cultivated professions in our country, and took a high position among the men of his time. He served several years in the legislature of his adopted state, Illinois, was elected a member of the national congress in 1847, was twice the candidate of his party for the United States senate, and was nominated for the presidency in May, 1860, and elected to that office on the 6th of November following. He was inaugurated on the 4th of March, in 1861. So well did he perform the duties of that high office, that he was reëlected on the 8th of November, 1864, by one of the largest majorities ever given to a candidate for that office.

When first he entered upon the duties of President, the country was in a most deplorable condition. Several of the states had seceded from the Union, others were threatening to do so; a large number of the forts, arsenals, custom houses, and military posts, had been wrested from the government; the southern confederacy had been formally organized; treason was rampant in the highest places of the government, and the rebellion had defiantly entered upon its career. He knew not whom he could trust, nor upon whose loyalty and support he could rely. Spies and agents of the rebellion were in the offices of the government, and scattered in all parts of the land. Such difficulties and dangers had never environed a President in the discharge of his duties. His own life even was not safe. He was calm, considerate, and conciliatory in his policy, yet firm, determined, and unswervingly loyal to the constitution and the country. His honesty, integrity and patriotism were above suspicion, and he drew the loyal heart of the country to him. He had been but a little more than a month in office, when the attack was made on Fort Sumter, which was followed by its surrender and the inauguration of the war. I will not follow the history of the war during these sad and bloody four years, nor his course in reference to it. The events are fresh in your memory. Suffice it to say, the war had been successful under his administration, and he lived long enough to see repossessed nearly all the posts and fortifications which had been wrested from the government by the plottings of treason, the national banner floating in every state in the Union, nearly all the rebel seaports in possession of the national forces, the surrender and dispersion of the principal army of the rebellion, and the overthrow of the main cause which produced it, *human slavery*. He died on the very day that the old flag, which four years before had been lowered by the force of armed treason from the walls of Sumter, was raised by loyal hands to its place again, and floated triumphantly in the breeze. He died with the dawnings of peace and reunion gladdening his eyes.

The work of ABRAHAM LINCOLN was done, and God permitted him to be removed. But so far as human hands and passions had to do with it, "the deep damnation of his taking off" we can never forget nor forgive. It was most atrocious in its character, combining the elements of horrid tragedy, as no like event recorded in human history had combined them — most shocking of all the acts which degraded human nature had produced. It was the consummation in full development of the demoniacal spirit of slavery and the rebellion, that spirit which had stricken down a SUMNER in the national Senate house, which had plotted to assassinate the President before his first inaguration, which had beat and shot down our soldiers in the streets of Baltimore, which had hanged and murdered Union men, which had starved prisoners to death in the foulest of human pens, which had applied the incendiary torch to our peaceful cities, and now crowned its hellish acts with this terrible deed. It was not the result of individual hate. It was not an individual act even. Its author was merely an agent, carrying out the plottings, abettings, and plans of the rebellion, impelled by the inherent barbarism of slavery. Toward such a spirit we can indulge no peace nor clemency.

And then, contemplate the folly and uselessness of the act. This government is not a one man power. The removal of no single individual, nor of several individuals, could stop its wheels or jostle its movement. This the conspirators well knew, or might have known. To strike down the President therefore, did not change the government nor weaken its power. It moved right on, and it would have moved right on, had they fully accomplished their plans. This they might have expected. No good could come to the rebellion in the accomplishment of their purposes. The assassination of the President, and especially at the time it occurred, could add no strength to their cause. It only weakens it and makes it the more odious. The act is, therefore, marked by the weakest *folly* as well as the foulest *crime*. It could only gratify the most malignant hate, and stamps the rebellion with a damnation and disgrace, that coming years and the judgment of the world, shall only make the more strong and emphatic.

In the death of ABRAHAM LINCOLN, the nation has lost one of the wisest, purest, best of rulers, and even the rebellious south, one of its truest friends. That he committed mistakes, he himself frankly acknowledged. And where is the man, that has the assurance to say, that in his circumstances, and environed by his difficulties, he should have committed less ones. Coming generations will estimate his character and appreciate his greatness and excellence, as we amid the passions, prejudices and excitements of the time, are unable to do. Says a foreign writer recently of him, "We all remember the animated eulogium on General Washington which Lord Macaulay passed parenthetically in his essay on Hampden. 'It was, when to the sullen tyranny of Laud and Charles had succeeded the fierce conflict of sects and factions, ambitious of ascendency or burning for revenge; it was, when the vices and ignorance which the old tyranny had engendered, threatened the new freedom with destruction, that England missed the sobriety, the self-command, the perfect rectitude of intention, to which the history of revolutions furnishes no parallel, or furnishes a parallel in Washington alone.' If that high eulogium was fully earned, as it was, by the first great President of the United States, we doubt if it has not been as well earned by the Illinois peasant proprietor and 'village lawyer,' whom, by some divine inspiration or providence, the republican caucus of 1860 substituted for Mr. Seward as their nominee for the President's chair. Mr. Lincoln has persevered through all, without ever giving way to anger, or despondency, or exultation, or popular arrogance, or sectarian fanaticism, or cast prejudice, visibly growing in force of character, in self possession, and in magnanimity, till in his last short message to congress on the fourth of March (the inaugural) we can detect no longer the rude and illiterate mould of a village lawyer's thought, but find it replaced by a grasp of principle, a dignity of manner, and a solemnity of purpose, which would have been unworthy neither of Hampden, nor of Cromwell, while his gentleness and generosity of feeling towards his foes, are almost greater than we should expect from either of them." This is high testimony to his goodness and greatness, but the statement is not overdrawn.

In his sterling good sense, in his profound knowledge of human nature, in his wise interpretation of passing events, in his adaptation to the demands of the time, in his ingenuous frankness, in his sturdy honesty, in his incorruptible integrity, in his unswerving patriotism, in his kindness to friends and magnanimity to foes, in his excellence and goodness of heart, he will rank among the foremost men and rulers of his time. He did not attempt to be what he could not be, the cultured scholar, the accomplished diplomatist, the eloquent orator: he was himself, original, practical, strong, a man of the people, a great and good President. And yet, some of the brightest gems of thought and language that ever flowed from human pen, or fell from human lips, have come from him. And the crowning thing of all is, ABRAHAM LINCOLN was a CHRISTIAN, a man of faith and of prayer. The recognition of God, and a reliance upon God, have been most marked characteristics of his presidential career, increasing and growing more prominent as the time passed on. We doubt not he has been called to a higher service, in the realms of eternal truth and life. Thus far in the history of our country, no name will so link itself to the name of WASHINGTON, as the name of ABRAHAM LINCOLN. So long as there is an emancipated bondman, or a descendant of his, in this land, so long will that name be revered and remembered, with devoutest gratitude to God.

We bow in the darkness and greatness of our grief submissively to Him, who has permitted our ruler to be taken from us. We trust Him still, for ourselves and for our country. May the example of the illustrious dead be a copy to our coming statesmen. May his life be a lesson to all the young men of our land, and may God sanctify his death, to the benefit of all.

"Thy converse drew us with delight,
   The men of rathe and riper years:
   The feeble soul, a haunt of fears,
Forgot his weakness in thy sight.

"On thee the loyal-hearted hung,
   The proud was half disarmed of pride,
   Nor cared the serpent at thy side
To flicker with his treble tongue.

"The stern were mild when thou wert by,
   The flippant put himself to school
   And heard thee, and the brazen fool
Was softened, and he knew not why.

*   *   *   *   *

> "And, doubtless, unto thee is given
> A life that bears immortal fruit
> In such great offices as suit
> The full-grown energies of heaven."

SERMON PREACHED AT THE NORTH SECOND STREET METHODIST EPISCOPAL CHURCH.

BY REV. J. WESLEY CARHART, D.D.

Trust in him at all times; ye people, pour out your heart before him: God is a refuge for us.—Psalm, lxii, 8.

Never, perhaps, in the history of the world, did the heart of any nation throb with such sorrow as does ours to day.

We have suffered great national bereavements before, in the death of Washington, Lafayette and others of less distinction; but these sorrows were under other and less aggravating circumstances. Then peace smiled on all the land. The great life-work of Washington and Lafayette seemed to be done. They went to the garner of the Lord, like the shock of corn fully ripe and ready for its master's use. They were permitted to die peacefully, surrounded by kindred and friends to soothe and comfort.

Not so with the martyr Abraham Lincoln. In the midst of years and usefulness he was struck down by the hand of a cowardly assassin, one who dared not meet him face to face. Severer is the wound, since hearts were already bleeding over loved and lost ones, in every city, village and town throughout the land.

LINCOLN MEMORIAL. 117

We mourn to day, not merely the Chief Magistrate of the nation, but each feels that he has lost a personal friend. It would seem as though in every house there was one dead. Abraham Lincoln was enshrined in the hearts of this great people as no other man ever was. Even his political enemies, how bitter soever they may have been, feel that a great and good man has fallen, and they hasten to pay that tribute to his memory which they feel his noble qualities merited, and are found mingling with the weeping multitudes every where. Tear drops glisten in the eyes of the little children, as they reverently speak his name.

Our sorrow is intensified by the peculiar combination of circumstances attending it. Four years ago, rebellion fired its first gun on Fort Sumter. That gun echoed and reëchoed throughout the land. It was heard in every valley and was returned with added thunder from every hillside, until the sons of freedom poured in almost endless columns, from New England, from the Empire state and from the boundless prairies of the west, to avenge the insult offered to our flag, and protect the altars of liberty. Never before did the world witness such an uprising of a great people. The strife raged, longer, louder and more bloody, until the gory folds of war hung over all our hearts. It was war in fearful earnest.

"'Twas war, war, war, with blood and woe;
  Widows in tears, and children without sires;
  Uncounted, trampling hosts—a ceaseless flow;

> Hearts burnt to dross by sorrow's quenchless fires—
> Brothers erecting brothers' funeral pyres,
> And lovers weeping o'er some portrait fair
> That tells of one whose noble heart aspires
> The victor's joy to know, his palm to bear,
> And on his honored brow the crown of conqueror wear."

At length, victory great and glorious blesses our arms. The dawn of peace paints the eastern sky. There are rifts in the cloud of war. The sound of battle recedes. The air is less sulphureous than before, and on every breeze is borne the victorious shout of freemen. Sumter is again ours. Four years from the day it fell, the same old flag, so gallantly defended by Major Anderson and his brave band, is again thrown to the breeze of heaven above those battered ramparts, amid the joyous acclamations of a delivered people. On that same day, when our hopes were so high and our joy so unbounded, the arrow enters our hearts again. The heaviest sorrow of the whole war falls upon us.

What extremes sometimes meet in our experiences here! What contrasts sometimes appear, in the history of individuals and nations! The news is flashed on the lightning's wing to every home and every heart—"The President is assassinated!" The whole nation bows itself in sorrow, and is draped in mourning. Never was a nation's grief sincerer! Never was such a spectacle, on such a scale, witnessed before!

Abraham Lincoln was born in Hardin county, Kentucky, February 12th, 1809. At an early age he removed with his father's family to Spencer county, Indiana, where, for ten years, he labored on his father's farm. His educational advantages were limited, he having attended school in all, only about a year.

On the breaking out of the Black Hawk war in 1832, he enlisted as a private, and was elected captain of a volunteer company. This event, he said, gave him more satisfaction than any other success of his life.

Such was his character for honesty, sobriety and intelligence, that he was soon called upon to hold responsible civil trusts. In such high esteem was he held by his countrymen, that in 1846 he was elected a representative in congress, and took his seat on the first Monday of December, 1847. On May 16th, 1860, the Republican National Convention met at Chicago, and on motion of the chairman of the New York delegation, the nomination of Abraham Lincoln for the presidency of the United States was made unanimous, and in November following, he was elected by a large majority.

He came to the presidential chair amid the threatenings of war and the greatest uncertainty as to who were the friends or the foes of the republic. With his administration of righteousness and wisdom during those four terrible years, we are familiar. Never before were such responsibilities imposed upon the chief magistrate of a nation. Never before were they met so manfully, and discharged with such fidelity.

With child-like trust in God, he was divinely led. Sustained by the prayers of a great people, he was made, under God, the benefactor of his race. Millions of freedmen rise up to call him blessed. As the ages roll on, his name will brighten. His was a mind of superior power. His a character of beautiful symmetry. The circumstances under which he was reared, as well as the natural disposition of his heart, made him preëminently one of the people. He thought as the people thought, felt as the people felt, and was, in the noblest sense, our brother.

The elevation of such an one from the humbler walks of life to the highest position in the gift of the people, shows the genius of our American institutions. Without material wealth, or family renown; without liberal advantages for learning; without literary attainments to distinguish him; enured to toil and hardship, he rose above his fellows by virtue of superior natural endowments of mind and heart.

It is the glory of American institutions that they open the way to greatness and renown to all however humble. "All men are created equal" shall be our motto forever. In what other land and nation could the elevation of one in such humble circumstances to such a position, have occurred? Trees of such luxuriant growth and maturity are indigenous to no soil but ours.

His was a noble and generous nature. He was true to the interests of his country, yet forgiving towards her foes. He was strict in the administration of justice, with no spirit of revenge to gratify. He shrank from war, with all the tenderness of a maiden, and yet, when all other hearts faltered and grew faint, his was undaunted. When others were desponding, he was hopeful.

He adopted no policy of his own, but with his finger on the popular pulse he watched the sentiment of the nation, knowing that the evil would be as great to be in advance of his times as to be behind. He kept pace with the times, and was governed by the sentiment of the people; taking as his motto, " *Vox populi, vox dei.*"

There were times when we thought him too slow and too lenient. But greater haste and severity might have ruined the nation. History will undoubtedly record, and indeed has already begun to do so, that his was the course of wisdom. His acts, as the Chief Magistrate of the nation, must live forever. Some of them — the crowning acts of his administration, are engrossed on the imperishable records of eternity. That act, whereby four millions of human beings were freed from bondage, is without a parallel in the history of sovereigns. The proclamation of freedom was like the angel in mid heaven, crying, "Behold, I bring you good tidings of great joy, which shall be to all people."

Intensely interesting has it been to watch the onward march of sentiment with reference to the sin and curse of human slavery. The strife was long and hard, but at length culminated, when God came in might to the rescue. It seemed that although atonement had already been made for individual sins, there could be no wiping out of our great national transgression without a further shedding of blood.

The immortal utterance of President Lincoln upon this subject in his late inaugural, brought the grateful applause of the good, and the scoffs of the vile and unappreciative. He said, "Woe unto the world because of offences, for it must needs be that offences come; but woe to that man by whom the offence cometh. If we shall suppose that American Slavery is one of these offences — which in the providence of God, must needs come, but which, having continued through His appointed time, He now wills to remove, and that He gives to both north and south this terrible war as the woe due to those by whom the offence came — shall we discern there is any departure from those Divine attributes which the believers in a living God always ascribe to Him? Fondly do we hope, fervently do we pray, that this mighty scourge of war may speedily pass away. Yet, if God wills that it continue until all the wealth piled by the bondman's two hundred and fifty years of unrequited toil shall be sunk, and until every drop of blood drawn with the lash shall be paid by another drawn with the sword, as was said three thousand years ago, so still it must be said that the judgments of the Lord are true and righteous altogether."

It took a long time for the people to come up to that position where they could without hesitancy say, "Let slavery perish, but save the nation." When the people said *that*, Abraham Lincoln said, "Open the prison doors, and let the captives go free!" And the millions went forth, and the tramp of freedom's hosts will resound throughout the coming ages.

One such act in the life of any man is enough for human greatness.

The world had scarcely yet come to regard Abraham Lincoln as among the truly great men of the earth, when the murderer's hand hurled him to the grave. Now, as seen in contrast with the renowned of the world, he outshines them all, and yet it can with truth be said of him, he was only great as he was good.

We wonder at the strange providence of God, that allowed such an event to occur at this time, and under these circumstances, and well we may, for His providences are profoundly mysterious. We know nothing of God's processes in providence, nature or grace.

The dew-drop that hangs in the bell of a flower, no less than the majestic mountain that rears its head above the clouds, or the mighty planet that whirls in space — is a world of wonder.

Man is equally lost in the contemplation of the earth-worm, or himself.

So in grace. "The wind bloweth where it listeth, and thou hearest the sound thereof, but canst not tell whence it cometh, and whither it goeth: so is every one that is born of the spirit." "Without controversy, great is the mystery of godliness." We need not then expect to understand the purposes of Jehovah when friends sicken and die, when the most prominent and useful are cut off in the bloom and vigor of their manhood, and the pauper, the inebriate, the felon is spared to be a burden, a curse to society.

> "God moves in a mysterious way,
> His wonders to perform;
> He plants his footsteps in the sea,
> And rides upon the storm."

There is one point connected with this subject upon which we would be especially guarded, and which we would impress upon all your hearts, and that is, God did not ordain this assassination. He did not, strictly speaking, permit, but *suffered* it. To say that he ordained it, is to say that the murderer committed no sin against God and no crime against humanity. To say that God permitted it, is to say that he sanctioned it. He suffered it. He does not see fit to prevent all that he may hate. With reference to many things, He doubtless sees it more to his glory to suffer them to be so, than to interfere and by almighty power, prevent them, and consequently he says of them, "Suffer it to be so now." So when the hellish work of conspiracy against the President's life was going on, he said, "Suffer it to be so now." And when the cowardly assassin, bent on the accomplishment of his fiendish purpose, entered that private box and aimed the deadly weapon at the head of the President, God said, "Suffer it to be so now," and it was done, the fearful deed was done!

Abraham Lincoln's mission to this people *may* have been at an end. His death may serve the purposes of God with reference to the nation better than his life. Not that his life was unimportant, but it may be that we had come to depend too much on him, and God suffered him to be taken away, to show us that the salvation of the nation was in His hands, and safe; that He can carry on His work though His workmen fall.

Leniency to traitors was once necessary, and unavoidable, to a great extent. And although mercy should be shown by the government to the mass of those in arms against us, yet the time has come when the leaders in the rebellion must be punished. Of them it may be said, "Mercy to the individual would be cruelty to the state." Leniency to such would prove the curse of the country. We have not yet begun to punish treason. We scarcely appreciate the nature of the crime.

All through the north as well as the south are men unpunished, who have not only expressed sympathy with traitors, but have rendered them aid and comfort. God deals with rebels in a sterner way. Every account in the bible of his dealings with rebels proves this.

It is God's purpose that treason against this government shall be punished. President Lincoln's position of leniency seemed to be a necessity from which he could not well recede. He was suffered to be removed from that position, by means the best calculated to excite, not a spirit of revenge but a desire and determination on the part of the people that the penalty of the law should be inflicted. Now justice can be measured out. I pray that it may be. The psalmist prays with reference to his enemies, "Let death seize upon them, and let them go down quick into hell." His enemies were incorrigible. He saw no chance for repentance, and that in view of the mischief they were working, hell and the grave were the fittest places for them. Is there not an analogy between his enemies and ours?

Let treason go unpunished, let the leaders be scattered and these branches of the deadly Upas will strike themselves into the soil, become rooted, and again bring forth their hellish fruit.

Andrew Johnson is President. Our duty is now plain. "Trust in God at all times." Such confidence will have the effect to calm our hearts and quiet our fears, to revive hope, to inspire confidence in our cause, and to insure the blessing of heaven. It will nerve the national heart for nobler achievements; and if need be, for deeper sorrow and intenser suffering and further sacrifice.

We have trusted too much in men and generals, in

numbers and skill. We have, to a great extent, ignored God. Let us now acknowledge Him. Our privilege is to pour out our hearts before Him. We are not merely to pray to Him, in the ordinary acceptation of the term, but to wrestle with Him. Did you ever go to God with any great desire? Did you feel that that desire was all absorbing, and uppermost in your heart? Did you feel that the granting of your request was in accordance with the will of God, and that you could not be denied? Did you allow no object to intervene between you and your God? Then you know what it is to wrestle with God. In like manner go to Him now. Pour out your heart before Him in behalf of the interests of this nation. God has already heard our prayer, and has averted many a sorrow that would otherwise have come upon us. He hath spared the nation for the righteous' sake.

Let those who have vilified the President and cursed the government, go before their Maker and repent as in dust and ashes at his feet, if haply they may find Him, and be forgiven.

Address Delivered in the Second Presbyterian Church.

By Rev. D. S. Gregory.

The event which has called us to these sad solemnities to-day, is one which has clothed the places of state in sackcloth and left a nation in mourning. It is always wise to give heed to the striking providences which from time to time startle the nations as with an audible voice of God. Not to give heed to such a providence as this, not to permit it to settle in the heart and to leave its impress upon the character and life, would be evidence of a degree of insensibility which should arouse and shock every Christian man. These hundreds of cities draped in mourning, the silence in these millions of homes, these busy scenes of traffic hushed and darkened, these ten thousand sanctuaries clad in sable, these many eyes to which tears are no longer strangers, proclaim to day the deep and solemn feeling of a bereaved people. The greatness, the suddenness of the calamity, accompanied at once with circumstances of the most tender and affecting interest and of the most horrifying and revolting nature, speaks to the heart in irresistible language. Death is always a solemn thing, opening up before us as it does visions of the grave, of the judgment, and of eternity with its rewards and retributions; but it is made a doubly solemn thing to-day, by the circumstances in which it is pressed upon our attention.

Nothing could bring home to us more forcibly the thought that *we can never be placed beyond the reach of death.* Greatness or eminence in position cannot give immunity from death. It would be vain to deny to him, whom this most atrocious murder of the modern ages has taken off, the title of *great*. True he may have had none of those qualities that dazzle, that awaken the enthusiasm of an hour, but there was something more substantial than these in his character which will cause his name to be written above all merely glittering names, on the scroll of fame. Called to preside in the grandest national crisis in the world's history, to guide this mighty nation in an overturning beside which all the other revolutions of the age are dwarfed into mere child's play, *he has nowhere been found wanting*. Entering upon his work in a capital, a very sink of corruption, he escaped the contamination. Beset from the first by political harpies, he cast them off and gathered around him the wisdom and strength of that party of many political creeds but of one heart, the mighty union party of the land. Slandered and maligned by radicals of every sort and all extremes, he took his stand like a rock for the right, seemingly insensible alike to censure and to flattery. And while the mighty struggle has been going on through the years, we have felt sometimes how keen and piercing an eye has been fixed upon it to interpret the march of events, and how mighty a hand has been constantly shaping the policy of the nation. Future generations alone will comprehend it fully.

But one thing is plain even now, and that is, that the man of whom it can be said in such a mighty struggle — almost mightier than the world has ever seen before — the man of whom it can be said that *he has not been found wanting*, not wanting in insight

17

and grasp of thought, not wanting in strength of will and power, not wanting in honesty and stern integrity, not wanting in a deep sense of his God-given mission, that man, however many and varied his faults, was *great*, not in position only but *in nature.* But this human greatness, felt at home, and beginning to be acknowledged everywhere abroad, this human greatness which under God had solved the problem which the nations had proclaimed insoluble, could not save its envied possessor from death — sudden and fearful death!

The *glory of the hour of triumph*, when that triumph is the success of a nation, of freedom, of humanity, of justice and of God, could not stay the mighty and universal conqueror. While the flag of freedom was being flung to the breeze again at Sumter, to assure blood-stained treason of the ascendency of the national authority on the very birth-ground of this wicked, treacherous rebellion, and while the news of the discomfiture and destruction of mighty rebel hosts was being borne on the wings of wind and lightning to the nations of the earth, this nation was roused by the news of his most horrible assassination.

The *grandest magnanimity* of soul cannot save from death. There must have been a grandeur of soul about the man who could pass through four years of such a struggle, and then come to a second inaugural address with those wonderful words, "with charity to all and malice for none," and so illustrate this in his life as did Abraham Lincoln. Four years, during which no day passed in which the organs and leaders of this rebellion, which is now passing away as chaff before the breath of Almighty justice, did not ferociously assail and malign, and strive to fix his name along with everything that is basest in nature and in history, in earth and in hell, and yet four years in which he did not utter one word of vindictiveness! Four such years, when the least demand of justice was death to every traitor, were crowned by that act of clemency which may well astonish the world, in which he showed how ready he was to forgive! Yet such magnanimity could not save him from death, and death too by so foul a murder, at the hand of those against whom God has written himself the eternal foe, though *he* had shown himself so ready to forgive and overlook the crime which cried out to heaven.

The *deepest affection of a great people* cannot save from death. Here is one before us, who against the strongest opposing influences, and in spite of all the bitterness of a great strife, had won his way to all honest hearts, adding, we trust, the Christian to the man. Here is one whose life had conquered political and partizan prejudices and made his love a delight to the nation. More and more unitedly, more and more firmly this people have gathered round him through the years of tumult and conflict, until the man who had emptied his coffers in the great and glorious cause, and the soldier who had faced death in a hundred battles, and the father and mother who had laid their son upon the altar of liberty, to be sacrificed and then buried in a nameless grave, and the widowed wife and the fatherless children who looked tearfully and anxiously into the darkened future, until all felt that in him they had a friend and son and brother and husband and father. At such an hour came the fearful blow, and it fell upon the nation like a death in every home. Even a nation's heart overflowing so with love, could not avert the blow. Death is an omnipotent and remorseless conqueror.

What a lesson of death then to the nation to-day. Death loves a shining mark. Nothing can guard against it, when the hour comes: no *position*, neither the lowliness of the hovel nor the exaltation of the president's mansion, neither the helplessness of the child nor the strength of the man : no *earthly love*, not a wife's with its tenderness, not a father's with its strength, not a mother's with its depth, not a nation's with the tenderness and strength and depth of all these. Death awaits you. It may come in an instant — without leaving time to ask, "Am I prepared to die?" It should impress this solemn thought upon every one in this nation. God has come into the high places that he might speak to each and all. Oh! will this people give heed?

But God has come to *teach us the vanity of man*, even at his best estate. "Altogether vanity!" How empty a trust is he. O people, "put not your trust in princes, nor in the son of man in whom is no help." What are all the great ones in God's plan after all but the most insignificant instruments? To-day there lies cold and low in yonder capital of the nation, one of these chosen instruments of the great King. God himself seemed strangely to point him out and to cling to him through the years. Selected as candidate for the chief magistracy in preference to our wisest statesman, called to fulfil a work to which a nation would have shrunk from calling an untried man, led on in ways the wisdom of which it has taken time to justify—Providence had seemed, like the nation, so to cling to the man! But suddenly he is cut down by the hand of a brutal murderer. The news flashes with lightning wings across the nation. A wail goes up to heaven from every house, and all eyes fill with blinding tears. Yonder where we looked upon our great and honored, and trusted, and beloved President, there is only dust and ashes—only dust and ashes! O nation, put not your trust in princes, nor in the son of man in whom there is no help! God's mighty work—the triumph of truth and justice and freedom and humanity, does not in the least depend upon any of these. The workmen perish but the work goes on—on—on through the ages—on—on through the nations,—on—on to final, complete and everlasting triumph. Whatever oppose, the day shall come when the grand principles of the gospel shall be everywhere acknowledged with their freedom, and no foot of earth be cursed by error, injustice, tyranny or oppression. These great ones at best are little more than dust and ashes, at most but the frail reeds with which God's omnipotence smites down the wicked and the oppressor. Of them we may say with the divinely inspired preacher, "Vanity of vanities; all is vanity."

But in speaking of mortality and vanity, God's voice to-day *calls again to repentance.* God forbid that we should forget that He has been chastising us for sin. Universal corruption added to the vow to consign man, made in God's own image, to perpetual bondage, called for Divine justice. The corruption which has fattened on even these million deaths demands rebuke. God has been smiting *us* as well as this iniquitous rebellion, smiting us on all these thousand battle fields. Now, again to-day He comes by this most startling voice, and demands of the nation, "Have you repented?" Oh! have we repented? God's heart is full, but, O! justice will have her way — eternal justice — until we repent. This event may teach us that God's storehouse is full. We know not what may await an impenitent people. God's ways are a mighty deep. Repent — repent at His fearfully solemn command.

But God speaks to us to-day of *justice*, as well as of death and nothingness and repentance. The innocent blood cries out to heaven for vengeance, not simply against the miserable, misguided, besotted tool of the traitor, who struck for him the blow that has bereaved a nation, but vengeance against the traitors all over the land who nerved and guided the fiendish blow; against the spirit of the savage and the fiend that has urged and upheld the cold-blooded butchery of these millions, which doomed to starvation the thousands in the prison-pens of Andersonville and Richmond, and which has drenched this whole land in blood and tears. Such men, wherever found, as the leaders of evil, are fit only for death; and while it is the great duty of the hour to extend the hand of forgiveness and love to all the misguided victims of such traitors, it is a duty stern as retribution itself to which this awfully solemn providence has called this nation, to see to it that there be no immunity to treason, no price paid for it in the future, that shall ensure destruction to the coming generations. Justice, at such times, justice to the murderer, justice without fear or passion, justice which abides by God's eternal word and God's eternal right is the only safety for the present, for the coming time and the coming generations: and to justice, this awful providence, this fearful crime has called this nation with a voice like a judgment trumpet.

God grant that we may not forget this justice, this repentance, this vanity and mortality of man, and in the coming future it will be seen that this bloodiest murder of the modern ages has not, in God's great providence, been in vain.

Address Delivered in the Second Street Presbyterian Church.

BY REV. DUNCAN KENNEDY, D.D.

At this hour, an event is occurring at the Capitol of the nation, upon which the gaze of the millions of our countrymen is intensely fixed. It is not what a few days since, we anticipated it would be, a scene of gladness, accompanied by every outward demonstration of rejoicing. On the contrary, it is one of funereal gloom, of tears, of unaffected grief. How abrupt the transition from the anticipated to the real, and how mighty the contrast between the two! How strange that amid circumstances well fitted to beget the loudest pæans of national joy; when numerous armies are yielding to the power of the government; when strong fortifications are crumbling at our feet; when skillful generals are stricken with despair, and veteran soldiers are scattering like the leaves of autumn; when treason is suffering a fatal exhaustion, and rebellion is in its dying struggle; when the drama of blood, with its fearful scenes of carnage, is culminating in the restoration of peace and concord; when the glorious banner of the Union has just been unfurled in the very place, where, four years since, it was stricken down by parricidal hands; how strange that amid such stirring and heart-thrilling events, the day should be one of unaffected sorrow, and that the whole country should be clothed in habiliments of mourning!

For a solution of this mystery, we ask you to look at what is now passing at the Capital. There is seen a densely formed procession made up of myriads of all classes of our fellow citizens, moving in slow and measured tread, marked by every token of sadness, bearing forth the mortal part of one, whose official life has commanded deeper feeling, stronger affection, fiercer animosity, and a more extended influence than have gathered around any other Chief Magistrate of this people, since the "Father of his Country" sunk to rest amid the hallowed shades of Mount Vernon! The true patriot has accomplished his mission; the loving heart has ceased to beat; the mild eye is forever closed; the friendly voice is silent; the head that had toiled so unremittingly for the integrity of the nation, and had so successfully planned for the reëstablishment of prosperity and peace, is being laid upon its pillow of earth, and we are taking our farewell look of all that remains of ABRAHAM LINCOLN, the latest, and among the best of the presidents of the United States! No wonder the nation is in tears! No wonder that every town and city and hamlet through all the loyal states are draped in emblems of grief! No wonder that universal joy, which was beginning to burst forth in various forms and expressions of outward gladness, has been repressed, yielding to the mightier claims of universal sorrow!

Had the event occurred in the usual course of providential dispensation, deep as the mystery might seem, and profound as the grief would be, the shock would not have been so great, nor the revulsion of feeling so abrupt and painful. Had he died as men ordinarily die, had we been apprised, day by day, of the progress of disease working its way, slowly but surely, toward the seat of life, we would have become nerved for the event, and the dread intelligence *he is dead*, would have been received with comparative composure. But no such premonitions prepared us for the catastrophe. We had not thought even, that such an event was possible. Had the blow been struck when he was in Richmond, it would have been scarcely a matter of surprise, for there, we knew him to have been surrounded by the bitterest enemies; but having returned in safety, we dismissed our transient fears, and yielded to the calmness of wonted security. But how soon has the spell been broken! How sudden and stunning the event! Ruthlessly stricken down in the fullness of his strength by the bloody hand of the assassin; at the period too, when beginning to realize the rewards of toil, anxiety and responsibility without parallel in official experience; when, having reached the point in the national struggle, from which, as from a lofty eminence, he could see the sun of peace and prosperity beginning to gild the darkened heavens, and contemplate the different states of the Union soon to enjoy undisturbed repose —at such a time, in the very capital of the nation, surrounded and protected by the most formidable defences, to be made the victim of that foul spirit of treason which he had so long and successfully battled, is well fitted to strike every heart with horror, and to cause the sternest spirits in the land to tremble with agitation and fear! In view of such an event, paralleled only by the assassination of Henry IV of France, and of the Prince of Orange of Holland, no wonder that an entire nation is in tears! And when the millions of the dusky children of the south shall have heard that "Father Abraham," the Moses of their deliverance from worse than Egyptian bondage, has fallen, their mourning will be even more deep than ours, it will be "as the mourning of Hadadrimmon in the valley of Megiddon."

For many of the disappointments and disasters which occurred at the commencement, and during the progress of the war to the army and the navy; for the conflicting theories and conduct of statesmen which perplexed the councils of the nation; and for the incompetency or treachery of military leaders which, at times, cast so deep a gloom over the loyal spirit of the people, we are able to discover satisfactory reasons. They were the necessary conditions in the evolution of a divine purpose, by which grand results have been wrought out for the permanent benefit of the nation. The contest was protracted in order to secure universal liberty, to mature and intensify the sentiment of nationality, and to demonstrate the power of self-government inherent in the republic, before the nations of the earth. All this is now obvious to every reflecting mind. But for the violent death of our Chief Magistrate at so important a crisis in our history, we cannot, as yet, discover the reason. That some wise design is to be answered by it, we do not doubt; but what it is we are unable to comprehend. Clouds and darkness enshroud the providential dispensation and it becomes us in Christian faith- and submission, to bow reverently before the inscrutable mystery.

In contemplating the career of Abraham Lincoln, we cannot but discover the fostering character of our institutions, and the encouragement held out to native talent and industry in whatever outward condition they may be found. Passing a portion of his earlier years in a section of Indiana which was then an almost uninhabited wilderness, he acquired among the hardships of frontier life, those habits of self-reliance and persistent energy which became the marked attributes of his subsequent character. He afterwards resided in the state of Illinois, where, in 1832, he took an active part in the Indian war which so sadly disturbed the western portion of the country. At the close of his brief military service he engaged in the study of the law, and by a natural transition, entered the political arena of the state. In 1847 he became a member of the congress of the United States, where he acquired honorable distinction among his compeers. His power as a statesman became more fully known, in 1858, when, opposed to Senator Douglas — no mean antagonist — he maintained on equal terms a protracted struggle, during which he evinced qualities of intellect, force of reasoning, comprehensiveness of judgment, and ability to grasp and master some of the most intricate questions of national policy, which attracted to him the attention of the nation, and prepared the way for his advancement to the high position which he so recently and honorably sustained. How humane and how efficient the character of that government, which thus takes charge of a child of penury and toil, opens the way for his intellectual and moral improvement, recognizes and fosters his true native worth, however rude the outward garb, and places within his reach the highest position of honor and trust, within the gift of a mighty people! Such is the genius of our institutions. It exercises a paternal care over all its children, seeking to qualify each for useful service. And how beautifully and forcibly is this feature illustrated in the history of him, for whose death the nation this day sits in the dust and refuses to be comforted! A few years since he was a plain man, comparatively obscure, and possessing little more than a mere local notoriety. But how by the discipline of native powers in the conflicts of public life, during which his mind was in contact with the profoundest questions and principles of national policy, was he prepared, when the great occasion demanded it, to loom up and become distinguished among the foremost statesmen of the world. What a sublime tribute to the character of our institutions! In this country distinction depends not upon contingencies of location or birth. The road to eminence is open equally to all, and there is no royal avenue to the summit. Here, intellect alone is the secret of success, intellect well cultivated and well balanced, and directed with persevering energy to the accomplishment of noble objects. Every American youth may aspire to become an American lord, a man who depends upon a higher distinction than an hereditary title, whose name is enrolled in nature's own peerage and who carries the patent of his nobility in his intellect and his heart.

Were I to attempt an analysis of the character of the lamented dead, I would not hesitate to accord to him a *high measure of intellectual power*. And by this I do not assert that he possessed either brilliancy of genius or extended literary acquirements, or vastness of research. He was, for the most part, a self-educated man, and was indebted to the schools for little more than the simplest rudiments of education. With natural capacities of a high order, his mind acquired, amid the struggles of public life, a culture, a vigor and a breadth which no institution of learning can ordinarily impart. He possessed, to a surprising degree, the faculty of penetrating deep into the intricacies of theories and arguments, detecting both the truth and the error that might be either magnified or concealed beneath the drapery of rhetoric, or the mystifications of false logic. He seems to have had an intuitive insight into the nature and relations of things, a ready perception of the bearings of measures and policies, and could anticipate results with a sort of prophetic foresight. His style was chaste, his words were few and well chosen, and his arguments pertinent and conclusive. Practical wisdom, or stern common sense, which always constitutes the basis of a sound judgment and of safe conclusions, was a preëminent attribute of his mind. He was patient and deliberate in investigating measures and in weighing the arguments for or against their adoption; and when he had reached a conclusion, it partook of the character of a positive unchangeable conviction, which resulted in corresponding action. No man ever had greater responsibilities resting upon him than he. No man was ever called to act in circumstances of greater perplexity, surrounded by counsellors of conflicting views and variant policies, and not certain always who were strictly loyal, and who were concealed traitors. Yet with a calm determination and an unwavering purpose he pursued one steady course, met every responsibility, and during the season of the most imminent peril, conducted the affairs of the nation in a manner which has elicited the admiration of the purest patriots and the wisest statesmen in all parts of the civilized world.

He possessed also a *well balanced character*. And here, I know not that I can do better than quote a brief passage from a recent writer who has pertinently expressed my views on this point.

"With a unanimity rarely equaled, a people who had fought eight years against a tax of three pence on the pound, and that was rapidly advancing to the front rank of nations through the victories of peace,— a people jealous of its liberties and proud of its prosperity, has reëlected to the chief magistracy a man under whose administration burdensome taxes have been levied, immense armies marshaled, imperative drafts ordered, and fearful suffering endured. They have done this because, in spite of possible mistakes and short-comings, they have seen his grasp ever tightening around the throat of slavery, his weapons ever seeking the vital point of the rebellion. They have beheld him standing always at his post, calm in the midst of peril, hopeful when all was dark, patient under every obloquy, courteous to his bitterest foes, conciliatory where conciliation was possible, inflexible where to yield was dishonor. Never have the passions of civil war betrayed him into cruelty or hurried him into revenge; nor has any hope of personal benefit or any fear of personal detriment stayed him when occasion beckoned. If he has erred, it has been on the side of leniency. If he has hesitated, it has been to assure himself of the right. Where there was censure, he claimed it for himself; where there was praise, he lavished it upon his subordinates. The strong he has braved, and the weak sheltered. He has rejected the counsels of his friends when they were inspired by partizanship, and adopted the suggestions of opponents when they were founded on wisdom. His ear has always been open to the people's voice, yet he has never suffered himself to be blindly driven by the storm of popular fury. He has consulted public opinion, as the public servant should; but he has not pandered to public prejudice, as only demagogues do. Not weakly impatient to secure the approval of the country, he has not scorned to explain his measures to the understanding of common people. Never bewildered by the solicitations of party, nor terrified by the menace of opposition, he has controlled with moderation, and yielded with dignity, as the exigencies of the time demanded. Entering upon office with the full share of the common incredulity, perceiving no more than his fellow-citizens the magnitude of the crisis, he has steadily risen to the height of the great argument. No suspicion of self-seeking stains his fair fame; but ever mindful of his solemn oath, he seeks with clean hands and a pure heart the welfare of the whole country. Future generations can alone do justice to his ability; his integrity is firmly established in the convictions of the present age."*

A just and noble tribute!

I add, again, that Abraham Lincoln was evidently controlled in his conduct by the high principles of morality and religion. The religious element seems to have marked his entire official career, and to have increased in strength and influence from the day he

* *Atlantic Monthly*, January, 1865.

left Springfield to assume the presidential chair to the hour when he resigned it, for, as we trust, a nobler destiny. None of his official predecessors have so frequently and devoutly acknowledged their dependence upon the God of nations, or have so earnestly requested the prayers of their countrymen, as he. He was a daily reader of the sacred scriptures, and seems to have been animated by the true spirit of the gospel. By its holy teachings he sought to be governed in all his outward relations. And I believe that no one, whether friend or foe, has ever questioned his moral honesty. No one has ever insinuated that he sought to use the vast power entrusted to him, for purposes of avarice or ambition. His integrity was of the nature of a holy, disciplined virtue: it was pure, unselfish and lofty. He was tried in the furnace, but was not burned; he breathed the malaria of corruption, intrigue and selfishness, but remained uncontaminated; he dealt with scheming men and heartless demagogues, who in their country's calamities sought the means of their own aggrandizement, but continued firm in the strength and simplicity of his uprightness. Irritated and insulted at home and abroad, he rendered just and equal dealings in return, with "malice for none, and charity for all." Few can read his last Inaugural Address, without being impressed with the deep religious tone which pervades it, and the simple scriptural phraseology in which portions of it are expressed. It would almost seem as if the shadow of his own tragic end had, for a moment, rested on him, and as if he were inspired to leave to posterity a document, which the highest Christian statesman might covet as the choicest memorial to attest his moral integrity and simple piety on the pages of history.

How consoling the hope we cherish at this hour of universal lamentation, when everything around us is veiled in emblems of sorrow, when every sanctuary is filled with weeping multitudes, and every family is stricken with a personal grief, that he, over whose tragic fate countless myriads are pouring forth their tears, has safely passed to that realm, where toil and care can never intrude, and where the traitor's bloody hand can never strike him more.

Such is the man whose career has been so sadly and abruptly terminated. Seldom do the robes of death gather over a nobler victim! The public loss is so great, and the chasm made in our national councils is so marked, that it is by no means surprising that every thoughtful mind becomes excited and appalled by the contemplation. And yet God, the God of our fathers, is the God of their children. Great as is the loss we have sustained, still the destiny of the country is not bound up in the fate of any one man. And perhaps we needed this stern admonition, to fix more deeply in our minds the salutary lesson of our absolute dependence upon the Most High, and to turn the hearts of the people more trustingly to Him. Perhaps also, in the midst of our triumphs, when about fully to realize results for which we had toiled and prayed and waited so long, we were beginning to lose our deep abhorrence of the crime of treason, and to cherish a weak and culpable clemency toward the miscreants who with fiend-like ferocity struck at the nation's life. It may have been necessary, therefore, that the nation should become aroused by this last demonstration of the spirit of rebellion, and should have a more tangible proof of its fierce and hellish character. And I cannot but think that the event of the President's assassination, has gone far toward curing us of a weak and criminal leniency toward that spirit which originated the bloody conflict of the last four years; which sought to wrap our cities in the devouring flames; which planned to diffuse the contagion of the yellow fever; which refused quarter to our troops at Fort Pillow; which deliberately murdered tens of thousands of our gallant soldiers by heat and cold and starvation; and which finally struck at the Ruler of the people, expecting that when he fell the government itself would sink into anarchy and ruin. And when we contemplate the horrid features of this spirit of rebellion, becoming darker and fiercer, and more cruel and devilish, through all its successive manifestations down to the catastrophe of this fearful tragedy, shall we hesitate to believe that we are bound, by its condign punishment, to vindicate the majesty of law, and sustain the principles of eternal justice? And while this day, we mourn the untimely fate of our beloved Chief Magistrate, have we not cause for gratitude that God has provided a worthy successor to the chair of state. He is one who from the commencement of the conflict, has stood "faithful among the faithless" in his loyalty to the Union. Sufferings and losses and deaths have served only to brighten and deepen and strengthen his patriotic devotion. He knows, by bitter experience, what the spirit of treason is; and I most confidently believe that he has been specially raised up, and inspired with adequate energy, to grapple with it, and mete out to it the penalty which the laws of God and of man have denounced against it. May He, who is Governor among the nations, guide and sustain the administration of Andrew Johnson!

Friends, this country is not destroyed, nor is it destined to ruin. The calamity which has for successive years fallen to our lot and which has just culminated in the death of our martyr President, is only purifying the national character, intensifying its spirit of loyalty, and preparing it for a higher destiny. The evil is only incidental and temporary; and in view of the unmistakeable omens of returning peace and prosperity, well may smiles of gladness shine this day through our tears of sorrow. We hail the near approach of the auspicious hour, which is to witness the adjustment of our national difficulties, and the period of repose which is to follow, when this fearful conflict shall be known only on the records of the distant past;

and when the ship of state, having safely weathered every shoal and tempest, shall be seen sailing majestically in a calm sea, with a law-abiding and exulting crew, and THE FLAG OF THE UNION NAILED TO HER MAST!

> "Sail on, O UNION, strong and great!
> Humanity with all its fears,
> With all the hopes of future years,
> Is hanging breathless on thy fate!
> In spite of rock and tempest's roar,
> In spite of false lights on the shore,
> Sail on, nor fear to breast the sea!
> Our hearts, our hopes, our prayers, our tears,
> Our faith triumphant o'er our fears,
> Are all with thee,—are all with thee!"

To the memory of the pilot whose strong arm guided the laboring vessel through the last four years of darkness and storm—during portions of which "neither sun nor stars appeared for many days," we dedicate this sacred hour. Abraham Lincoln! thy work on earth is done, and thy country awards thee the verdict, "good and faithful servant!" Thy place is secure in the affections of a grateful people! Thy name will live untarnished on the records of history, so long as the world shall continue to appreciate devoted patriotism, elevated wisdom, unbending integrity, and sublime virtue! Abraham Lincoln! the good, the noble, and the true, fare thee well!

> "Thy grave shall be a hallowed shrine,
> Adorned with nature's brightest wreath;

Each glowing season will combine
Its incense there to breathe;
And oft upon the midnight air,
Shall viewless harps be murmuring there."

Sermon Preached in the Liberty Street Presbyterian Church (Colored).

BY REV. JOSEPH A. PRIME.

And Saul also went home to Gibeah; and there went with him a band of men, whose hearts God had touched.
But the children of Belial said, how shall this man save us? And they despised him, and brought him no presents. But he held his peace.—1 Samuel, x, 26, 27.

The events of the past repeat themselves in the history of the present. What happened in the days of Saul, has taken place in our own day, only modified and varied in some of its circumstances. In the case of Saul, we have every reason to believe that he was God-appointed, to accomplish a certain work. We have equal reason also, to believe that Abraham Lincoln was designated by the same divine power, to perform a certain service, namely, the redemption of the colored race from slavery.

As in the days of Saul "there went with him a band of men, whose hearts God had touched," so in our own time, there has been a faithful company which has stood by Abraham Lincoln in his struggle for right and truth. As in those days there were men who asked concerning Saul, "How shall this man save us?" and despised him, so have we seen, within the past four years, multitudes who have queried in like manner as to Abraham Lincoln, and have refused to recognize in him the man commissioned by God to work out His great and divine purpose.

The occasion for which we have met to-day, is to do honor to our martyred President. A great and good man has been murdered by the hand of an assassin! What crime had he committed? What law had he violated? Neither crime nor the violation of law could be laid to his charge, still he was foully slaughtered. There is nothing new in this. The events of all history teach us that the innocent are frequently sacrificed by the hands of the guilty.

From the story of Saul, as narrated in the Scriptures, we learn that he was a member of the smallest of the tribes of Israel, and his family the least of all the families of that tribe, yet was he chosen king. The ancestors of Abraham Lincoln were not distinguished among men, yet was he made President of the United States. Our greatest men whose lives and labors and influence have done most to bless the world, have but rarely been found among those who have been rocked in the cradle of ease and supplied with every luxury. No, the men who carry the welfare of a nation in their hearts, and stoop down to lift up crushed and bleeding humanity, are oftener reared in humbleness and obscurity. If we look at Mr. Lincoln's early history, we shall find that he had a rough training, but at the same time a training that fitted him for the duties he was called to perform, inasmuch as it made him self-reliant. This preparation was not obtained in the halls of education, but amid the plainer and more active business of life, where mind and muscle aid each other. In this combined strength lies the true element of human greatness. Abraham Lincoln, the father and preserver of our nation, who lifted up the despised and the degraded out of that wretched condition to which pride and caste had consigned them, is to be ranked with Washington the successful exponent of another holy but different mission.

Slavery, that cruel system, had not only degraded the black man of the south, but had rendered the poor whites even more degraded and less hopeful of future elevation than the slaves themselves. Just at this crisis when the nation was in its greatest peril, God sent forth the modern Moses to deliver this people from that curse which was sapping the foundation of our public. The southern heart was wedded to slavery. Abraham Lincoln saw what constituted the strength of the rebellion, and he proclaimed "liberty to the captives, and the opening of the prison to them that are bound." This act increased the bitter spirit of the south, and his overthrow was determined from that hour. In fulfillment of this determination, Abraham Lincoln, the nation's Chief Magistrate, was murdered by the hands of an assassin. Had he been a usurper of the place he occupied; had he exercised his power in the spirit of tyranny; had he inflicted heavy blows upon the innocent; had he refused to listen to the cry for mercy, there might have been mitigating circumstances to lessen the enormity of this hellish and God forbidden crime. But instead of his being guilty of any of these acts, he must be regarded as one of the best and purest of men, having the most benevolent feelings for the welfare of the entire race of mankind, of any of those who have filled the presidential chair since our American independence was declared. Washington was the Father of our country, Lincoln was the Father of our nation.

In some things Abraham Lincoln is to be regarded as superior to Washington.. Especially is this so in the comprehensive plans he instituted for the happiness of the inhabitants of these United States, irrespective of class or condition. He was strictly moral, untiring in his labors of incorruptible integrity, and free from selfishness. He was simple and yet wonderfully firm and independent in his manner. He was blessed with great intuitive perception of truth. He was sagacious and farseeing in his plans, amiable in disposition and meek in temper. These qualities prepared him for almost any emergency. He was truly the friend of man. The high and the low, the rich and the poor, the learned and the unlearned, could all approach him upon a common level and find him ready to hear their statements, and sympathize with them, and they would depart with minds impressed in his favor. He had an appropriate word for every man. With an even balance he maintained the affairs of the nation in its life struggle. As an exponent of American principles, a man occupied the seat of power who was incapable of being a tyrant, and his virtues commended him to the people. His fame has become universal, and I do not know but it may be said, that he was the centre of observation for all foreign nations and countries. He had the sympathy of millions upon millions who only judged him by his acts. No deeper gloom ever fell upon any people than has fallen upon this nation on this occasion. No deeper sorrow ever filled the universal heart of the country than that caused by the death of our beloved President. The heart of the nation has been pierced to its very centre.

But there is a class who feel this death more keenly than all the other classes combined. It is the colored people. None mourn or lament more sincerely than they. None feel that they have lost so true and tried a friend as the millions of bond and freed men of the south. He was hailed as their great deliverer. So deeply had he taken the cause of the oppressed into his heart, and so clearly did this fact appear to the mind of the slaves, that they declared him their savior, sent to set them free from the cruel yoke of oppression. The rebellion was the direct out-growth of slavery, and the murder of the President, is only the intensified spirit of slavery personified. It was slavery that killed our President, and the blood of the murdered President will cry out against slavery as long as there is a bondman to sigh for freedom.

But pause a moment. Cast your thoughts back to the home of our departed President, on the eve of his leaving for Washington. Behold the immense assemblage who have gathered to bid him farewell. Well might he look forward with deep apprehension and say, " A duty devolves upon me which is perhaps greater than that which has devolved upon any other man since the days of Washington." How well he understood that duty, how conscientious he was in discharging it, how fully he relied upon that Divine assistance without which human effort is vain, all know who have traced his career and watched the progresss of events. If the American people have reason to rejoice in the life and labors of a Washington, then the colored people of our country have a much greater reason to rejoice that Abraham Lincoln was permitted to occupy the executive chair, as Chief Ruler of this nation.

Let the name of Abraham Lincoln ever be dear to the colored race, for he, above all other presidents, dared to open his mouth for the down-trodden and despised. Let his acts, his noble deeds, be stamped upon your inmost minds. But you are not alone the recipients of these benefits bestowed by this great and good man. He was the world's benefactor, Heaven's gift to mankind. In the death he died, he has drawn all mankind to behold the deeds he has done. Abraham Lincoln still lives, though murdered by the foulest spirit of the lowest pit. Let us pray that the mantle of our beloved and lamented President may fall upon his successor. And let the prayers of all good men ascend to God for the thorough healing of the nation. Amen and Amen.

SERVICE AT THE JEWISH SYNAGOGUE.

The synagogue of the Jewish congregation, Anshe Chesed, was draped in mourning. A large audience assembled, comprising all the Hebrews living in the city and a great number of Germans of other denominations. After the introductory prayer in Hebrew, the Thora (Law scrolls) were unfolded, and the Rev. Dr. H. G. Salomon, the Rabbi of the congregation, delivered a most solemn sermon, in which he set forth the virtues of the late President and directed attention to the fact that the whole north, though divided in political views, was united in bewailing the loss of the Chief Magistrate of the nation and in expressions of respect for his character and patriotic conduct. He alluded to the law of Judaism, which made it incumbent upon every one professing that faith to pray daily for the welfare of the chieftain of the country, and to the effect produced by this injunction in making Israelites true and loyal citizens. He closed by drawing a picture of the desolation and anarchy into which the nation would have been plunged if the designs of the conspirators had not been checked by providence.

Mr. Frank Hartsfeld then ascended the pulpit and addressed the audience in substance, as follows. He said there was no parallel to be found in history to the great crime over which we mourn, except the assassination of Henry the Fourth of France, by Ravaillac. Lincoln ruled at a time when the United States were divided by conspiracy and rebellion. Henry reigned when France was torn in pieces by dissensions. When the former was inaugurated he was obliged to guard his way to Washington, the seat of the government. The latter was compelled to take Paris by force before he was crowned a king. Each was a chieftain who was full of love for his country and strove to reconcile contending parties and establish peace on a firm and lasting basis. When Henry was assassinated he was riding in a carriage through one of the public streets of Paris accompanied by several of his friends, and surrounded by gentlemen on horseback and running footmen, any of whom would have sacrificed life for him. Lincoln was shot while seated in a private box at a theatre, in company with a party of friends and surrounded by hundreds of people who would have defended him unto death. So sudden was the attack on Henry, that those with him did not perceive the state of the case, until he fell forward after the second blow was struck. The fearful fate of Lincoln was not recognized until after the murderer had escaped. Ravaillac was put to the most frightful tortures and was condemned to the most horrible death. Booth died miserably, but before the decrees of the law could overtake him, and the spot desecrated by his foul body is unknown. Lincoln was acknowledged to be a good man, even by his enemies. Henry possessed the love of all classes, even of the Jesuits who opposed him. It was Henry's wish, often expressed, that every peasant in France might have a chicken in his pot. Lincoln's regard for the people was ever manifesting itself in deeds of mercy and love. As France dates its greatness from the time of Henry's reign, so will the United States come out of the struggle now ending, in which Lincoln's name has been preëminent, the first nation of the world. Washington's name is identified with our liberty and independence. The name of Lincoln will be identified with our nationality and greatness.

At the close of this address, prayers were read in Hebrew, for the immortal part of the dead. A translation of these prayers follows. The prayers by the mourner, were read by the Rabbi.

Mourner. O Lord our God, King of the universe, who art merciful and gracious to the living, be merciful and gracious to the soul of thy servant Abraham Lincoln, who has been called from this world to appear before the throne of thy holiness. Remember him with a good memorial before thee. Visit him with the visitation of salvation and mercy. Let him dwell amongst those just and pious who dwell in the secret place of thy holiness and abide under the shadow of thy glory. Have compassion upon him and inspect him with thy benevolent goodness. Return unto him with the multitude of thy mercy for the sake of the just who performed thy will. Be gracious to him, guard him with thy endless kindness, and grant him immortality.

Congregation. Blessed art thou, O Lord, our God! King of the Universe, who art a judge.

Blessed art thou, O Lord, our God! King of the Universe, who createst in justice, maintainest in justice, slayest in justice, and bringest again into life in justice. Blessed art thou, O Lord, who revivest the dead.

Mourner. Thou art righteous to slay and to revive, thou in whose hand is the custody of all spirits; blessed be then the righteous Judge who slayeth and reviveth.

Congregation. We know, O Lord, that thy judgment is righteous; thou art righteous when thou speakest, justified when thou judgest, and no one can find fault with thy manner of judging; for thou art righteous and thy judgment is just. The Lord gave and the Lord hath taken; blessed be the name of the Lord.

OTHER SERVICES.

At the First Baptist Church, Rev. Dr. George C. Baldwin, the pastor, spoke in eulogistic terms of the deceased President, and took occasion to draw the parallel between the lessons taught by this event and the lessons taught by somewhat similar events in the scriptures.

The Rev. Dr. E. Wentworth, in his discourse, at the State Street Methodist Episcopal Church, reminded his hearers that no cup of the Divine providence is unmixed, that good and evil travel hand in hand. "The death of Abraham Lincoln" said he, "resulted from the death struggle, the expiring desperation of rebellion, slavery and secession. We rejoice at the destruction of these heresies, as much as we mourn for the loss of our revered head. But slavery dies even if it throttles the Chief Magistrate with its last convulsive clutch." An address was also made on this occasion by the Rev. S. Parks.

In his sermon at the First Presbyterian Church, the pastor, Rev. Marvin R. Vincent reminded his congregation that neither men nor communities must fix their faith upon any one man, but remember that it is God who preserves nations. He expressed the hope, that coming as this death came, at an hour when the President was winning almost universal favor, the event might serve as a lessson to recall us to our sole source of dependence — our dependence on God.

In the Roman Catholic Churches the occasion was solemnly observed.

At St. Mary's Church, the services conducted by Rev. Peter Havermans were similar to those on Holy Saturday, and the prayers *pro quacunque tribulatione,* prescribed by the rubrics for public calamities were read in addition to the usual collects of the day. These prayers are as follows:

"Despise not Almighty God, thy people crying to thee in affliction: but for the glory of thy name come to their succour."

"Receive mercifully O Lord the sacrifices by which it hath pleased thee to be reconciled, and by thy powerful goodness, to have restored safety to us."

"Look down mercifully, we beseech thee O Lord, upon our tribulation, and turn away the anger of thy indignation which we have so justly deserved, through our Lord Jesus Christ, thy Son, who liveth and reigneth with thee, for ever and ever. *Amen.*"

At the end of the high mass, the psalm *Miserere* was chanted, supplicating God's mercy upon the congregation and upon all people.

The service at St. Peter's Church consisted of solemn and plaintive chants by the choir, and public prayers and litanies by the pastor, the Rev. James Keveny, for the safety and triumph of our beloved country and the defeat and confusion of its enemies. Appropriate remarks were also made by the pastor, sympathizing with our nation in this the hour of her trial and sad bereavement, but expressing sentiments of encouragement also, at the prospect of a bright and glorious future.

The services at St. Joseph's Church were as follows:
"The altars were draped in black. A catafalque was

placed opposite the main altar in the centre aisle. Everything in the church bespoke mourning and sorrow, as befitted the solemn occasion. The bell tolled, and the people assembled in the church to assist at a service which the fell stroke of the assassin's hand made imperative. The pastor, the Rev. Aug. J. Thebaud, delivered a lengthy discourse to his sorrowing flock. He spoke of the enormity of the crime of murder, which was much aggravated when committed against a man invested with the highest authority in the land. He said the crime had been such, as to make it incumbent on all to endeavor to appease the wrath of God, and to supplicate Him to spare the people. Catholics especially should mourn on this occasion, because in losing Mr. Lincoln, they had lost a sincere friend and a true lover of civil and religious liberty: they should mourn, because murder is a crime crying to heaven for vengeance. Gratitude likewise called upon the Catholics to give expression to their sorrow, for, through the magnanimity of the people, and through the wisdom and enlightenment of their chief magistrates, the Catholic church has been always free in her action in America.

"When the pastor had ended his discourse, the church choir chanted in solemn and mournful notes, the psalm *Miserere*. At its conclusion, the Rev. Father Thebaud read aloud, prayers for the President, for congress, for the state legislature, and lastly for the peace, happiness and prosperity of the country.

When service had been concluded, the people left the church, deeply impressed with what they had heard, and more fully persuaded of the loss they and the country at large had sustained in the death of the lamented President."

No service was held at St. John's Episcopal Church, the rector being absent at the bedside of a wounded brother, and at another church the service was postponed to the day following. With these exceptions, it is believed that impressive exercises were held in every place of worship in the city. These exercises were similar in their main features, consisting of prayer, hymns, solemn music, scripture lessons and addresses or sermons suited to the occasion. The black draperies which covered the pulpit and the desk and the altar, which swung festooned about the galleries, or hung in volumnious masses from the ceiling, or twined in spiral bands around the columns, or flowed over the facade of the organ, added to the impressiveness of the scene and the solemnity of the worship.

The observance of the day was quiet, but heartfelt and earnest. The solemn tolling of the numerous bells of the city broke out upon the stillness in saddest harmony with human feeling and human thought. Emblems of mourning, flags bordered with black, crape from the small fragment placed by the hand of love on the poor man's cottage to the heavy folds draping in dark masses the dwelling of his richer neighbor, gave an appearance to the city never before witnessed. Sentences taken from the loved President's last inaugural address, shields, stars, tablets inscribed with words of patriotism or religion, pictures of the great departed — these were some of the devices that appeared on buildings both public and private.

All shops and warehouses and offices, the schools and courts, places of business and amusement all were closed. There was no military or other parade, and the citizens who walked in groups through the streets appeared like the separated detachments of a grand company of mourners. Never before was there witnessed such a spontaneous expression of the grief of the nation's heart, as on this solemn occasion. The day with its ceremonies, its humiliation, its religious feeling will pass down on the page of history as a fitting memorial of the love of the people for one whom they respected for his noble character and devoted patriotism while living, and embalmed with their prayers and tears when dead.

THURSDAY, APRIL 20TH, 1865.

This day, which prior to the assassination of the President had been designated by the governor of the state as a day of thanksgiving for national victories, and which by a subsequent proclamation* had been set apart to services appropriate to a season of national bereavement, was not as generally observed

---

* This proclamation is printed at pages 28 and 29.

in the manner designed, as it would have been had not the services of the day previous anticipated its character and solemnities. Places of business, however, were generally closed, and emblems of mourning were apparent on buildings both public and private.

At the United Presbyterian Church, the occasion was solemnized as one of humiliation, praise and prayer. After the reading of the forty-fourth Psalm, the pastor, the Rev. H. P. McAdam, preached a sermon, taking as his text the first verse of the one hundred and first Psalm, "I will sing of mercy and judgment."

A service similar in character was conducted by the Rev. D. S. Gregory, at the Second Presbyterian Church, and in several other churches the day was solemnized by acts of worship.

FRIDAY, APRIL 21ST, 1865.

Resolutions of the Board of Supervisors of Rensselaer County.

A special meeting of the Board of Supervisors was held on Friday, April 21st, 1865, for the purpose of signing tax-warrants. Previous to adjourning, Gen. Martin Miller offered the following resolutions, which were adopted.

Whereas, We are all aware of the murder of Abraham Lincoln, Chief Magistrate of the United States, and of the attempted assassination of Wm. H. Seward, Secretary of State. And

Whereas, It becomes us as a public body to give expression to those sentiments of sorrow and profound regret which fill the heart of each individual of this community. Therefore, be it

Resolved, That by this unmitigated and unparalleled atrocity our nation is called upon to mourn the untimely end of one in whom were centered the highest hopes of an anxious and expectant people, one who gave bright promise through his meritorious, wise and liberal action to bring to a speedy termination those difficulties which have agitated this great and powerful nation for the past four years. But He who controlleth the destinies of all, willed it otherwise, before whom let us bow with meek submission, knowing that this event has been permitted for some wise purpose as yet unintelligible to man.

Resolved, That instead of accomplishing the fell purpose at which the instigators and perpetrators of this foul and damnable deed aimed, they have opened the eyes of those who might otherwise have remained blind to the interests and welfare of our beloved country, strengthened the hands of those who to-day are defending its cause and consigned themselves to an inglorious and infamous end.

Resolved, That the foregoing preambles and resolutions be spread upon the journal of this board, and published in the papers of the county.

On motion, the Board resolved to attend the obsequies of President Lincoln when his remains should pass through Albany, and a committee was appointed to make the necessary arrangements for such attendance. The Board adjourned to meet on the morning of the 26th inst., at nine o'clock, at the Court House.

HIRAM D. HULL, Chairman.

T. S. BANKER, Clerk.

SATURDAY, APRIL 22D, 1865.

"SIC SEMPER TYRANNIS."

BY E. H. G. CLARK.

"*Sic semper tyrannis*," vile southron?
You murdered your own truest friend!
And may God now have pity for traitors —
Man's patience has come to an end!

"*Sic semper tyrannis*," O madman?
He marshalled to freedom a race!
He led us to battle with tyrants;
To dare look the right in the face!

"*Sic semper tyrannis*," assassin?
Behold a whole nation in black!
And hark to the curse of its millions
That rumbles along your track!

"*Sic semper tyrannis*,"— O Heaven!
That motto for slavery's knife;
While died the great servant of freedom,
As martyrdom sainted his life!

"*Sic semper tyrannis,*"— God help us
To bear it — the deed and the loss;
The crime that has scarcely been mated
Since Jesus was nailed to the cross!

"*Sic semper tyrannis*"— Our Father
In Heaven, we swear unto Thee,
Once more over him thou hast taken,
All men shall be equally free!

Troy Daily Times.

ABRAHAM LINCOLN.

BY JULIA ADELAIDE BURDICK.

"*Hung be the heavens with black.*"

Bring the censer and shake it gently, bring the bell and toll it solemnly, bring the psalm and chant it mournfully. Bring the flag and lower it, bring the drum and muffle it, bring the fife, the bugle and the instruments all, and pour out a requiem over him who has fallen in the morning of his glory.

Our foes are flying, but our chieftain has fallen. It is a shame not to rejoice when victory perches upon our banners, but it is a sin not to weep when our standard bearer is slain. It is base not to greet with acclamations the living who lived to witness their triumphs, but it is cruel not to mourn the dead who died in sight of what they died for. It is right to sing and shout in honor of those who have passed the furnace without the smell of fire on their garments, but it is no less just to sigh and carry cypress in memory of those whom the flames consumed.

In the entrenchments, along the banks of the James, on the field before Richmond our heroes have fallen, while bullets whistled, blood gushed, hearts broke, the heavens blackened, and the earth shook with the wrestle of mad armies thundering and clashing together in deadly combat. Not a hero suffered there for naught, not a precious breath fluttered out from its frail tenement in vain, for thus were our great but costly victories won. But he, the pride, the hope, and the glory of the nation; in the midst of an assembly radiant with beauty, glorious in intellect, and full-hearted with happiness, without an instant's warning, saw the unstable earth melt and vanish away, and the golden portals of eternity open before the dissolving pageantry of life. With laurels nobly won yet green on his brow, at a moment when the angel of peace was spreading her white wings over the land, and it seemed that the last victim had been sacrificed on the altar of liberty, God in his infinite wisdom saw fit to remove from among us, him who for four weary years of war and desolation had been our buckler and our shield, our fortress and our strong defence.

Alas that I can say nothing of Abraham Lincoln, which will not be far better said many times, ere the shudder of this sad calamity will have passed from our hearts! But it is no less a blessed privilege to me than to others, to be permitted to offer my simple tribute of love and sorrow to the memory of departed greatness; and while the anguish of my soul refuses to be allayed in silence, it would be hard indeed, were I forced to crush back the rising tears, or repress the lamentations crowding to my lips. Who that loves his country, but will weep in this, her hour of deep distress? What heart so insensible to the claims of unaffected greatness, or so unmoved by the example of a patriotism so exalted as his, that it will refuse to mourn that a cruel and violent death has taken from the nation he served so faithfully, the greatest and best man of the age?

Never within the memory of living man has a President been so loved. Despite the ridicule of little minds, in the face of every injurious device that malignity could conceive, and tried by every test that constant, harrassing hatred could invent or apply, surrounded by enemies at home, and menaced by foes from abroad, he conquered every prejudice, surmounted every obstacle and enshrined himself in the very hearts of the people. The respect he won the first year became admiration the second, warmed into confidence the third, and finally culminated in something almost sinfully allied to adoration the fourth and last. Not only did he compel those who thought ill of him to think well, and those who thought well to think better; but, in many a notable instance, his bitterest opponents he converted into staunch supporters. Every candid mind acknowledged his worth, every loyal tongue spoke his praise. He lived to see the day dawn when the wisdom of the course he had unwaveringly pursued was becoming apparent to the world; but it is reserved for the light of the future to illuminate the mighty intellect which was just beginning to make its latent strength felt when its great plans were suddenly arrested, and its giant working stilled forever.

It is no discredit to his memory to say that four years ago many an anxious heart trembled for the strength of the untried arm that was to pilot the ship of state in her perilous course against the head winds already whistling through her canvass, and over the breakers even then angrily hurling themselves athwart her pathway. The farmer boy, the rail splitter, the flat boatman, the humble western lawyer, would he stand unaffrighted when the shock of war should come and he should know not friend from foe, and his enemies should be they of his own household? How needless were our fears! Of just such rugged material are heroes made. When the storm burst in all its fury, when the heavens hurled their doom in thunderbolts and lightning flashes, which fell, not harmless, as thousands of known and unknown graves and the countless host of broken lives and mourning hearthstones will attest, but impotent to work the evil they sought, he for whom our fears were marshalled in dread array stood undaunted amid the smoking ruins. From that hour to this, our trust has never for a single moment faltered nor sought any other source of support.

How wise and conciliatory were the offers of pardon he tendered to the rebellious states during the first year of the war, yet how firmly again and again was the determination repeated to forcibly subdue them if they would not peacefully return to their allegiance. The hand held out to the penitent proffered the gentle clasp of a friend, but the finger tightening around the heart of the traitor had the hardness of steel. Futile was each generous appeal, and futile he doubtless felt they would be, but they were the fitting expressions of that thoughtful care for friends, and boundless magnanimity to foes, which would have provided for the safety of the loyal by the same humane measure which would instigate the punishment of the disloyal. It was this broad humanity more than anything else except the purity of his motives, and the rare simplicity of his nature, which endeared him to the hearts of his countrymen. The same clemency that marked the first acts of his official life characterized them until the day of his death. Even when the fatal bullet was being made ready for its unconscious victim, his noble heart was busy planning and providing for the future welfare of his enemies. Even when the brutal plot that terminated his existence was in process of completion, he was seeking the guidance of heaven, and the assistance of the best counsels of the nation to enable him to decide how far consistently with his duty as the dispenser of righteous punishment, he could exercise the power of restoring to their olden privileges the misguided foes of the country their madness so nearly destroyed.

Oh, when shall we see his like again? There has no good thing ever been spoken of any man living or dead which may not truly be said of him. What if the casket were plain and unpolished? The jewel it enclosed was as pure as the Mountain of Light. Firm, yet gentle; severe, yet just; inflexible in the right, yet never obstinate in the wrong; pure minded, unselfish; grateful to his friends; magnanimous to his foes; true to himself and true to his country; so might we go on enumerating his virtues, and still leave some grace of spirit unmentioned though the catalogue were never so long. "Honest Abe," homely though the title may be, there was never a truer one bestowed upon man, or one more surely destined to immortality. When they who have spoken ill of him are the dust of the earth; when his maligners are mouldering in their forgotten graves; when oblivion rests upon the memory of those who heaped sorrow upon his head; when they who wrought his destruction are remembered only with loathing, and their names uttered with a shudder, then, side by side with that of George Washington will the unsullied name of Abraham Lincoln be written, and while the one remains the great and good Father of his Country, the other will bear the no less illustrious title of the Saviour of his Country.

How is our joy turned into mourning! The bells that have been ringing the notes of gladness, are clanging in consonance with the unutterable woe that fills every heart. The flags that have been flaunting the glorious tidings of victory, are draped with the gloomy emblems of mourning. All, all is sorrow and gloom. Bring the censer and shake it gently, bring the bell and toll it solemnly, bring the psalm and chant it mournfully. Bring the flag and lower it, bring the drum and muffle it, bring the fife, the bugle and the instruments all, and pour out a requiem over the noblest victim ever sacrificed to appease fiendish hate.— *Troy Daily Times.*

A DIRGE FOR WEDNESDAY, APRIL 19, 1865.

BY A. S. PEASE.

Toll! toll! the solemn bell!
And as the dirges swell
   On the sad air,
Let every voice be dumb.
Let every heart be still;
Let every bosom thrill
   Only with prayer.

Great God of Liberty!
Humbly we pray to Thee:
   Hear us to-day:
Save Thou our native land.
Save by Thy mighty power.
Cheer us. In this dark hour,
   Turn not away.

Drape every heart in grief,
Sad that our Nation's chief,
    Loved and revered,
Dead from the Capitol,
Goes to his silent rest,
By all the people blest,
    Solemnly bier'd.

Muffle the rousing drum;
Stifle the busy hum
    Of daily strife.
Keep down the bitter thought.
Out of this fearful grief
(God give our hopes relief,)
    Get we new life.

High let our eagle soar;
Loud let the cannon roar,
    No more to cease.
Shrill blow the bugle blast.
Plain in the air are heard,
By every leaf that's stirred,
    Whispers of peace.

Great God of Liberty!
God of Prosperity!
    Hear us, we pray:
Spare us our life and laws.
Empty all hearts of hate;
All of War's ills abate.
    Bless us to-day.

Troy Daily Press.

During the afternoon of this day, the Hon. Uri Gilbert, Mayor of the city, received the following note.

Albany, April 22.

To the Mayor of Troy:

The common council committee of this city, having in charge the arrangements for the obsequies of the late President Lincoln, on Wednesday next, have directed that an invitation be extended to your municipal authorities, and through you, to the various military and fire companies, and also the civic and religious associations of your city, to unite in the ceremonies. You will please communicate your intention to John Tracey, chairman of the committee.

J. C. CUYLER, Secretary.

The mayor caused this note to be published soon after its reception, and announced generally to those named in it, the invitation it contained. He also notified a meeting of the common council, to be held on the Monday next following.

ORDER OF THE NATIONAL GUARD.

HEAD QRS., 24TH REGT., N. Y. S. N. G.,
Troy, N. Y., April 22d, 1865.

GENERAL ORDER NO. 12.

The regiment will parade on Wednesday, the 26th inst., for the purpose of participating in the obsequies of the late lamented President of the United States.

Commandants of companies will report with their commands at their armories, fully uniformed and equipped, at 8 o'clock A. M. of that day. Field and staff will report at the colonel's quarters at the same hour. The regimental band, Capt. Doring, and the drum corps, Drum Major Perkins, will report to the Adjutant, at the hour before mentioned. Commandants of companies will be notified by the Adjutant on the morning of the parade as to the the formation of the line. Quartermaster Church will provide the transportation.

The regimental battery will accompany the parade. Capt. Landon, commanding A Co., will make such arrangements as may be necessary.

Commandants of armories will cause the colors to be displayed at half-staff at 8 o'clock A. M. on the 26th inst., and to remain at half-staff till their commands return to their quarters.

The attention of officers is again called to General Order No. 10. By order.

ISAAC McCONIHE JR.,

GURDON G. MOORE, Adj.   Col. Com.

SUNDAY, APRIL 23D, 1865.

In Memoriam
A. L.

BY B. H. HALL.

Strong in the strength of common sense :
  Fettered by naught but right's own rules ;
  With wisdom blessed above the schools,
And void of sham and false pretence ;

Finding in every human face
  Some image of the source of all,
  Hearing in every bondman's call
The suppliance of a common race ;—

Thus armed, in blackest hour of hate,
  Obedient to a people's voice
  And sacred by a people's choice,
He came to guard and save the state.

He waited, suffering long the rage
  That strove the nation's heart to pierce,
  And watched, till treason's madness fierce
At Sumter cast the rebel gage.

Then to his summons forth there came
  Brave Northern men with hurrying tread,
  Fired with a vengeance grand and dread,
To vindicate the nation's fame.

They left the busy marts of trade,
  They left the anvil and the plough,
  And their sweet lives, with solemn vow,
On their dear country's altar laid.

Then through long years of deadliest strife —
  Our banner trodden in the dust—
  Lincoln, with simple, childlike trust,
Stood firm to save the nation's life.

He never yielded hope nor heart.
  Pierced with the shaft of bitter hate,
  He chose with kindest soul to wait,
And hide the venom of the dart.

He could not sink to motives base,
  Nor seek a good by doubtful ends ;

But weighed the counsel of his friends,
And looked above for light and grace.

Then Truth revealed her godlike form,
   And Slavery fell, no more to rise,
   Crushed by the fiat of the skies,
Dying amid the battle storm.

Man, bound in gyves of grief and pain
   For crime of color or of birth,
   Rose from the common mother earth,
Freed from the dark, inhuman stain.

Out from unnumbered voices poured
   The anthem sweet of freedom's song,
   Of right triumphant over wrong,
From man redeemed to God adored.

Then one by one the strongholds fell
   Where treason long had held her seat,
   While he, so calm amid defeat,
In triumph, checked the exultant swell.

Thus victory came to be our friend,
   And hope inspired the longing view
   With vision of a heavenly hue—
The omen of a peaceful end.

Then sped that midnight message dread,
   Borne madly on the electric wire,
   Burning its way on wings of fire,
That he who loved us all was dead.

On that black day that saw thee slain
   Oh Christ! that sinful man might live,
   That noble soul which thou did'st give
Passed from a murdered body's pain!

On that white day, when to the sun
    Again from Sumter's ruins rose
    Our country's flag, by fiercest foes
This deed of damning guilt was done!

Crowned with a never ending fame,
    Encircled by a nation's love,
    A martyr here, a saint above,
Be every honor done his name.

Oh God! a nation prostrate lies,
    And supplicates Thy favoring care:
    Make answer to its wrestling prayer,
And bid it in Thy strength arise.

Then shall these brooding clouds of night,
    That cast their shadow o'er our way,
    Dissolve before the brightening day,
And leave us in Thy blessed light.

Troy News.

April 19, 1865.

SERMON PREACHED IN THE FIRST PRESBYTERIAN CHURCH.

BY REV. MARVIN R. VINCENT.

Know ye not that there is a prince and a great man fallen this day in Israel?—2 SAMUEL, iii, 38.

The events of history are often like figures in relief. We see but one side of them, that which the artist chooses to represent. But this is not an *universal* truth. Some events have a dramatic interest inherent in them. They are independent of the artist. Though, like the sculptor who would hew Mount Athos into the figure of a recumbent giant, the historian may mould and drape and soften the lines, yet as the mountain, spite of the sculptor's work, would have been a mountain still, so such events stand out from their age, bearing their own character and speaking for themselves under all the misrepresentations of history. They convey their own great lesson. They resolutely strip from themselves all palliations.

Concurrent events, moreover, have often much to do with the sharpness with which these historic eras or incidents are cut. Often the accumulated sentiment and action of a whole cycle concentrate and find expression in a single event which henceforth becomes typical of the cycle. Often the condensed power of a century is behind a word or a blow. Often, too, contemporary events are so disposed as to heighten to the utmost the effect of a single deed, and to form a background against which its lines come out with preternatural sharpness.

If these characteristics ever united in any event, they do so in that which brings us here to-day. Death is not a new event. Death in high places is not a strange thing, even to us who, twice before this, have been called to mourn over the nation's chief magistrate. Even death under such circumstances is not unheard of nor uncommon. Not to us alone attaches the stigma of a murdered ruler. But this event is nevertheless instinct with a horror and with a significance independent of our nearness to it, and our practical connection with it. It concentrates in itself the elements of one fearful phase of our national life.

It is its natural offshoot, its pet child, its crowning development of horror, its grand expression before the civilized world. And, at the same time, concurrent circumstances are such as to define its lines more sharply. In many instances, as I have already said, even the assassination of a man in power does not impress us like this event. In so many instances the man owes his consequence only to his position. So much coloring is given to the deed by his tyranny or inefficiency. So many conflicting interests, whose claims history gives us no means of estimating, have been eddying round him, and the moral basis of the age has been so rotten and wavering, the moral sentiment of the age so perverted, that *that* event seems but in harmony with surrounding events. But here it is otherwise. The nation since its rise, and more rapidly within the last four years, has been developing a process of grouping. On one side of the line have been ranging themselves order, the government of reason and not of passion, fair and open discussion, patriotism, loyalty, devotion to the morals rather than to the politics of government. As an exponent of these principles, a man occupied the seat of power who could not, if he would, have been a tyrant, and who would not if he could; a man whose virtues commended themselves to the people, whose policy commanded their confidence and their endorsement. Breaking sharply off from such sentiments appeared another group, representing treason, disloyalty, impatience of control, passion, disregard of the principle of majority rule, oppression of the weak, deeper degradation of the degraded, its principles represented by factious demagogues who would rather "rule in hell than serve in heaven." No distinction was ever clearer. Ever diverging more and more, these two developments have gone on since the foundation of the republic, until at last the distinction has culminated. The one side has exhausted its venom in this crowning atrocity, and placed it in such startling relief against the virtues of the victim and the great order-loving, liberty-loving, rebellion-hating, humanity-cherishing sentiment of the nation, as henceforth to stamp the act and that of which it was the product with a character which no future historian will dare to palliate, and to insure to them a detestation the bitterness of which shall be intensified with every succeeding generation. God has forestalled the judgment of history, and on this act, at least, its decision shall be unanimous.

There then stands the fact in its terrific proportions. *Abraham Lincoln, President of the United States, has been foully murdered by an assassin.* Truly the murderer must have well studied the effect of contrasts. Had the deed been done when, as it is said, it was first contemplated, it might have harmonized somewhat better with the confusion which swayed the popular mind, with the anxiety respecting the still unfinished conflict, and the still menacing rebellion.

But this had passed. Victory had perched upon the banners of our brave generals. The routed army of the confederacy had laid down its arms. The pseudo president had abandoned his capital and fled, none knew whither. The land was gay with waving banners and vocal with the thunder of cannon and the pealing of bells; and the President, a man of the people, was rejoicing with the people. For the moment

"Grim visaged war had smoothed his wrinkled front."

For a moment the nation that had sailed so long under the gloomy, bristling headlands of war, had caught a glimpse of a calm, open bay, with the sun of peace shining down on its green encircling hills. And for an hour the man whose shoulders had borne, for over four years, the heaviest burden ever placed upon any ruler, the man whose unceasing vigilance had been in demand to guide the vessel of state through such tortuous channels and around such reefs as never threatened nation before, for an hour he had laid aside the cares of state: for an hour he had said "Good bye to pain and care:" for an hour he had forgotten the nation's burden and given himself up to the current of the nation's joy. And in that hour of grateful relaxation the blow fell. The assassin, inspired with hellish daring, threw his life upon the issue, and to-day the nation mourns his success.

I will not dwell upon the horrible fact. It is my

duty to-day to gather up its lessons as far as may be; and I go back now to my introductory thought, that some of the deeds of history are the concentrated expression of a long train of previous events, giving in their expression a typical character to the whole. It were easy enough to cite illustrations, did time permit; yet it is unnecessary with such an illustration before our eyes. To repeat once more what I have already said from this place, I go back of the deed and of its perpetrator. I remind you only of the words of the assassin as he leaped to the floor — "*Sic semper tyrannis. Virginia is avenged*" — as showing that the fatal blow was struck in the spirit of hatred to constituted authority, in the spirit of devotion to that pestilent heresy of state sovereignty, in the interest of rebellion. The rebellion was the direct outgrowth of slavery, and the assassination of the President is the grand consummate expression of the *spirit of slavery*. This is not the first time it has struck from behind. It is full of the instinct of its own meanness. It knows it is a vile thing, a suspected thing, a dangerous, false and cruel thing, and it would fain call itself by other names, and make its way under a mask. But thank God its name is written, and to-day it stands baptized in the name of the devil and all his angels as the spirit of *assassination and murder*.

For, look you calmly at this thing. I ask the most strenuous advocate of slavery, if there be one left, whether, in reason, we could expect any other development? Go back to the fundamental principle of this institution which enables a man to own another, and tell me if that is a safe right to entrust to any man. Tell me if the testimony of history is not uniform on this point? Tell me if the principle which permits one man to regard another as a chattel is not destructive in the end of respect for all human right, even the inalienable right of life? You may put restriction upon a master, forbidding him to kill his slave; but the spirit which thinks nothing of whipping a man or degrading a woman, will only be restrained by policy or penalty or want of opportunity from going further. The moment you admit in *any case* the absolute right of one man over another's person or property or family, that moment you remove the question from its only substantial basis, and put it upon varying circumstances, such as distinctions of social position or color. Be what you are to-day, mentally and morally, only black, and the planter will sell you, or whip you, or degrade you as readily as he would the African fresh from the Guinea coast. The man who is taught that he is at liberty to disregard *any* right of another, is in a fair way to disregard *all*. It is dangerous to set such a principle in motion. You cannot stop it where or when you will. It laughs at statutes. It is like the demons in the old story, which were called to draw water by one who knew the spell to set them at work, but had forgotten how to lay them again; and which drew and drew until they flooded his dwelling. You can confine the application of this principle to no one class. Begin with distinction of color, and gradually it will have come to overleap all distinction of color, as it has done already; for you know that men and women have been sold in the slave marts with skins as white as yours. Assume that a slave women is rightfully the toy and property of her master, and you lessen the respect for female virtue everywhere, and stop not short of that state of society which this is no place to lay bare, but which has been for years existing at the south, and than which hell itself can present nothing more revolting. Begin with right over a slave's person, and insensibly the master spirit will assert itself over other persons; and if it dare not strike, will affect contempt of wise and virtuous men, and come with its slave-driving airs and its talk of "mudsills" into the national councils. Begin with killing a negro in the heat of passion, or by the administration of a few dozen lashes too many, and under a system which finds it most politic to wink at such deeds, and the transition is easy to holding the life of a white man in light esteem. The hot blood, the childish view of honor which sends the hand of the southern desperado to his knife-hilt or pistol-handle on the first fancied provocation, and which has made the south the favorite arena of the duelling code, are but other cases in point showing how disregard of one class of rights has begotten disregard of all. The spirit which shot the President in his chair is the same spirit which has been inflicting mutilation and death upon men and women who dared open their mouths to condemn the benignant institution of slavery, and sometimes on mere suspicion of their sentiments. It is the same spirit that struck down Charles Sumner in his place in the United States senate for daring to hold the mirror up to slavery, and to call things by their right names, and which gave public ovations to the miscreant who did the deed. And if you want a catalogue without end, turn over the history of this war, leaf by leaf, and see whether the spirit of slavery can be expected to respect *any* right. Rights! even the grave has had no rights. We have lived to see enacted on this land which we have claimed for Christian civilization, the feats that were deemed heroic, centuries ago by barbarians who could quench their rage only in draughts from the skulls of their slain foes. We have driven the Indian from his native forest, and wept sentimentally over the horrors of the scalping knife, only to see the mutilation of the dead incorporated into the civilized warfare of the chivalrous south, and to have our murdered sons and brothers dug from their graves, and their bones hacked into pieces to furnish amulets for dainty southern dames. We have lived not only to read of the inquisition as history, but to see it revived with refinements of cruelty in southern prisons. We have seen even the hard mercies of civilized warfare ignored, and the policy deliberately inaugurated of maiming and disabling hundreds and thousands of northern men. Have you seen the photographer's work? Have you marked the idiotic stare, the ghastly features, the protruding bones, the swollen joints? Have you studied the horrors of fever in the stockades of Andersonville? Do you think it a small cause that will send men deliberately across the dead-line to be shot rather than pine longer amid such misery? Did you see the bread which George Stuart brought here a year ago, the staple of our imprisoned soldiers' fare? Do you know that Libby Prison was undermined when the authorities of Richmond anticipated the approach of our troops, and that the hellish machinery was all in readiness to blow the prison into the air with its whole living tenantry? Have your minds sounded the black depths of the villainy that, under the shadow of English neutrality plotted the propagation of pestilence in the north, and the burning and pillage of northern cities, and the poisoning of the reservoirs whence a million of human beings drew their daily supply? Do you remember that this very act of murder over which we grieve was in contemplation four years ago, and that only a superintending Providence saved Abraham Lincoln to the United States, and Baltimore from adding another crime to the murder of Massachusetts troops? And are you to think this last event strange? Is an assassination out of keeping with the antecedents of slave barbarism? No, no! Slavery has done this deed, and upon it I call down the curse of heaven. I invoke it in the name of a down-trodden race; I invoke it in the name of the hearts it has torn, the domestic ties it has severed, the virtue it has corrupted, the ignorance it has fostered; in the name of man robbed of the image of his Maker, and of woman shorn of her dearest and most sacred rights; in the name of slave mothers sitting like Niobes all over the wasted heritage of the south; in the name of the blighted hopes and desolate hearths of the north; in the name of the emaciated skeletons in our hospitals, and the maimed forms that crawl along our streets; in the name of the mutilated and pillaged dead; in the name of that bereaved widow and her fatherless children, and of the bereaved nation lying to-day in sackcloth and ashes; I call down upon it the blight of heaven; I brand it as the *representative trampler upon human rights.* Oh! that when its vile head shall have been crushed, as crushed it will be ere long, its vestiges might be obliterated forever. But this cannot be: They will remain to bear testimony against the southern lords who have fostered and fought for it, and against the northern men who, in admiration of its patriarchal beauties, have lavished upon it their sympathy, and truckled to its imperious demands. The reminders are written all over the land. The white tablets gleaming from a thousand hill-side churchyards shall tell the story. The rough boards that mark the thousands of graves by the Rappahannock and Potomac and Chickahominy shall moulder, but the grass shall grow more greenly there, and flowers bloom more luxuriantly; and even in their summer loveliness, the voice of brothers' blood shall cry from the ground. The plow shall turn up mute witnesses, and the fields, with their multitudinous relics of battle, be vocal with slavery's reproach.

And the west shall remember it. It shall keep the lesson to whet its good sword, and to fire its heart, if ever traitors attempt a like experiment; for there, in one of its quiet cemeteries, shall rise the monument of slave treason's last and greatest victim. To the home of his early struggles and successes, to the home from which he went with prayer and faith to assume his high destiny, to it shall be the honored task of cherishing his loved remains, and his obelisk shall stand when our beloved land shall have emerged purified and triumphant from this bloody ordeal, with its marble finger ever pointing to heaven in protest against the barbarism which tore him from the hearts of a loving people.

But I turn now from the authorship of this calamity to the illustrious dead himself.

Our late beloved President, while in no sense a sectional President, represented nevertheless a peculiar phase of our national life—its youngest, its most progressive side. The west was his birth-place; the west, that grand theatre where the pent up energy and glowing aspiration of all other portions of the land find ample room for development. While the west furnishes types of the best growths of other soils, it superadds to them a character peculiarly its own. It exhibits the shrewdness of New England without its rigidity; the geniality of the south without its passion. It combines the impulsiveness of the Carolinas, and the caution of Maine and Connecticut. In its more thinly settled districts men are obliged to fill larger spaces. The circumstances are more favorable for the development of strong individualities. A man cannot merge himself in a multitude or retire into a convenient obscurity. He must fill a place, do a work, assert himself, bring out the best that is in him, or suffer the consequent odium. The early life of the President was well adapted to call out the practical shrewdness, the strong common sense, and the knowledge of men which characterized him. In such societies men's culture, except in its practical adaptations, would have been wasted. Men's knowledge was estimated according to its visible practical contributions to the common weal. The emergencies of that pioneer life called for tact, readiness, practical ability. In the development of these the future President was not wanting in mental stimulus and training. The very meagreness of the sources of knowledge sharpened his appetite for it, and perhaps contributed to that characteristic thoroughness which placed what knowledge he had so thoroughly at his command. The conscientious carefulness so early exhibited marked him throughout his official life; so that whatever men may think of his expressed sentiments on any subject, his discussions always show an opinion laboriously and conscientiously formed. The freedom and geniality of western life, its rough but genuine familiarity, tended to deepen a naturally sunny and affectionate disposition. No less were the circumstances under which he appeared in political life adapted to sharpen his intellect and fit him for the wider arena upon which he was destined to enter. That close contact of political leaders with the people, requiring that the representatives of opposite parties should discuss the great questions of the day in their presence, was unfavorable to superficial knowledge or evasive logic. No point must be shirked, however difficult. In the sword play of debate before the people, exposed to a running fire of question and comment, with the keenest interest and the most intense feeling excited, he who evaded, if not exposed by his adversary, was discovered by the people, and compelled to meet the issue or blush for his ignorance or cowardice. From such a school he came to the executive chair. You know well how exciting and alarming was the crisis at which he assumed it. His own election had been connived at by the opposite party to gain a pretext for the execution of their long cherished scheme of secession. South Carolina had begun the pestilent work and had turned her guns upon a government fortress. The executive, too timid, too imbecile, or too much in sympathy with the treason, to act, refused to lift a finger to strangle the infant rebellion. States were falling into line under the new confederacy. Its agents had pilfered the public treasury and scattered the public munitions. The border states hung wavering in the balance, an object of apprehension and desire to either party. The slavery question was presenting itself under the most complicated aspect—the acknowledged source of the difficulty, yet incapable of being assailed for the time. Foreign nations were prepared to extend their sympathy only on the ground of a crusade against slavery, and we were compelled by fidelity to the Constitution, to deal only with the overt act of treason, at the risk of forfeiting sympathy and insuring foreign intervention. The conspirators were jubilant over their first success, and boasting that their flag would soon wave over the Capitol. On this scene of turmoil and danger Abraham Lincoln entered at his inauguration. Well might he look forward with apprehension. Well might he say on leaving his western home: "A duty devolves upon me which is perhaps greater than that which has devolved upon any other man since the days of Washington." But once committed to his duty he was not the man to shrink. He had been used to meeting emergencies. He had been trained in the school of difficulty; and gathering up his manhood with a calm dignity and a childlike trust in God, he went forth to give his labor and his life for his country. It is, of course, foreign to my purpose to follow him through that administration so fruitful in events, in which the nation has made history faster than in all the rest of her life together. I desire only to bring out a few of those traits which most clearly illustrate the man, and with which the nation has been made familiar in his late position. His qualities of heart were such as commended him to all men. He was in the real sense of that term a hearty man. The expression of this characteristic was with him something more than that assumed cordiality and familiarity which is counted one of the politician's necessary weapons. It went beyond mere hand-shakings and expressions of good fellowship. He was naturally disposed to think well of his race. His prepossessions were generally in favor of a man. He would rather love than hate him; and hence his feeling was literally *cordial*—the spontaneous outgoing of a frank and manly nature. In the theatre of his earlier victories, he was a man whose intellectual power his adversaries feared; but *he* would rather disarm an opponent with a good natured jest than with a sarcasm or denunciation. With such a nature, backed by a keen appreciation of the ludicrous, a ready memory, a quick perception, a wide experience, his power of anecdote and repartee has become proverbial. This feature of his character, which has provoked the sneers of the starched magnates of Europe, has ever appeared to my mind as a special gift for a special emergency. As already remarked, such a burden rested upon him as seldom or never fell to any ruler's lot. Added to the intricacy and number of the state questions constantly before him, his natural kindness of heart rendered him accessible to numberless petty, personal applications which he would have been fully justified in committing to subordinates; and that never-failing fund of cheerfulness, that exhaustless humor which the most complicated problem would so often "remind of a story," that elasticity which suffered him to bate not one jot of heart or hope in those times when the strongest held their breath, were God's own gifts to the care-worn man, blessed springs of refreshing and strength gushing up all along the dusty road of official duty.

But this element of his character had yet a deeper and more practical bearing upon his official life. Official brusqueness is by no means a rare quality, and, in a position where, as in the executive seat, it is so often necessary to say "NO!" decidedly and sternly, is not an altogether valueless one. Many men of kindly natures rapidly acquire it under the ceaseless rasping of official duty. But upon Mr. Lincoln the effect of his constant and wearing intercourse with the people was, if anything, rather to open his heart to them, and to make him more unwilling to refuse any reasonable request. Haughty and cold he could not be, but in his never failing humor he found a shield as well as a sword, a medium of refusal which relieved the task of half its pain to himself and effectually tempered its bitterness to the disappointed applicant. His kindly satire covered the evasion of many an intrusive question, and the denial of many a petition which duty forbade kindness to grant. As it was, his deep conscientiousness, his keen sense of justice, his unwillingness to wrong anything human, and perhaps his too great faith in the natural goodness of mankind, led him at times to be lenient and forgiving, when many thought that severity would have been but justice. His personal kindness had extended to his own assassin. His mind, at the time of his death, was full of schemes for the forgiveness and restoration of the traitors who had struck at the nation's heart; and if it be, that the south is avenged in his death, she will find it to be a vengeance that will recoil upon her own head; for in him she has lost her best friend, and however little *we* could afford to spare him, *she* could afford it still less.

The lightness and jocularity of which I have spoken, were but a veil for sterner traits. They were but as the waving verdure, flecked with passing shadows, and toyed with by every wind, yet growing upon the everlasting hills whose heart is rock, and whose foundations are in the depths of the earth. His uprightness has passed into a proverb. His jest and story covered a strength of purpose, a rigid determination, an adherence to principle which no crooked policy could undermine, and which no bribe was great enough to tempt. In the real old Roman sense of the term he was an *honest* man — an embodiment of manly worth and honor. Where men or measures stood in the way of principle they must go down. When even plausible views of moral right on certain great questions were urged upon him by reformers, he could even consent for the time to be deemed false to the great objects of philanthropy, rather than swerve from his conscientiously chosen policy. He did not consult personal popularity. He regarded himself as the people's servant; and to do their work in the best way, and in accordance with his sworn obligation to the Constitution, was his sole care. And the secret of this lay in his *religiousness*. From the time of his assumption of his office to his death, his words on all public occasions breathe a spirit of trust in the God of nations. After his assumption of office, he became the subject of deeper religious experience. Amid the graves of the fallen heroes of Gettysburg, the weary and heavy laden heart which the impending cares of state and the bitterness of bereavement had failed to bring to the cross, accepted Christ as its guide and His yoke and burden as its portion. This sentiment is the key-note of the few words spoken by him on leaving his home for Washington. "Washington would never have succeeded except for the aid of Divine Providence, upon which he at all times relied. I feel that I cannot succeed without the same Divine aid which sustained him, and on the same Almighty being I place my reliance for support." Of him it might be justly said, as of William of Orange, to whose character his own presents some points of similarity: "From his trust in God, he ever derived support and consolation in the darkest hours. Implicitly relying upon Almighty wisdom and goodness, he looked danger in the face with a constant smile, and endured incessant labors and trials with a serenity which seemed more than human;" and, in the beautiful words of him who pronounced his funeral eulogy, "While we admired and loved him on many accounts, more suitable than any or all of these, more holy and influential, more beautiful and strong and sustaining, was his habitual confidence in God, and in the final triumph of truth and righteousness through him and for His sake. This was his noblest virtue and grandest principle, the secret alike of his strength, his patriotism and his success. And this, it seems to me, after being near him steadily, and with him often for more than four years, is the principle by which, more than by any other, he being dead yet speaketh."

Oh! were it my lot to speak this day to men in high places, I would commend to him who comes to Abraham Lincoln's place, this trait above any in Abraham Lincoln's character. I would implore him by the great interests of humanity now committed to him, in view of the fact that the questions which sway the nation to-day have risen far above the realm of politics, into that of morals and religion; in view of the insignificance of all human power and wisdom, in an arena where God is so manifestly exercising control, and shaping the age's destiny, to look to this first of all. I would implore him to let the wave of prayer that sweeps toward him from every hearthstone in the land, bear him to the secret places of the Most High, there to seek the leadings of that higher will, there to have his thought drawn into sympathy with the Divine purposes, there to be clad in the mantle of Lincoln's unswerving faith, and thence to come forth and place himself at the nation's head, girt with a sublimer strength, a purer patriotism, and a holier wisdom.

The elements of the President's intellectual character were not complex. It has been taken for granted that he did not exhibit the characteristics of a great statesman. But without presuming to deny this, I would not be too certain that he was wanting in the capacities for the highest statesmanship. His discernment was quick; his power of generalizing not inferior; his grasp of a subject firm; his knowledge of political machinery extensive, though gathered from experience more than from study. His policy, as exhibited in his administration, was cautious and far-reaching. To his sterling integrity and frankness he added the wiliness of a Talleyrand. Under other influences, and in a foreign court, he might have developed into a diplomat of the first order. After all that has been said of his statesmanship, it cannot be denied that he piloted the nation through one of the most difficult of all possible junctures with consummate skill and tact, and, the result will probably show, with as few mistakes as any man would have been likely to make under similar circumstances. His ignorance or rejection of mere technicalities may, in some instances, have blinded superficial observers to the statesmanlike qualities of his mind. He was one of those to whom it was given to show the courts of Europe that the difference between the administrators of the old and new world is in the *polish* rather than in the temper of the blade. He laid no claim to the rhetorician's laurels, yet his public documents were strongly, clearly and vigorously written. His state papers were eminently popular documents. The discussions of political issues introduced into them were set forth ofttimes with familiar illustrations, which, while they might provoke a smile from the sticklers for official stateliness, imparted to them a wonderful freshness, and tended to root their principles deep in the popular mind. No president has ever surpassed him, if any has equalled him, in clearly defining his policy to the masses. His strong, practical common sense was the basis of his intellectual character. In his political discussions he had a rare faculty of detecting and exposing sophistry. He seized intuitively upon the vital point of every question, clearly stated the real issue, ranged all subordinate facts round this, and summarily discarded everything which had no relation to it. This faculty proved especially valuable in the class of questions with which his administration so largely dealt. His strong sense saved the Constitution from its greatest danger, the danger of tying its own hands; and this was what enabled him to cut the Gordian knot where some men would have found themselves embarrassed by a mere technicality or formula.

Perhaps one of the chief elements of his success in this respect was what I may call his *docility*. This feature of his character stamps him as truly great, when viewed in relation to the facts of his administration. For a man may be truly willing to learn, without the ability to profit by his acquisitions. But when a man not only learns of passing events in the spirit of a child, but out of his learning draws a power which equals him to whatever emergency they develop,— when he grows in wisdom and majesty and power with his task, we may no longer refuse him the meed of greatness. Lincoln's simplicity here, was wiser than many another man's wisdom. A less teachable, more conceited man, coming to the executive chair at that crisis, with a determination to make events bend to a definite inflexible policy, might have plunged the nation in ruin. I have heard it said more than once since the war began, "would that Jackson, or a man of his mould were at the helm."

But I question now, whether it would have been well. The stern old hero would scarcely have fallen so readily into the track of events as the more pliable, but not less courageous Lincoln. God knew his instrument better than we did. The crisis was one which no preconceived human policy could fit. A policy had to develop itself out of the crisis, and it is not the least of Abraham Lincoln's claims to greatness, that he had the humility to accept this fact, and the power to use it so successfully.

> "No hasty fool of stubborn will,
> But prudent, cautious, pliant still,
> Who, since his work was good,
> Would do it as he could,
> Doubting, was not ashamed to doubt,
> And lacking prescience went without."

He was willing to learn not only from events but from the people. He, as already remarked, recognized himself as the people's choice: as the exponent of their will. His words on this subject as reported by a late writer, are important as illustrating a rule of his action, and to some extent perhaps, the representative character of his mind and of his administration. When some one remonstrated with him for giving so much of his time to petty applications, and not referring them to subordinates, he replied. "Ah, yes! such things do very well for you military people, with your arbitrary rule, and in your camps. But the office of President is essentially a civil one, and the affair is very different. For myself, I feel—though the tax on my time is heavy—that no hours of my day are better employed than those which thus bring me again within the direct contact and atmosphere of the average of our whole people. Men moving only in an official circle are apt to become merely official—not to say arbitrary—in their ideas; and are apter and apter, with each passing day, to forget that they only hold power in a representative capacity. Now this is all wrong. I go into these promiscuous receptions of all, who claim to have business with me twice each week, and every applicant for audience has to take his turn as if waiting to be shaved in a barber's shop. Many of the matters brought to my notice are utterly frivolous; but others are of more or less importance; and all serve to renew in me a clearer and more vivid image of that great popular assemblage out of which I sprang, and to which at the end of two years I must return. I tell you, Major," he said—appearing at this point to recollect I was in the room, for the former part of these remarks had been made with half shut eyes, as if in soliloquy—"I tell you that I call these receptions my public-opinion baths, for I have little time to read the papers and gather public opinion that way; and though they may not be pleasant in all their particulars, the effect, as a whole, is renovating and invigorating to my perceptions of responsibility and duty. It would never do for a president to have guards with drawn sabres at his door, as if he fancied he were, or were trying to be, or were assuming to be, an emperor."

And out of this grew as a consequence that direct *personal* interest of the people in him which has honored his tomb with the most magnificent demonstration of public sorrow ever paid to a ruler. The reverence of the people for Washington might have equalled if not surpassed that conceded to Lincoln. I doubt if the Nation's *love* for its first president equalled its love for the last. The more stately revolutionary regime, the circumstance of birth, the condition of society, even the character of the Father of his Country, did not tend to bring the hearts of president and people in as close contact then as now. We never knew this until he was taken from us. For four years the hearts and eyes of the nation had unconciously rested on him as the central figure of every public movement; for four years he has been demonstrating by continuous testimony his personal interest in every man, woman and child of the American people that came into contact with him. Those who had never seen him, knew nevertheless that the same cordial welcome, the same affectionate sympathy with their cares and wishes awaited them if their time should come: and when he died, it was as if the light had gone out of every eye. Every hand instinctively groped for a support, and little children wept because Abraham Lincoln was dead.

A recent article from the *London Spectator* so forcibly illustrates some of these views that I may be pardoned for quoting an extract:

"But without the advantages of Washington's education or training, Mr. Lincoln was called from a humble station at the opening of a mighty civil war to form a government out of a party in which the habits and traditions of official life did not exist. Finding himself the object of southern abuse so fierce and so foul that in any man less passionless it would long ago have stirred up an implacable animosity; mocked at for his official awkwardness and denounced for his steadfast policy by all the Democratic section of the loyal states; tried by years of failure before that policy achieved a single great success; further tried by a series of successes so rapid and brilliant that they would have puffed up a smaller mind and overset its balance; embarrassed by the boastfulness of his people and of his subordinates no less than by his own inexperience in his relations with foreign states; beset by fanatics of principle on one side, who would pay no attention to his obligations as a constitutional ruler, and by fanatics of caste on the other, who were not only deaf to the claims of justice but would hear of no policy large enough for a revolutionary emergency, Mr. Lincoln has persevered through all without ever giving way to anger, or despondency, or exultation, or popular arrogance, or sectarian fanaticism, or caste prejudice, visibly growing in force of character, in self-possession, and in magnanimity, till, in his last short message to Congress on the fourth of March, we can detect no longer the rude and illiterate mould of a village lawyer's thought, but find it replaced by a grasp of principle, a dignity of manner, and a solemnity of purpose which would have been unworthy neither of Hampden nor of Cromwell, while his gentleness and generosity of feeling towards his foes are almost greater than we should expect from either of them."

At once the representative fact of his administration, and that which distinguished it above any other in our history, is its relations to the great question of human bondage. In this respect his administration forms an era in the history of the race. The status of the question at the time of his inauguration, and for a long time after, was peculiar and difficult. The moral and political aspects of the contest were brought into apparent antagonism; and the foreign emissaries of secession had no dearer object than to prove this antagonism real, and thus alienate from us the sympathy of Europe. Europe, knowing slavery to lie at the root of our trouble, expected us to strike at once at slavery. *We*, knowing the fact equally well, could, at the time, strike only at treason. We could deal only with the immediate development, not with the ultimate cause. The provisions of the Constitution, the divided sentiment of the north, the hesitating attitude of the border states, the general ignorance of the extent and maturity of the conspiracy, made it a matter of the utmost difficulty and delicacy. The President clearly appreciated the source of the difficulty, and, as the result showed, had its removal as deeply at heart as any man. Hence, at Philadelphia, prior to his inauguration, he remarked: "I have often inquired of myself what great principle or idea it was that kept this confederacy so long together. It was something in the Declaration of Independence, giving liberty not only to the people of this country, but hope to the world for all coming time. It was that which gave promise that in due time the weights should be lifted from the shoulders of all men, and that all should have an equal chance. If this country cannot be saved without giving up that principle, I was about to say *I would rather be assassinated upon the spot than surrender it.*" I need not follow the great question through the history of its solution. The world will bear testimony to the cautious, far-seeing wisdom with which he dealt with it. History will do justice to the man who could make impulse, however high and generous, stand back for duty. It will bear witness to the faith which could wait as well as labor; which was content to let the result come out in the slow grinding of the mills of God, without putting forth his hand to quicken the machinery. It will record how sacredly he respected the constitutional rights of the south; how timely were his warnings; how liberal his solicitations, until at last, when he saw that God's purpose was ripe, when, having kept adroitly in the rear of events, yet having so employed them as to make the full power of the popular wave bear him to his goal, he rose in his might, and with a word that echoed through the world, the fetters fell forever from the slave. How a great moral act like this looms up amid the political developments of the age, and those things which more directly touch us as individuals— questions of financial policy, learned diplomatic correspondence, generals, victories, deeds of individual heroism, party triumphs. For when state volumes shall be mouldering in libraries, and the soldiers' children's children playing with his rusty sword and asking its story, when the names of old political parties shall be obsolete, and the issues which created them forgotten, this fact shall be fresh in the nation's memory. Abraham Lincoln signed the death warrant of American slavery. Thank God, "the past at least is secure." What he has done in this matter will not be undone. The moral sentiment of the nation, educated by the stern discipline of war and sorrow, has followed up the blow and clinched the nail, and to-day one mighty will pulsates from east to west, that this curse shall be no more. Shut close thine accursed door, oh! slave mart. Stand in the midst of the southern cities, a monument of a past barbarism, a haunted place past which the belated wayfarer shall hasten, and whose story of horror shall be told with bated breath. Where the auctioneer's hammer sealed the doom of humanity and virtue, let the rank grass grow, and scorpions lurk, and silence brood, and over its door let it be written —"*Aceldama.*" Lie still, oh! slave ship, in thy port, thou whose every plank and timber is seasoned with bitter tears; lie still and rot in the blistering sun; let the foul slime and ooze gather about thy keel, and the crawling things of the deep, foul shapes that fishers' line never brought to light, lurk in thy shadow; and let the breeze refuse to fill thine idle sails, and no traitorous wind ever send thee lessening down the west on thy mission of woe. Pile the fetters into the furnace, and let the molten flood pour forth into moulds of plow and pruning-hook wherewith the ransomed man shall bring beauty out of the wilderness, and train the clustering vines of the south over his cabin, his home, his castle, on whose threshold he shall have a *man's* right to stand and keep the destroyer from his flock. This land at least cannot, dare not renew the curse. It dare not cancel the charter to which Abraham Lincoln set his hand. His great shade would rise from the grave in its fiery indignation. No, the hand cannot be found that shall rivet the chains again, and this deed of his shall stand in time to come, a monument more enduring than brass, whose inscription angels shall pause to read on their messages of peace.

But he could not be spared to us longer. His work

here was done. Heaven had new and higher purposes concerning him which it does not reveal to us; and now that he has been so mysteriously and suddenly snatched from us, it becomes us to ask with all due reverence, "What does it mean?"

He must be presumptuous indeed who shall assume to interpret such a providence, and to say for what end this blow hath fallen. We can do little more than sit reverently at God's closed gates, and wait until He shall tell us more. Yet there are some thoughts so naturally suggested to us that we should not be justified in wholly passing them by.

The juncture at which the event occurred is significant. The President was fully committed to a vigorous prosecution of the war, and to the submission of the rebels as the first condition of peace. He was reëlected on this basis over a man who, in all human probability, would have stopped the war where it was, patched up an unrighteous peace, and left the whole fundamental question open for our children to settle. Lincoln lived to see his policy carried out — the military power of the rebellion broken; and almost at the very hour of this consummation his life was cut short. I accept this as an indication that his work as an instrument of Providence ended here, and that the work of reconstruction belonged to other and doubtless fitter instruments. I will not positively assert that his policy toward traitors was so much too lenient that God replaced him by a man who, we have good reason to think, will not err in this direction. Yet I say that this *may* be so, and that it looks like it. Mr. Lincoln was a man whose policy was formed in the light of events, and in this instance it had not had time to develop itself fully; but I have no hesitation in saying that in so far as it had developed itself, it was setting, in my opinion, much too strongly in the direction of lenity and conciliation. We may talk as we will about the great right of freedom of speech, but if this right be admitted to be unlimited at all times, I cannot see but that a popular government like this deliberately exposes itself to the most mischievous of all results, a perverted public opinion. I see nothing in the letter or spirit of the Constitution which should prevent such men as Vallandigham and the Woods, and others who might be named, whose treason was open and blatant, and who, from their public position and influence, were enabled to divide the north, and give aid and comfort to our enemies — nothing which should prevent their mouths being stopped, and they themselves being put beyond the possibility of doing further mischief. And as for the leading traitors of the south — the men who struck their blow deliberately and with malice aforethought— who, for years before the overt act, were digging their mines and laying their train, I call upon the Christian justice and common sense of this nation to show cause why they should not suffer the extreme penalty of the law? Do we not yet realize the full significance of their crime? Have we been so free from the damning crime of treason, that we do not yet recognize it, even when it comes to us without pretence of disguise? Do we realize the murder and outrage and desolation that have followed in its track, and are we to stand here to-day and clasp their blood-stained hands in ours, and welcome back to fellowship those who only want the opportunity to renew their devilish work? For one, I say *no!* In simple justice *no!* We have been all along discussing this question on the basis of the right or wrong of retaliation, forgetting that that question does not enter into the consideration at all. The question is simply whether we will put in force the laws against treason which we have made for our own protection. We need to understand a little more clearly the true relations of the divine law to individuals and to states in forming a correct view of this question. It is clear enough that revenge is to have no place in an individual Christian's creed. If thine enemy hunger feed him. If he thirst give him drink. Love is to be the ruling principle of action between man and man. In God's law for the regulation of communities the same principle rules, but under different manifestations; manifestations which sometimes blind us to the principle. Let government proceed upon the principle of blessing those that curse it, and doing good to those that despitefully use it, and on the instant you convert government into the great foster mother of crime and society into a city of refuge for the most depraved villains upon earth; you forbid war in self defence: you put society at the mercy of evil. Now I say that in social regulations the principle of love operates just as really as in individual relations. But it operates under the limitation that God consults for the greatest good of the greatest number, and therefore it exhibits itself in those protections and retributions, which are inseparable from law. The highest exhibition of mercy in such cases is through strict retributive justice. So, if Jefferson Davis comes to my door disguised for flight, and says, I am hungry, weary, thirsty, though I remember that my brother was starved at Libby, or my father shot at Andersonville, or my home burned and my property ruined by the myrmidons of this arch traitor, as a man I am bound to feed him and rest him. But I am a citizen also; and I shall deserve to be hanged myself if I do not say to him, you may eat of my bread, you may drink of my cup, you may rest on my couch, but from this place you shall not go if I have power to stop you, until you go in company of the provost marshal and his guards. We cannot afford to be lenient to these men. It has been said that we have triumphed gloriously enough, and are strong enough to forgive. I grant the fact, but deny the inference. We do not want our first great public act after our victories to be a wholesale violation of our own law in favor of the men who have left no means untried to ruin us. In the words of our present executive, lenity of the few may be injustice to the many. By an indiscriminate lenity we shall only be setting so many vipers loose to sting and to poison. It was the spirit of the *conquered* south that smote down the President. The hatred of free institutions, and the spirit of revenge and malice have not died out with the military power of the rebellion. They are as strong to-day in the crushed and humbled south as on the morning when its bastard palmetto first waved over Sumter. The snake is scotched, but not killed. We owe something to justice as well as to mercy. Something to self protection as well as to forgiveness; and in the name of this bleeding country, in the name of our maimed and starved soldiers, in the name of our blighted hearts and homes, I call upon government to put in force against these leading traitors the penalty of the law.. And I would their gibbet were so high that every man north and south might see it from his housetop, and learn as he looks that treason is not safe for the perpetrator: high enough for the despots of Europe, and its statesmen who have longed for the fall of the republic, to learn that the republic has yet strength enough and self respect enough to punish terribly those who strike at her vitals. Citizens of this community, gathered here to-day, let this be our last experience in the toleration of treason. It has been allowed too much liberty heretofore. It is time its mouth was stopped. If we cannot stop it at the south, we can at least stop it here. Nothing less than this is our duty; and let us go forth from this place resolved to foster a public sentiment that shall from this time forth, sternly though calmly and legally silence the press or the man, no matter what his position, that dares to lift up a voice in favor of extenuation of treason.

As another lesson, we are taught to respect our own government more; to cherish it more fondly than ever. What has it done for us in the present crisis? There are nations where such an event would have blocked the wheels of legislation, and thrown all things into direst confusion: To-day government moves on without a break or jar. Ere the nation's ruler is scarce cold in death, his successor steps quietly into his vacant place, without a movement or a remonstrance from the great nation. And the nation itself but falls back a pace to let the retiring leader's bier pass out, to look for one moment on his beloved face, to exchange a word on his many virtues, and then closes up fast and firm round his successor, with a sterner determination to push its great work to its completion.

Again we are reminded "Little children keep yourselves from idols." As much as any other people we are hero worshipers. With all our vaunted independence, popular leaders sway us mightily. All through this conflict God's voice has been saying to us, as one after another of our trusted champions bit the dust, "Put not your trust in princes." I tremble when I hear men say, "Grant is left. Sherman is left. Sheridan and Thomas are left." God wants this nation to trust in Him, and in Him only. He comes to us to-day in our heart-sickness, and asks us if we think any man or body of men is indispensable, and dictates to us our lesson again, "*The Lord reigneth! Let the earth rejoice!*" And when our leaders fall, he bids us not to be looking back to the ranks, anxiously and tearfully asking: "What shall we do now?" but foward to where his pillar of fire moves steadily on through the night in solemn and mysterious majesty, and saying to our fainting hearts, "*God is left!* and in the name of the Lord will we set up our banners."

And this event draws us more closely together. Around the coffin of our beloved dead we clasp hands, and feel shoulder touch shoulder, and even amid the bitterness of this bereavement it is a blessed thing to know that we are more nearly one than ever. If the south had striven to select the act which of all others should concentrate the sentiment of the north against her, which should commit the whole people irrevocably to the completion of the work they have taken in hand, they could not have made a happier choice. If anything were needed to teach a certain class of northern men the true nature and tendencies of the cause they have been secretly favoring, this deed has supplied the want. Henceforth, brothers, we go forth more unitedly to our work. Henceforth the lines are more sharply drawn. Henceforth we know but two classes—loyal men and traitors. Northern men with southern principles, I tell you your skirts are not clear of the President's blood. You have fostered the spirit which struck the blow. You have apologized for it. You have fretted and been angry at those who would insist that slavery was at the root of that carelessness of human right and human life, that mad ambition, that aristocratic folly which precipitated the country into war. And now the result has justified them. This last deed has crowned the catalogue which has been running up so rapidly for four years past; and I do most of you the credit to believe that from this, its last work, you shrink aghast. I do you the justice to believe that your hearts equally with mine condemn this deed. I could not believe otherwise and believe you men. And now, by the open grave of the nation's President, amid the tears of the people, by every consideration of national honor and self-respect, I entreat you to look upon the legitimate fruit of southern principles, and from this time forth, in the name of God and humanity, come out from among them and be separate, and touch not the unclean thing.

And still we linger by the open grave. One look more ere the clods fall and the tomb enfolds him in its cold embrace. Is it not some ghastly nightmare — some dreadful dream from which we shall awake by and by to find the nation still undisgraced by murder, and him still at the helm? Alas, alas! the cold reality will not depart at our bidding. Abraham Lincoln is dead. Gone from a nation's burdens and a nation's love. Stricken down in the fore front of the battle; his great work done, yet with his armor on, in the high noon of a noble, successful, God-fearing manhood. And by that sterling worth, that simple piety, that kindness and tenderness, that never faltering faith in God and humanity, he, being dead, yet speaketh. Aye, speaketh. I hear his voice come down to us from the tranquil heights of his eternal rest bidding us be true to ourselves, true to our national idea, true to freedom, true to God, daring to be just though the heavens fall. I hear him saying to the nation: "Away with these idle tears, these vain regrets; ye have no time now for lamentation;

'The day of the Lord is at hand, at hand,
   Its storms roll up the sky,'

and the meekest of saints may find stern work to do. Up and be doing!"

We hear thee beloved leader, and here, beside thy tomb, we put off our sackcloth and ashes and take our armor to ourselves again. We turn our faces to the future, and from under the shadow of this dispensation we go forth with girded loins and trimmed lamps and in God's strength to work out our destiny. We leave thee with God on thy mount of vision, and press on at the beck of our new leader to that promised land which thou sawest from afar, but wert not permitted to enter; press on, bearing the inspiration of thy courage into battles yet to come. And thou shalt be gloriously avenged one day. Thou shalt be avenged when our Union, the object of thy dearest desire, shall stand cemented anew, "now and forever, one and inseparable." Thou shalt be avenged in every look which down-trodden humanity shall send across the sea to our land, then, as never before, the home of the oppressed. Thou shalt be avenged when one heart and one mind shall animate the people; when Americans shall know no north, no south, and one starry flag, the dear old banner which was the joy of thine eyes, covers with its ample folds the children of those who now thirst for each others blood. Thou shalt be avenged when the echo of war shall have died out from our hillsides, and the war desolated land be blossoming like a paradise beneath the willing hand of free industry. Thou shalt be avenged when, beneath the palmetto's shade, Africa's sons shall teach their children to lisp thy name, and bedew thine immortal charter with their grateful tears. Oh! even amid the grand realities which ere this have dawned upon thy vision, thou shalt not surely be so far removed from sympathy with the land thou lovedst and diedst for, that thou wilt not follow her career with thy spirit gaze, and smile with heavenly joy, when thou shalt see peace within her walls and prosperity within her palaces. And so, till our work be done, and we follow thee into the silence, we bid thee farewell. Sleep! beloved ruler! Rest! great, tender, careworn heart! Sleep sweetly in the bosom of the West, while the gratitude of the down-trodden and the love of the nation gather like clustering vines round thy tomb, and thy monument points through the years to heaven, telling the oppressed of a liberator and the tyrant of an avenger.

> "Uplifted high in heart and hope are we,
> Until we doubt not that, for one so true
> There must be other, nobler work to do,
> And victor he must ever be.
> For tho' the giant ages heave the hill,
> And break the shore, and evermore
> Make and break and work their will;
> Tho' worlds on worlds in myriad myriads roll
> Round us, each with different powers,
> And other forms of life than ours,
> What know we greater than the soul?
> On God and godlike men we build our trust.
> Hush! The dead-march wails in the people's ears:
> The dark crowd moves, and there are sobs and tears;
> The black earth yawns; the mortal disappears;
> Ashes to ashes, dust to dust:
> He is gone who seemed so great,
> Gone, but nothing can bereave him
> Of the force he made his own
> Being here, and we believe him
> Something far advanced in state
> And that he wears a truer crown
> Than any wreath that man can weave him.
> But speak no more of his renown,
> Lay your earthly fancies down
> And in the vast cathedral leave him;
> God accept him — Christ receive him."

The Nation's Sorrow. — Substance of a Sermon Preached in the State Street Methodist Episcopal Church.

BY REV. ERASTUS WENTWORTH, D.D.

And devout men carried Stephen to his burial, and made great lamentation over him.—Acts, viii, 2.

Rendering funeral honors to the dead is an immemorial custom as widespread as the human race. The oldest records, poetic and historical, throw abundant light upon the burial usages of the ancients. Iu Homer's Iliad an entire book is devoted to the description of the rites and games celebrated by the Greeks in honor of the slain Patroclus. The funeral panegyrics of Pericles and Demosthenes were gems of eloquence and ranked with the most admired compositions of classical antiquity.

The honors paid by Abraham to the remains of Sarah, are chronicled in the book of Genesis, in an account as minute, and almost as long as that of the creation by the same author.

Jacob, when led by his treacherous sons to believe that Joseph was dead, rent his clothes, put sackcloth upon his loins, mourned for his son many days and said, "I will go down into the grave unto my son mourning."

When this patriarch died at a great age in Egypt, he was embalmed with care, mourned by the Egyptians seventy days, escorted to Canaan with a grand funeral procession and there bewailed with such sore lamentation, that the wondering Canaanites said "this is a grievous mourning to the Egyptians," and the place of their seven days' weeping was thenceforward popularly designated as the "Egyptians' Mourning."

The bones of Joseph accompanied the Israelites as a sacred deposit during all their forty years' wandering. "The children of Israel wept for Moses in the plains of Moab thirty days." "Samuel died; and all the Israelites were gathered together, and lamented him, and buried him in his house at Ramah."

David pronounced eulogies full of pathos and beauty over the murdered Abner and the slaughtered Jonathan and Saul, though the latter was a suicide, who would have been condemned in our days to "maim-ed rites," and "ground unsanctified," "without requiem" and the "bringing home of bell and burial."

In honor of the dead, the ancient Jews rent their clothes, dressed in sackcloth and black, put ashes and dust on their heads, shaved their heads, removed their ornaments, diminished their temple offerings, went half naked, wept, wailed and fasted, beat their breasts, lay on the ground, and employed hired mourners. Customs like these are common throughout Asia at the present day, and in modified forms they exist throughout the world. They were not condemned by the great Author of Christianity. On the eve of his betrayal, when, in the house of Simon of Bethany, the gentle Mary, with impatient haste, broke the beautiful alabaster casket and lavished its precious odors upon the person of her beloved master, the disciples were indignant at the costly waste, but Christ defended her devotion, saying, "Let her alone; she hath wrought a good work on me, she is come aforehand to anoint my body to the burying!"

The devoted Arimathean sepulchered the body of Jesus with every honor that night and secrecy would allow, and the Marys prepared spices and ointments with which to embalm the sacred remains of the revered Master. Of the first Christian martyr it is recorded, "Devout men carried Stephen to his burial, and made great lamentation over him." From these Scripture examples we infer that it is not unchristian to honor the dead; that tears, lamentations, weeds of woe, and words of eulogy are alike in the order of nature and the order of God, sanctioned by universal custom and not forbidden by the Christian religion.

It is true that Christianity, by its genius, inculcates moderation in grief, economy in expenditure, and truthfulness in eulogy. We need not beat our breasts and tear our hair or howl like savages. We need not lavish such sums upon monuments and mausoleums as to require penal restrictions like the ancient Greeks. We need not use such words of fulsome adulation, lying eulogy and panegyric as have been the custom with other countries and other ages. We need not make a wholesale application of the motto, "De mortuis nil nisi bonum," concerning the dead say nothing but good, but we may and should bury our dead with a suitable amount of that respect that has been shown to the dead in all ages and countries. It is this attention to the dead that distinguishes man from the animal races, that vindicates his claim to superior reason in this life and points to immortality.

Honors paid to the dead are a stimulus to every one so to live as to deserve eulogy at his death. It was a wholesome custom, that of some of our Indian tribes, not to bury a man unless somebody could say something good of him. It was a fearful curse, that of Jehovah upon Jehoiakim king of Judah. "They shall not lament for him, saying Ah, my brother! Ah, Lord! or, Ah, his glory! He shall be buried with the burial of an ass, drawn and cast forth beyond the gates of Jerusalem."

Eulogies after death will avail nothing unless we have deserved them while living. The best of eulogies is a good life. It is impossible to cover up a bad life with a speech at a funeral or a lying epitaph. It may not be said of us "a great man and a prince hath fallen," but it may be said by every passer by, this is the grave of a good man. Character is immortal. It dies not, it will not lie down in the ground. Ghosts in graveyards is an exploded superstition, but, about the costly obelisks of the cities of the dead, springing up in the green wood, in the suburbs of every city and village, reputations flit, like troubled ghosts about the shores of Styx and Acheron in the ancient Hades.

To-day we are a nation of mourners. The horror that brooded over our hearts like a pall of hell's own weaving, as the telegraph winged over the land the news of the assassination, has given place to grief and tears.

On Wednesday last, at high noon, the people of the United States assembled in their places of worship to celebrate the funeral services of their murdered Chief. Never before was such universal and spontaneous homage paid to the memory of mortal. Never before were so many millions gathered at the same hour to honor the obsequies of one man. The funerals of other days have been celebrated piecemeal or as an after thought. Here, thanks to the telegraph, our entire nation stood around the bier and over the open coffin of our common head. And that wonderful funeral procession! to reach, without figure, from the capital of the nation to the capital of Illinois,—sixteen hundred miles! When did the world ever before witness such a funeral cortege! It is true, only the hearse with nine cars flies along the rails, but everywhere, from city and hamlet, mountain, vale and prairie, it raises and carries along with it a mighty tide wave of mourning humanity. Everywhere it rolls through an avenue walled on either side with silent crowds, uncovered, unsurging, tearful; its approach heralded and its departure signaled by tolling bells and booming cannon. By day it flies through cities and villages covered with weeds of woe, and by night, flaming torches mark its course and show the tears glittering like blood drops on the bronzed cheeks of rural populations. Everywhere flags at half mast, dirges by martial bands, and requiems at the stations sung by young men and maidens. Everywhere weeping and eulogies, music and flowers. Was there ever such attendance upon the relics of one not regally born? It is a nation's tribute to a citizen ruler whose firmness and integrity, quaint shrewdness and blunt common sense have carried it through a terrible crisis in its history and given liberty to millions.

The nation is right in paying the highest funeral honors to our late departed Chief Magistrate. We owe it to our national self respect. Shall the head of the family, the father, the Saviour of the nation die, and the children not mourn?

The nation thus reproves crime. Slavery, secession, treason, assassination, barbarism, stand aghast in the presence of this sublime outburst of national sorrow. The bloody corpse of Lucretia expelled the Tarquins from Rome. The bloody fragments of the murdered wife of a Levite thrilled all Israel with horror, and they well-nigh exterminated the tribe of Benjamin for abetting the murder. The bloody corpse of our murdered chief, carried in solemn procession through the country, will leave in its funeral train the solemn purpose to visit vengeance upon traitors and treason. By these rites the nation honors goodness, honesty, integrity. Abraham Lincoln was not a church member, but he was a Christian and led a life of virtue and a life of prayer. He was the Christian head of a Christian nation, and deserves Christian burial.

His sudden and tragical death has inspired the nation with mutual forbearance, sympathy, unity, fraternity. Political papers have moderated their acerbity. Opposing parties shake hands over the coffin of their common father, and agree to bury past animosities and to stand nobly by his successor in this hour of trial. It is due to the idiocy and malignity of human nature, that a few pitiful souls spit upon his bier, and trample on these universal weeds of mourning, but the grand record of history will be "A devout nation carried ABRAHAM LINCOLN to his burial, and made great lamentation over him."

SUBSTANCE OF A SERMON PREACHED AT THE UNITARIAN CHURCH.

BY REV. EDGAR BUCKINGHAM.

We trusted that it had been he which should have redeemed Israel.—
LUKE, xxiv, 21.

We are not required by public proclamation, nor induced by general expectation to spend again our Sunday hour in lessons drawn directly from the death of the President. The hearts of the people are full with this single subject of thought, and it is well to continue our more careful consideration of it. I have drawn a text from the disappointment experienced by the veneration, the love and tenderness of the disciples, at the death of Jesus Christ. Not that a comparison could be suggested with the Divine Master. The great hopes which are before us, and the pleasure we should have enjoyed in arriving at the fulfillment of them with him for our leader who has been our leader through the depths of our anxieties, call to mind peculiarly the sad disappointment of great hopes expressed in the language of the text.

The minds of the people cannot fail to be long and deeply affected. From so lofty a position, such a sudden removal! So great responsibilities, so suddenly laid down! Prospects so bright, to human view so suddenly darkened! The great dependence of the nation, so suddenly transferred to another, who had never expected to bear it! An event so sudden in private life, or to a man respected only for superior powers of mind, would have been fearfully impressive. If the President had been no more to us than a common statesman, or one only in the common line of the chief-magistracy, or if he had died wearied out with his great labors, after long sickness at the executive mansion, the community would have been religiously impressed. How much more are we likely to be so, under the existing circumstances, and for such a man!

I do not mean to speak additional words of eulogy.

But few men in public station have ever inspired so much confidence and secured so much attachment and love. We cast about in our minds, to study into the feelings with which he has affected us. Prominent among the influences with which his exalted life and character have wrought upon us, seems this:— in his justice, he made integrity seem more true. If, in the rivalships of the world, its covetousness, its over-reachings, its other various transgressions, we have ever indulged the common sentiment, that honesty was rare, or that it was feebly lived, or have felt that, perhaps, because it was rare, it had less intrinsic worth than nature or religion seemed to assign to it, we felt, on the other hand, that Mr. Lincoln was a living example of the value of it. Through him, it seemed to be gaining a new life for the world. The life of it, which he lived, outweighed in our minds the example of millions on the other side. In this way, he, with the broad bulwark of his personal character, helped to sustain the general morality. Temptation has less power, honesty arrives at more honor, integrity holds a more substantial life.

There circulates, we have found, through the public prints, some mention of professions or acknowledgments made by him, corresponding to the usual professions in the church, of religious faith or religious experience. Of the full truth of such accounts, or whether only partially or in some sense true, we have to-day and here no means of determining. But this may be known by all. A spirit of religion, not a conventional religiousness, not one artificial or imitative, but a simple, natural appeal to God, to his presence and his law, we find underflowing through all his conduct, and making its appearance in all his public writings. And such has been the impressiveness of his simplicity, and such is the confidence reposed in his truth, that thousands will become reverential and obedient through the influence of his public religiousness.

In the homeliness of his conversation, the playfulness of his talk has endeared him to people's hearts. Much as his jests have been questioned about, they have had a great value. They have showed to us that he was at home with himself, not acting a part. For though laughter is sometimes affected, yet it is among the sincerest of all things; and when it is not assumed for show, to secure applause, or made use of for ridicule or bitterness (and when it it is used for such purposes, its character is easily seen through), it is like sunrise on the brook, which proves that the ripples are not frozen, or flowers of the forest, that prove the richness of the soil. It cannot indeed be financially reckoned, or arithmetically, nor can the sweep of the swallow, or the chattering on the trees, which tell the beauty of the year and announce the summer. So in the nature of man, the overabundance of power in the ease of his work shows itself, at last, in playfulness. When a friend smiles upon us, we know that he loves us. The playful jests of the social circle reveal character. Formality and hypocrisy, art and concealment, they show to be at an end. They put people in natural relations; they unite them in cordial intimacies. And the homely conversation of our late President has enabled the people to see him as a man of truth, not a mask; not an abstraction, but a human being; not an official magistrate, not an incarnation of diplomatic intrigue, or a state machine, but a man; an honest man; and a friend.

* * * * * * *

The suddenness of the death of one so distinguished quickens our sense of the unsubstantial condition of earthly things; it makes many highest earthly hopes seem of little importance. How many persons have paused, in the midst of daily occupations, this last week, in worldly ambitions and in household cares, seeming to think for a moment, 'all is worthless.' His death has cheapened many things. How many affectations it has rebuked! how many false desires it has unmasked! how much of the love of power it has shaken! how it has appeased the fever of the world! How it has renewedly taught us, impressing the common thought, gain what you will, wealth, position, applause or opportunity, all will end. Your house you shall leave behind you; your wealth, another shall spend; your power you shall lay down in the grave; you shall breathe out your last breath, and never breathe more.

Is life a breath? Is nothing abiding? "We are such stuff as dreams are made of, and our little life is rounded with a sleep." Yes; though substantial man seems to fade as doth a leaf, or like a cloud exhale, we rest, and we cannot fail to rest in the sense that there are realities. And though we do not find them where we thought to, yet to our feelings, never were the realities of existence more sure, more trusted in, more dear than now. Personal vices, moral corruption, the infidelity of the heart, the spirit of selfishness, these have gained no new power. But a good life, a pure character, a loving spirit, appear more valuable, in the great account we make of the estimate of existence. Patriotism is real; sincerity is real; goodness and love never seemed more real than now. The infinite distinction between right and wrong does not pass into the order of the insubstantialities. Crime never was more abhorrent; vice never was more repulsive. We love our kindred and our friends to-day, with a tenderer, truer love; for true life and human souls appear possessed of a reality we never so clearly saw in them before. Our own soul's existence, our immortal being, our sense of responsibility to the eternal Law, all that God has taught us of life and of Himself, these show themselves real now. We gaze, in spirit, through the opening, by which the departed rises to eternity, and worship before the revelation of the throne of God. The music of angels breaks upon our ear. We return to daily occupations, if startled at unrealities here, comforted, strengthened, blessed in the sense of a universal and infinite reality.

By this distinguished, sudden death, we are renewedly impressed with the sense of the superiority of the greatest virtues to men's appreciation, and the constant refusal of the world to receive and endure exalted worth. We have thought it mysterious in the providence of God, that martyrs must shed their blood as the seed of the church, and the precious life of the patriot be given for his country and humanity. Yet do not gaze at this common truth with wonder, nor consider the appointment too hard, nor lament as inexplicable the danger of virtue, the persecution of the great and good. It seems the universal law, just, and sublime, and a part of nature's order. The soul tends to break through all mortal confines. Neither with the body, nor among mortal men does it find its most appropriate or final home. As it exerts itself more highly and laboriously, see how thin becomes its fleshly covering. The thinker's eye is never that of the unthinking clown. The face illumined by love, sanctified by purity, impressed with holy and sublime resolution, shows to the world the power of the soul within. No artist can depict on canvass, or cut in marble, or describe in words the expression we behold. It is the soul. We recognize it; and stand awed at its power and its loveliness. The body cannot confine it, or cover and conceal it.

So men cannot, with their confining, controlling power, hold in the virtue that is too large for human comprehension. They bind it; they resist its growth and expansion in the good man's soul and its influence in the world, as the husk binds in the tender leaf, the sprouting branches in the spring of the year. Men forbid advancement beyond their own. They seek to silence the free speech of patriotism and religion, to prevent the thought even that reaches out beyond their knowledge and their view. Littleness is safe with them. It may be prosperous and honored. It is understood. The world, in looking at the common thought and common virtue, sees what it sees, knows what it knows, and fears no danger from what it has long been acquainted with, whose limitations it understands, whose thought and power do not interfere with its ambitions, its possessions and its pleasures. But every highest thought frightens it with fear of danger, even when the great man's thought is only doing it most good. So, reverently, Christ died what may be termed a natural death. Patriots and saints, before and since, bruise themselves against the world that surround them; for the antagonism is natural and inevitable.

And we ourselves, of humblest life, in every humblest duty, illustrate the same great law. The spirit too pure for earthly principles, consents to break through mortal barriers, to deny pleasure, to resist the world, to refuse honor,—the same law of suffering,—(if it must be called by such a name)—the same law of suffering in duty being everywhere met with, because earth and the world are too narrow for the soul.

But do we lament the conditions? The buried seed bursts through into the darkness of earth and the soil, before it pushes its way above the superincumbent clod, to rise to air and sunlight to grow in freshness, life and beauty.

* * * * * * *

MEETING OF THE CONCORDIA SOCIETY.

The Concordia society, a German literary and social union, met at their hall on River street for the purpose of commemorating the sad and untimely death of President Lincoln. The room which was filled with an attentive audience, was draped in mourning. Mr. Frank Hartsfeld, the president of the association, began the exercises of the evening with a few introductory remarks, saying that as there were in the lives of individuals certain days more important than others, so in the lives of nations there were days distinguished by great events. In the latter portion of the life of this nation two of the important days were the fourteenth of April, 1861, when Sumter fell and the war began, and that same day four years later, when the flag of our country was again raised over that redeemed fortress and the war was ended. This last day obtains even greater significance, from the fact that during its passing hours, Abraham Lincoln, the most distinguished of our citizens and the President of this nation, was assassinated.

Prof. P. H. Baermann, in a very forcible speech, urged his hearers to take warning from the past, and under all circumstances and on all occasions to record themselves on the side of right and humanity. He spoke at length concerning the solution effected by the war, of some of the most momentous difficulties in the problem of our national life. In referring to the event which had stirred so deeply the hearts of the people, he said that although we had lost in Abraham Lincoln, one of the greatest men of his time, God in His providence had preserved his life long enough to see the end, virtually, of the rebellion and of the accursed institution of slavery.

Short addresses were also made by the Rev. H. G. Salomon, Rev. Jonas Heilbron, and Mr. Henry Staude, after which the meeting was dissolved.

MONDAY, APRIL 24TH, 1865.

The proclamation of the President of the United States, recommending to the nation the observance of a day of humiliation and mourning, forms a part of the history of the times, and is here presented.

PROCLAMATION BY THE PRESIDENT.

Whereas, By my direction, the acting secretary of state, in a notice to the public on the seventeenth of

April, requested the various religious denominations to assemble on the nineteenth of April, on the occasion of the obsequies of Abraham Lincoln, late President of the United States, and to observe the same with appropriate ceremonies; and

Whereas, Our country has become one great house of mourning, where the head of the family has been taken away, and believing that a special period should be assigned for again humbling ourselves before Almighty God, in order that the bereavement may be sanctified to the nation;

Now, therefore, in order to mitigate that grief on earth which can only be assuaged by communion with the Father in heaven, and in compliance with the wishes of senators and representatives in congress, communicated to me by a resolution adopted at the national Capitol, I, Andrew Johnson, President of the United States, do hereby appoint Thursday, the twenty-fifth day of May next, to be observed wherever in the United States the flag of the country may be respected as a day of humiliation and mourning, and I recommend my fellow citizens then to assemble in their respective places of worship, there to unite in solemn service to Almighty God, in memory of the good man who has been removed, so that all shall be occupied at the same time in contemplation of his virtues, and sorrow for his sudden and violent end.

In witness whereof, I have hereunto set my hand and caused the seal of the United States to be affixed.

Done at the city of Washington, the twenty-fourth day of April, in the year of our Lord one thousand eight hundred and sixty-five, and of the independence of the United States the eighty-ninth.

By the President:

ANDREW JOHNSON.

W. HUNTER, Acting Secretary of State.*

COMMON COUNCIL PROCEEDINGS.

SPECIAL MEETING.

Monday, April 24th, 1865.

Members present:—Hon. Uri Gilbert, mayor; Hon. John Moran, recorder, and Aldermen Cox, Fales, Fitzgerald, Hay, Hislop, Haight, Harrity, Kemp, McManus, Morris, Prentice, Stanton, Smart, Starbuck, Sears, Stannard.

The mayor stated that he had received an invitation from the Albany common council for the board to take part in the obsequies of the late President Lincoln, on Wednesday next; that he had communicated with the authorities at Albany, and tendered an invitation, as requested, to Col. McConihe, of the twenty-fourth regiment, which had been accepted. He had called the board together to take further action.

On motion of the recorder, the invitation of the

---

* The first day of June was afterwards substituted for the day recommended in this proclamation.

Albany common council was accepted, and a committee of five was appointed to make arrangements for the board to attend the funeral. Aldermen Kemp, McManus, Morris, Prentice and Hay were appointed as such committee. Mayor Gilbert was added to the committee, to extend invitations to any distinguished guests whom it might be desirable to invite.

On motion of Alderman Starbuck, the mayor was desired to request citizens to close their places of business from twelve to four o'clock on Wednesday next.

Then, on motion, the board adjourned.

JAMES S. THORN, City Clerk.

THE GUARD OF HONOR.

Officers who have served in the war, with those at present in the service, and private soldiers who have taken part in putting down the rebellion, are to form a guard of honor next Wednesday at the obsequies. The Albany officers held a meeting, this morning, and resolved to invite Troy officers and soldiers to take part with them: All who accept the invitation are requested to meet at the City Hall, Albany, on Wednesday, at ten A. M. Officers to appear in full dress uniform, and side arms.

TUESDAY, APRIL 25TH, 1865.

In accordance with the request of the common council, set forth in their proceedings on the twenty-fourth instant, the mayor of the city published the following

ANNOUNCEMENT.

To the Citizens of Troy:

In respect for the memory of the illustrious dead, whose obsequies will take place in our neighboring city of Albany, on Wednesday, April twenty-sixth, our citizens are respectfully requested to display the usual emblems of mourning, and to close their places of business from twelve to four o'clock on that day.

URI GILBERT, Mayor.

Troy, April 25th, 1865.

INVITATION.

HEAD QRS., 24TH REGT., N. Y. S. N. G., }
Troy, April 25, 1865. }

The commissioned officers of returned regiments, together with all officers of the army and navy in this city and vicinity are cordially invited to accompany this regiment to Albany to-morrow. Those so desiring will please report at the colonel's quarters, regimental armory, at nine o'clock A. M.

I. McCONIHE JR., Colonel.

G. G. MOORE, Adjutant.

Proceedings of the Executive Committee of the Troy Young Men's Association.

Special Meeting.

Troy, April 25th, 1865.

Present — Clarence Willard, Esq., president, in the chair, and the following members: Henry Galusha, Wm. W. Rousseau, J. Spencer Garnsey, T. Henry Bussey, Josiah L. Young, Martin L. Hollister, Geo. C. Baldwin Jr., Jas. S. Thorn, H. C. Folger, J. E. Schoonmaker, Wm. E. Gilbert, Benj. D. Benson.

The President stated the object of the meeting to be, to take action on an invitation which had been received from the Albany Young Men's Association to our association, to take part in the obsequies of the late President Lincoln at Albany.

Mr. Galusha moved that the president appoint a committee of as many members of the executive committee as could attend the obsequies, to represent the association. This motion was adopted.

The president appointed Wm. E. Gilbert chairman of said committee, with authority to select his associates from the members of the executive committee.

On motion, adjourned.

T. Henry Bussey, Rec. Sec'y.

Meeting of Veteran Officers.

At a meeting of the veteran officers held at the Mansion House, on Tuesday evening, the meeting was organized by calling to the chair Maj. Joseph Egolf and the appointment of Capt. Thomas B. Eaton as secretary. Maj. Egolf stated the object of the meeting.

Capt. McConihe offered the following resolution, which was adopted:

Resolved, That we, the old officers of the volunteer army and navy, fully sympathize with the public in the death of our lamented President, and that we appear in a body at the obsequies at Albany on the twenty-sixth instant.

An invitation was presented from the adjutant of the twenty-fourth regiment to the veteran officers of Troy and vicinity, to accompany said regiment to Albany and return on the steamer Vanderbilt. On motion their invitation was accepted, and Capt. Eaton was instructed to inform the adjutant of the fact. On motion,

Resolved, That the veteran officers of Troy and vicinity be requested to wear the usual badge of mourning for thirty days.

Resolved, That all the veteran officers of the army and navy in Troy and vicinity, not present at this meeting, be requested to participate in the obsequies of the late President, and that all veteran officers who design to join in the solemnities of the day be requested to meet at the armory of the twenty-fourth regiment at half past eight o'clock to-morrow morning, in full uniform so far as possible.

Resolved, That the proceedings of this meeting be published.

Maj. JOSEPH EGOLF, Chairman.

Capt. T. B. EATON, Secretary.

OFFICERS' MEETING.

At a meeting of the discharged and present officers in the city, convened for the purpose of paying the last tribute of respect to the remains of the late President, a motion was made and unanimously adopted, generally inviting the officers and enlisted men of the city of Troy and elsewhere to participate.

WILLIAM E. WHITE, late Capt. 43d N. Y.

WEDNESDAY, APRIL 26TH, 1865.

AN ACCOUNT OF THE PARTICIPATION OF CITIZENS OF TROY IN THE OBSEQUIES OF ABRAHAM LINCOLN, AT ALBANY.

The funeral train conveying the remains of the lamented President reached Albany at eleven o'clock on the evening of the twenty-fifth of April. Escorted by an immense and imposing procession, the coffin was borne to the Capitol, where, at half past one o'clock on the morning of this day, it was opened, and the dead features of Abraham Lincoln were exposed to the reverent gaze of thousands. From this time until two o'clock in the afternoon, a guard of honor surrounded the coffin in conjunction with the military companies detailed for special service on this occasion.

The body lay in state in the Assembly Chamber, which was tastefully draped, and from the floor of which the desks and chairs had been removed. In the centre of the space thus made, was a dais covered with black cloth beautifully festooned, and adorned with heavy silver mountings. Upon this dais the coffin was placed. The military companies, three in number, were on guard alternately, for two hours each. The guard of honor was composed of the officers named in the following order:

GUARD OF HONOR.

HEAD QUARTERS DISTRICTS OF NORTHERN
AND WESTERN NEW YORK.
Albany, April 25, 1865.

The following officers have been detailed as a Guard of Honor to the remains of the late President of the United States:—

First Watch—12 M. till 3 A. M. Brigadier General John F. Rathbone, Colonel B. F. Baker, Colonel W. H. Young, Colonel J. J. De Forrest, Colonel R. C. Bentley, Major W. C. Beardsley.

Second Watch—3 A. M. till 6 A. M. Brigadier Generál Darius Allén, Colonel Ira Ainsworth, Colonel A. S. Baker, Colonel C. S. Peak, Colonel John Hastings, Lieutenant Colonel Chas. H. Thompson.

Third Watch—6 A. M. till 9 A. M. Brevet Colonel Frederick Townsend, Major H. C. Pratt, Major George Pomeroy, Brevet Major H. A. Swartwout, Captain F. P. Muhlenberg, Captain George H. Weeks.

Fourth Watch—9 A. M. till 12 M. Major General John T. Cooper, Colonel James Hendrick, Colonel Charles Strong, Colonel George Beach, Captain M. L. Norton, Assistant Surgeon James H. Armsby.

Fifth Watch—12 M. till 2 P. M. Major General T. R. Pratt, Colonel J. B. Stonehouse, Colonel B. C. Gilbert, Colonel S. E. Marvin, Colonel M. A. Farrell, Major John Manly.

JNO. C. ROBINSON, Brev. Major General.

The preparations in Troy, which had been in progress several days, for attending the obsequies at Albany, were renewed at an early hour this morning. Soon after nine o'clock the Twenty-fourth Regiment, New York State National Guard, formed on First street, its right resting on Congress street. The field, staff and line officers of this regiment were as follows:

Colonel, Isaac McConihe Jr.; Lieutenant Colonel, John I. Le Roy; Major, George T. Steenbergh; Surgeon, Le Roy McLean; Chaplain, Rev. Henry C. Potter; Engineer, Captain Martin Payne; Adjutant, Gurdon G. Moore; Quartermaster, Henry S. Church; Assistant Surgeon, Nathan H. Camp.

Co. A. — Captain, John M. Landon; Lieutenants, Henry A. Merritt, William A. Daniels; Junior Second Lieutenant, James E. Curran, commanding battery.

Co. H. — Captain, William F. Calder; Lieutenants, Charles E. Hawley, Gabriel T. Winne.

Co. G. — Captain, James W. Cusack; Lieutenants, Gurdon G. Wolfe, John M. Cary.

Co. F. — Captain, John H. Quackenbush; Lieutenants, Wallace F. Bullis, Ezra R. Vail.

Co. E. — Captain, Michael Timpane; Lieutenants, William O'Brien, Patrick Conners.

Co. B. — Captain, Timothy McAuliffe; First Lieutenant, John Duke; Second Lieutenant, vacant.

Co. I. — Captain, Moses A. Upham; Lieutenants, John Myers, Michael Riley.

Co. D. — Captain, I. Seymour Scott; Lieutenants, Sidney T. Cary, Minott A. Thomas.

Co. C. — Captain, Edward A. Ives; Lieutenants, George S. Thompson, Le Grand Cramer.

Co. K. — Captain, Christian W. Rapp; Lieutenants, Albert E. Berger, Philip Dorr.

The regiment numbered seven hundred and twelve men, rank and file, and its fine appearance elicited the comment and admiration of all. Preceded by the regimental band, under the the direction of Charles

Doring, and the drum corps of Henry Perkins, it marched up First street to the wharf at the foot of Broadway, whence at ten o'clock it embarked for Albany on board the steamboat Vanderbilt, which had been chartered by the city for the occasion. On the same boat, as the guests of the twenty-fourth regiment, were nearly thirty veteran officers who had seen service in the field, and who were commanded by Lieutenant Colonel Charles E. Brintnall; besides officers of other regiments that had served or were now serving in the war, together with representatives of the navy service. By the same conveyance a number of the members of the Troy Young Men's Association proceeded to Albany to take part in the services of the day. The rest of the company on board consisted of members of the press and a few specially invited guests, the whole number of civilians being about two hundred.

The battery of the twenty-fourth regiment, consisting of four brass howitzers with their caissons complete, under the command of Lieutenant James E. Curran, of the artillery company A, went by the road to Albany.

The mayor and common council and the board of fire commissioners of the city, together with the board of supervisors of Rensselaer county proceeded to Albany in carriages. The members of the Loyal League and the fire companies and other civic associations, besides hundreds of citizens not connected with any organization, went by rail.

On reaching Albany the twenty-fourth regiment was met at Columbia street wharf, by the twenty-fifth regiment, N. Y. S. N. G., commanded by Col. Walter S. Church, and having formed on South Broadway, was escorted to its position on Eagle street in the line of the forming procession. The city and county officials were received at the mayor's office in the City Hall by the mayor of Albany and a committee of the Albany common council. To other organizations appropriate places were assigned in the funeral cortege. Most of the civilians wore badges designating them as the Rensselaer county delegation.

At two o'clock P. M. the procession began to move in the following order:

Advance of Police Force.
Gen. Rathbone's Brigade of the New York State National Guard, composed of the tenth, twenty-fourth and twenty-fifth regiments, constituting the Local Military Guard.
The Washington Military Escort.
Officers accompanying the remains.
Officers of the Army and Navy of the United States.
Major General John Tayler Cooper and Staff, and other Officers of the National Guard.
Ex-Officers of United States Volunteers.
The Congressional and other delegates accompanying the remains.
Pall Bearers — Hearse — Pall Bearers.
The Governor and Staff, Lieutenant Governor.

State Officers and Judges of the Court of Appeals.
Members of the Senate and Assembly.
The Albany Burgesses Corps.
The Mayor and Common Council and Officials of the City
and County of Albany.
The Mayor and Common Council of the City of Troy, and
Officials and Citizens of neighboring
Cities and Counties.
Citizens of Albany.
Board of Trade.
Young Men's Associations of Albany, Troy and West Troy.
German Literary Society.
Officers and members of the Albany Institute.
St. Andrew's Society.
St. George's Society.
Fenian Brotherhood.
Hibernian Provident Society.
Beaverwyck Club.
Typographical Union.
Union League of Albany, Troy and other places.
Iron Moulders' Union.
St. Peter's Society.
Brother Band.
St. Joseph's Society.
City Philanthropic Grove, No. 5, Order of Druids.
Schiller Grove, No. 4, Order of Druids.
William Tell Lodge.
Harmony Lodge, No. 12, Order of Harugarie.
Free Brother Lodge, No. 6, Order of Harugarie.
Bethust Society.
German Brothers Association.

Albany Turner Verein.
Independent Order of Odd Fellows.
The Fire Department of the City of Albany.
Fire companies of neighboring Cities and Towns.

The military moved in platoons, with solemn tread, their arms reversed, and formed one of the principal features in the imposing display.

The route of the procession was as follows: From State street, on which the main line was formed, up State street to Dove street, through Dove street to Washington avenue, down the avenue to State street, down State street to North Broadway, and thence to the Central rail road crossing.

At this point the remains of the late President were placed in the hearse car, and the funeral train resumed its westward course. The civic procession returned to State street, where it was dismissed. A few minutes later the twenty-fourth regiment was returning to Troy on the Vanderbilt. On reaching this city at five o'clock, the regiment proceeded to the Court House in front of which a dress parade took place, in the presence of the mayor and common council. The following order was then read by the adjutant and soon after the regiment was dismissed.

Order of the National Guard.

Head Qrs. 24th Regt., N. Y. S. N. G.,
Troy, *April* 26*th*, 1865.

General Order No. 18.

The colonel commanding, on behalf of this command, tenders his thanks to Col. Walter S. Church and his fine regiment, the Twenty-fifth N. Y. S. N. G., for a proper escort and other attentions and courtesies while this regiment was in Albany to-day; also to his honor the mayor, and common council of Troy, for generous coöperation; and to Chief of Police Barron, for efficient service, in Albany and Troy. By order,

I. McConihe Jr.,
Colonel Commanding.

G. G. Moore, Adjutant.

In sympathy with the solemn and imposing ceremonies at Albany, the day was observed in Troy by an almost total suspension of business. No church services were held, but with this exception the manifestations of sorrow and respect were similar to those apparent on the day of the funeral at Washington. It was estimated that not less than five thousand of the citizens of Troy were present at the obsequies solemnized at the capital of the state of New York. A mourning such as was this, was never before witnessed on this continent, and the days which intervened between the morning of that fatal Saturday when the announcement was made that Abraham Lincoln was dead and the close of this day, will be remembered by all, as the most notable, in many respects, of the passing century.

THURSDAY, APRIL, 27TH, 1865.

RESOLUTIONS OF THE TROY YOUNG MEN'S ASSOCIATION.

At a regular meeting of the executive committee of the Troy Young Men's Association, held at their rooms, on the evening of the twenty-seventh of April, 1865, on motion of Mr. Benj. D. Benson, it was

Resolved, that a committee be appointed with Mr. James S. Thorn as chairman, to draft resolutions in regard to the late President of the United States.

The chair appointed Mr. Benj. D. Benson and Mr. Wm. E. Gilbert on such committee. Subsequently the committee, through their chairman, reported the following preamble and resolutions, which were unanimously adopted.

In joining our voice of lamentation to the mourning wail that is rising from a continent, we only wish to swell by a single note the solemn chorus that comes from hearts desolated by a crushing blow. Yet as young men, members of a literary association, we deem it not inappropriate to record our profound participation in the common sorrow, and to testify that the gloom is not only general, but universal. Therefore

Resolved, That in the assassination of our beloved President, the late Abraham Lincoln, we see the last dying relic of a fell spirit which, subdued on the battle field, seeks to gain its end by means at which the spirit of the age must shudder. And yet in the universal execration with which the deed has been received, we recognize the impulse of a virtuous manhood which time cannot lessen, nor barbarism destroy.

Resolved, That in the spread of free institutions, and in the increase of societies such as ours, we shall find the surest guaranties of peace, order and happiness, amid which, society, created anew, shall never more know a parricidal deed. Then shall this tragic blot upon America's fair fame be succeeded by unending years of tranquility, till the present generation passes from the stage of action, and the oblivion of the future swallows the very names of the assassins of to-day.

FRIDAY, APRIL 28TH, 1865.

DECLINE OF AMUSEMENTS.

BY F. B. HUBBELL.

Since the death of the President, public amusements have been at a discount. In New York the theatres have reopened, but the audiences have been very slim. Traveling bands of minstrels, concert people, etc., etc., say they never experienced such a lack of patronage, and it seems impossible for them to reëstablish their old-time magnetism with the great public. In this city—not by any means backward, usually, in patronizing amusements—the halls heretofore nightly filled and often crowded, are well nigh deserted, no matter what the attraction.

This is to be taken as an evidence of the real soberness of the public mind at the present juncture. Men and women feel the country is under a deep cloud. The future is dark and uncertain. In place of craving diversion, there is a proneness to reflection, quiet consultation with friends, and even absolute seclusion. We shall doubtless soon recover from all this. Our people are so volatile and recuperative, it would be strange if we did not—unless indeed fresh sources of sorrow are opened. These, if not really anticipated, are more or less apprehended.

There has been a great deal of ostentation, a great deal of affected grief, over the national calamity; but it is doubtless true that the event, more than any other known to our national history, has caused deep, heartfelt and abiding sorrow, and it is a sorrow which as yet refuses to be comforted.— *Troy Daily Press.*

SATURDAY, APRIL 29TH, 1865.

PROCLAMATION BY THE PRESIDENT.

Whereas, By my proclamation of the twenty-fifth inst., Thursday, the twenty-fifth day of the next month, was recommended as a day for special humiliation and prayer, in consequence of the assassination of Abraham Lincoln, late President of the United States; but

Whereas, My attention has been called to the fact that the day aforesaid is sacred to a large number of Christians as one of rejoicing;

Now, therefore, be it known that I, Andrew Johnson, President of the United States, do hereby suggest that the religious services recommended as aforesaid, should be postponed until Thursday, the first day of June next.

In testimony whereof I have hereunto set my hand, and caused the seal of the United States to be affixed. Done at the City of Washington, this twenty-ninth day of April, A. D. 1865, and of the Inde-
[L. S.] pendence of the United States of America the eighty-ninth.

By the President,   ANDREW JOHNSON.

W. HUNTER, Acting Secretary of State.

THE MONTH OF MAY, 1865.

"TO EVERYTHING THERE IS A SEASON."

BY JAMES S. THORN.

Correspondents are asking us how soon it would be proper to remove the mourning emblems from the streets. When we recollect how deep and heartfelt has been the sorrow, and how profuse its outward expression, we think its effect would rather be lessened by continuing these manifestations for any longer period. Abraham Lincoln has been mourned as few men were ever before thus honored in the history of the world. Mammon has forgotten the pursuit of wealth, and pleasure has assumed a sober mein. Men who opposed him while living have become the champions of his memory when dead. Not only have the good elements of society done him honor, but even the volatile and the rougher portions have seemed to appreciate the magnitude of the tragedy. But one of the chief teachings of the terrible event is the lesson that the life of the American republic does not depend upon the existence of any one leader. We lament him, but the next in order takes his place, and even he is but the representative man temporarily placed at the helm of state. So while we mourn Abraham Lincoln, dead, we must recollect that the President can never die. At the commencement of the third week since the great tragedy, no one can accuse any community of a lack of feeling, if the streets resume their ordinary appearance; and it has been well suggested that such of the mourning cloth as can be made available, be given to the poor.— *Troy Daily Times, May 1st.*

A Dirge on the Death of Abraham Lincoln.

BY JOSIAH L. YOUNG.

Rest, thy noble work is done:
Sleep among the hallowed dead:
Golden buds encrown thy head,
  Evermore.

Distant far from mortal rage,
From the envy of thy power,
Perfect triumph is thy dower,
        Evermore.

No more sorrow, no more pain,
Sleepless nights nor days of toil:
Safe, above the rude turmoil,
        Evermore.

Costly tears are shed for thee,
Envy dareth not to rave,
Millions bend above thy grave,
        Evermore.

Weep, oh sobbing nation, weep!
Hallowed sunshine guards his rest,
Cradled in the golden West,
        Evermore.

He is thine, thy chosen son,
Naught can rob thee of his fame,
Naught can dim his deathless name,
        Evermore.

Down the ages it will glow
Mid the shining stars of time,
Paling those of every clime,
        Evermore.

None, through all the peopled past,
Has been loved like thee, save one,
He, the blessed Virgin's son,
        Sacred evermore.

No such sepulchre as thine,
Greener for a Nation's tears,

Green throughout a thousand years,
To the outmost flank of time.
Sleep, impassive silence reign!
No assassin can invade
Where thy precious dust is laid,
    Evermore.

Bloom, oh prairie, verdure sweet!
All your rare redundance spread,
Sprinkling perfume o'er his head,
    Evermore.
    Troy Daily Whig, May 2d.

LINCOLN AND CICERO.

BY B. H. HALL.

The juxtaposition of these two names may excite a smile in those who do not at the first thought perceive anything in common in the life or character of the Roman orator and the American ruler. In fact one would be apt to think that their names could only be brought together save for the sake of contrast. It is true, doubtless, that the differences between them are more marked than the similarities, still there are points of resemblance, and to these we desire to call attention. Cicero died by violence, so did Lincoln. Cicero was slain by the hands of traitors. Lincoln was the victim of treason. The manner of their death was different but equally affecting. On hearing that he had been proscribed, Cicero sought safety in flight. As his servants were carrying him in his litter or portable chair, the soldiers appeared. His servants prepared to fight, but Cicero commanded them to set him down and to make no resistance. "Then looking upon his executioners," as says Middleton in his Life of Cicero, "with a presence and firmness, which almost daunted them, and thrusting his neck, as forwardly as he could, out of the litter, he bade them do their work and take what they wantdd, upon which they presently cut off his head and both his hands." The sad story of Mr. Lincoln's assassination is too fresh in our minds to require a repetition.

The world has been moved as never before, wherever a spark of civilization glows, with sympathy at the loss we have sustained. Governments of all kinds, whether republican or monarchical, limited as to the power of the ruler or autocratical, Protestant or Roman Catholic, obeying the laws of Mahomet or based on Indian superstitions — all have evinced their horror at and declared their detestation of the fearful crime. Time will not weaken the impression. As the full antecedent history of the foul transaction becomes known, the terrible meaning of the act of assassination will appear, and after ages will recognize the fact as proved beyond cavil, that the blow which struck down their leader was intended for the heart of a free people. Already has the place where the deed was done become marked with an interest heretofore unimagined of any locality in our land. Already has the city named from the Father of his country become sacred as the place where fell time's noblest and latest martyr for Liberty and Truth. And so was it measurably with Cicero. The story of his death continued fresh in the minds of the Romans for many ages after the event and was delivered down to posterity with all its circumstances, as one of the most affecting and memorable of their history. The spot on which he was slain became famous, and was visited by travelers with a kind of religious reverence and awe.

But it is to the similarity between these two illustrious men, in certain traits of character, we desire to call particular attention. The language of the historian already alluded to, concerning Cicero's ideas of friendship, applies with equal force to Lincoln: "He entertained very high notions of friendship, and of its excellent use and benefit to human life. In all the variety of friendships in which his eminent rank engaged him, he was never charged with deceiving, deserting, or even slighting any one, whom he had once called his friend, or esteemed an honest man." So too did Lincoln resemble Cicero in his kindness to his enemies. The record which is left of the latter, on this point, is equally true of the former: "He was not more generous to his friends, than placable to his enemies, readily pardoning the greatest injuries, upon the slightest submission; and though no man ever had greater abilities or opportunities of revenging himself, yet when it was in his power to hurt, he sought out reasons to forgive, and whenever he was invited to it, never declined a reconciliation with his most inveterate enemies, of which there are numerous instances in his history. He declared nothing to be more laudable and worthy of a great man, than placability, and laid it down for a natural duty, to moderate our revenge, and observe a temper in punishing; and held repentance to be a sufficient ground for remitting it." As Cicero once said of himself so may it with equal truth be said of Lincoln, that his enmities were mortal, his friendships immortal.

In one other trait of character — a trait the possession and manifestation of which has brought upon Lincoln the slander of being a ribald jester — namely, that of pleasantry in conversation; in this characteristic did Lincoln especially resemble the great Roman. In the quaint language of Middleton, from whom citations have already been made, we give the picture of the humorous side of Cicero's life, and find in it much to remind us of him whose "little story" has grown a proverb. He was "of a nature remarkably facetious, and singularly turned to raillery, a talent, which was of great service to him at the bar, to correct the petulance of an adversary, relieve the satiety of a tedious cause, divert the minds of the judges, and mitigate the rigor of a sentence, by making both the bench and audience merry at the expense of the accuser.

"This use of it was always thought fair, and greatly applauded in public trials, but in private conversations, he was charged sometimes with pushing his raillery too far, and, through a consciousness of his superior wit, exerting it often intemperately, without reflecting what cruel wounds his lashes inflicted. Yet of all his sarcastical jokes, which are transmitted to us by antiquity, we shall not observe any, but what were pointed against characters, either ridiculous or profligate, such as he despised for their follies, or hated for their vices; and though he might provoke the spleen, and quicken the malice of enemies, more than was consistent with a regard to his own ease, yet he never appears to have hurt or lost a friend, or any one whom he valued, by the levity of jesting.

"It is certain that the fame of his wit was as celebrated as that of his eloquence; and that several spurious collections of his sayings were handed about in Rome in his life time; till his friend Trebonius, after he had been consul, thought it worth while to publish an authentic edition of them, in a volume which he addressed to Cicero himself. Cæsar likewise, in the height of his power, having taken a fancy to collect the apophthegms or memorable sayings of eminent men, gave strict orders to all his friends who used to frequent Cicero, to bring him everything of that sort, which happened to drop from him in their company. But Tiro, Cicero's freedman, who served him chiefly in his studies and literary affairs, published after his death, the most perfect collections of his sayings in three books."

Such is the account of some of the traits of Cicero's character in which Lincoln resembled him. The parallelism might be further continued, and other particulars adduced which were common to the two men. As Tiro preserved the sayings of Cicero, and as Boswell never failed to secure every chance thought that fell from the lips of Johnson, so too, there will be men who will collect the stories that have been accredited to Lincoln; and the pleasantry which was employed by him to relieve the tedium of the hour and to serve as an escape valve to his feelings, may hereafter be preserved in volumes as elaborate as those perfected by the freedman of the orator, and the follower of the lexicographer.

Troy Daily Whig, May 22d.

Agreeably to the spirit of the proclamation of the President of the United States, appointing the first day of June, as a day of mourning in view of the bereavement sustained by the nation, the Rev. Dr. Horatio Potter, the bishop of New York, issued on the twenty-fourth of May, a letter and an order of services for that occasion. They are here inserted, as they served to give direction to the religious worship of a portion of the people.

LETTER, AND ORDER OF SERVICES.

To the Clergy and Laity of the Diocese of New York:

DEAR BRETHREN: Thursday, the first day of June,

having been designated and set apart by the President of the United States, as a day of National Humiliation, Fasting and Prayer, the following order of services is set forth to be used in this Diocese on that day.

Commending you, dear Brethren to the blessing of God, I remain your faithful friend and

    Brother in Christ,

        HORATIO POTTER,

            Bishop of New York.

New York, May 24, 1865.

ORDER OF SERVICES SET FORTH BY THE BISHOP, TO BE USED IN THE DIOCESE OF NEW YORK ON THURSDAY, JUNE 1ST, 1865:

¶ The Morning Service shall be the same with the usual Office, except where it is hereby otherwise appointed.

¶ Instead of the Anthem, *Venite, Exultemus Domino:* Psalm cxxx, *De profundis clamavi*, shall be said or sung.

Proper Psalms.—Psalm xc, and Psalm xci.

Proper Lessons.—The first Lesson, Isaiah, i.; The second Lesson, Hebrews, xii to v. 15.

¶ After the second Lesson the Hymn, *Benedictus.*

¶ The *Litany* shall be said entire.

¶ In the end of the *Litany*, immediately before the General Thanksgiving, shall be said the Prayer *For a Person under Affliction*, the phrase "sorrows of thy servants," being altered so as to read "sorrows of the people of this land."

¶ The *Litany* being ended, there shall be sung from

the Selection of Psalms in metre, *Selection* 30, *verses* 1, 2, and 3; or *Selection* 40; or some other Selection, at the discretion of the Minister.

¶ In the *Communion Service*, the Collect, the Epistle, and the Gospel, shall be those for the Week (The Sunday after Ascension Day), with the addition of the Collect for the Fifth Sunday in Lent, after the Collect for the day.

¶ After the Gospel, shall be sung the 12th, or 202d Hymn; or some other Hymn at the discretion of the Minister.

¶ Immediately before the Blessing, the two final prayers *In the Order for the Burial of the Dead*, one or both, may be said.

Proclamation by the Mayor.

The President of the United States having, by Proclamation, set apart Thursday, the first day of June, to be observed as a day of humiliation and prayer, in view of the great national calamity suffered by reason of the assassination of Abraham Lincoln, President of the United States, I do hereby respectfully recommend to the citizens of Troy that they pay due respect and make proper observance of the day, by suspending labor, closing their places of business, and by assembling at the stated places of worship.

Done in the city of Troy, this thirty-first day of May, 1865.

Uri Gilbert, Mayor.

JUNE 1st, 1865.

"The Sword of the Lord," A Discourse Delivered in St. Paul's Church.

BY REV. THOMAS W. COIT, D.D.

O, thou sword of the Lord, How long will it be ere thou be quiet? Put up thyself into thy scabbard, rest, and be still.— JEREMIAH, xlvii, 6.

This is not the first time, my brethren, that I have selected this text for a National Fast-Day. The very same text was long since chosen for a sermon to be addressed to you on a national occasion; but circumstances, not necessary to mention, prevented its completion. In making it a theme for the present occasion, I resume some thoughts which have long been suspended.

The imagery of the Hebrews is, you know, very strong; is, to us, seemingly excessive and extravagant. But we must take it as we find it; it would not be oriental, if it were not apparently romantic. The text depicts God as a warrior, with a sword in his hand, equipped for bloodshed and extermination. But to a Hebrew, this would be no more than our saying, that war as well as peace was under the control of the Almighty; and that he could govern the destinies of both, with a sovereignty none can dispute. As controlling the destinies of the former, God is pronounced by Moses, in just so many words, "a man of war;"* while, in the visions of St. John,

* Exodus, xv, 3.

even the Prince of Peace is represented with a sharp two-edged sword proceeding out of a mouth, which would fain utter nothing but benedictions.*

But if God is thus an arbiter, and a supreme arbiter, for that which more than any thing else puts the destinies of a nation in peril — war, and of all wars a civil war — then in relation to war, one of the best things we can do is to appeal to Him, *in that character*, and pour our supplications at his feet, for forbearance and compassion, for mercy, sustenance and direction. It is such a supplication as this, which the Prophet Jeremiah gives us an instance of, when — as I doubt not — he raised a tearful eye to Heaven, and exclaimed :

> O, thou sword of the Lord,
> How long will it be, ere thou be quiet?
> Put up thyself into thy scabbard,
> Rest, and be still.

Such a resource, however, as *that*, is not one which our human preferences would put forth, as a commanding, as a transcending one, when war smokes and thunders around us, and threatens to overwhelm us with its fires and earthquakes. No; the *mind* of man would look rather to the *hand* of man for extrication in such formidable exigencies — to the sagacity of statesmen, to the bravery of soldiers, to thronging armies and encircling fleets, and all war's enginery of

* Revelations, i, 16.

mischief. The greatest, grandest warrior of all is apt to be forgotten, amid such circumstances — the sword which He wields is all unthought of — and though the actual arbiter of every destiny, the resistless decider of every battle, He is treated as if a fiction of the fancy, the creation of cloud-painting hopes.

Our Prophet, you perceive, did *not* forget such a dread and resistless personage — the only genuine Lord paramount of human fates. And I do believe, I cannot help believing, when I look at the issue of our late tremendous conflict, that such an example was not forgotten by our countrymen, as it has been by those who laugh to scorn the idea, that the bending of human knees can influence a will that sways the universe — that a whisper from this earth's dust can be heard in the courts of the Eternal, the Immortal, the Invisible. But when the struggle deepened — when our country's fortunes trembled in the balance — then, I am persuaded, multitudes began to pray, as they had never done, to that "High and Mighty Ruler of the Universe," to whom the prayer book teaches us constantly to appeal for public men. And then too, as I am recently informed, and am most glad to be informed, the late Head of the nation began to imitate his countrymen, and to plead daily at God's footstool, for the pressing necessities and calamities of the land entrusted to his guardianship. There is to me, no brighter spot in all his history — a history which the future will glorify more perhaps than we do, since it will judge him by *results* perfectly incredible to ordinary calculation — no brighter spot, I say, in all his history; and one can follow him, in view of it into the world whither he was hurried with such appalling haste, with hopes outweighing immensely all his human honors.

But if things are so, then why are we this day called to mourn the utterly unlooked for, the paralyzing catastrophe, which removed him from the midst of us?

Perhaps, my brethren, our rapid success was too exhilirating, too flattering, too intoxicating. Like Israel, on the banks of the Jordan, we had vanquished all essential opposition. We stood, as they did, upon the borders of a promised land, and were bewildered, as they were, with prospective triumphs which opened around on all sides, and with radiant brilliancy. Our hearts were lifted up, and we were beginning to forget Him, who, and who alone, had wrought such a series of wonders, that as one looks back, he feels tempted to call them not phenomena but miracles; we were forgetting that it was virtually the sheathing of *His* sword, and not the taking as spoil the swords of our opponents — that *this* was the true cause, which had obtained our exemption from war's blighting horrors, and brought back omens of peace and plenty — and were inclining to say, with self-satisfied Israel, "My power, and the might of mine hand, hath gotten me this wealth." *

* Deuteronomy, viii, 17.

So the sword of the Almighty was again drawn forth, so far as to make us feel, most smartingly, that our destinies were no more in our own keeping than before. The nation was touched, where it could most ill afford to bear it, in a Head upon whom such expectations rested, as have not rested upon any one, save the Father of his country, the immortal Washington. I say *such* expectations, including not our portion of the land alone, but that which has arrayed itself against the laws and constitution of *their* fathers as well as *ours*. Well did one of the chiefs in that land say, in terms of bitter lamentation, "The south has lost its best friend." And well may the south keep this day, with a depth of earnestness exceeding our own; for a madder act was never perpetrated, since the days of Cain, than by him who slew for the south, as he thought, a tyrant, when he slew one, who, sooner than have been a tyrant, would have died as he did a martyr. If I could believe the south might supply many such utter madmen, I could believe that the age of demoniacal possessions had returned, and that we needed exorcisms which would cast out seven devils from a single human breast!

But I must make this address a short one, brethren, and therefore turn to a question, which naturally suggests itself, when we are in the midst of mourning and fasting, namely: How shall we conduct ourselves, so that we may not be called to mourn and fast *again ?*

We might easily have had much more to mourn

and fast for, than we have now. Had the sword of the Lord been drawn but a little further from its scabbard — in other words, had not God restrained the wrath of man in its devouring malignity — the very wheels of government might have been arrested, and the nation resembled a vessel in the trough of the sea, amid the billows of a storm. God only knows, how little of non-interference on his part might have brought us to the verge of anarchy, or dashed us upon its breakers.

So to God then let us go for the future, as we *have* done for the past: to God let us still lift the plaintive cry of the prophet,

> O, thou sword of the Lord,
> How long will it be, ere thou be quiet?
> Put up thyself into thy scabbard,
> Rest, and be still.

This is our best security against future evils, as it has been against the evils from which we have been so singularly redeemed. Problems of the deepest and most anxious concernment are before the nation, which should be decided by that union of the wisdom of the serpent with the gentleness of the dove, which God only can impart and regulate. Widespread destruction is an easy work — as easy, sometimes, as individual self-ruin. We have virtually destroyed what attempted to be a nation, and which now lies before us as Lisbon lay before the King of Portugal, after the earthquake of 1755. Such almost immeasurable ruin accompanied that enormous convulsion of the ground, whose undulations spread over four millions of square miles, that the monarch cried to his prime minister in an agony of consternation, "What, oh what, is to be done?" "Bury the dead, and feed the living," was the calm, ever memorable reply. And beyond all question, our great crowning work is to be much the same. We must bury the past, as well as justice, attempered and softened by charity, will permit. We must consider this,

> "That, in the course of justice, none of us
> Should see salvation. We do pray for mercy;
> And that same prayer doth teach us all to render
> The deeds of mercy."*

And in providing for the future, we must act under such sacred cautions, as our church addresses to her bishops, at the moment of their consecration: "Be so merciful, that you be not too remiss; so minister discipline, that you forget not mercy." May such cautions ever guide our rulers in the state, as well as in the church; and that they may, and may continually, let us pray for them, as we do for those about to be confirmed, that God would daily increase in them His manifold gifts of grace, the spirit of wisdom and understanding, the spirit of counsel and ghostly strength, the spirit of knowledge and true godliness, and fill them with the spirit of His holy fear.

* Merchant of Venice, Act iv, scene 1.

Happily, by universal consent, one hitherto impracticable difficulty in the reconstruction of the southern social state has been obliterated; and Christanity has now the fairest of opportunities to accomplish for the colored race, all which it could ever accomplish for the freest of human beings. I say Christianity; since it is a grievous mistake to suppose that Christianity has ever sanctioned slavery, though it has endured it, and not interfered with it, as a civil institution. So our Saviour endured the system of Roman taxation, and paid his tribute punctually to a Roman emperor; while in direct reference to another Roman emperor, one of his apostles—the very chiefest of them, as some will have it—said most explicitly, "Honor the King."* Did our Saviour approve the laws, which governed the collection of internal revenue in the Roman Empire? Did St. Peter approve the tyranny and bloodthirstiness of Nero? No more did Christianity approve of slavery, when it bade those in bondage obey their masters. The real sentiments of Christianity respecting slavery can be seen in the antidote, which it offered a baptized slave for his sad subjection—an antidote such as no system of philosophy, or ethics, or political economy, ever gave him, or ever could give him. It pronounced him the freeman of his God!† This was a comfort, which no

---

* 1 Peter, ii, 17.

† See 1 Corinthians, vii, 22. St. Paul could scarcely pronounce, to my mind, a higher condemnation of slavery, *per se*, than by maintaining

earthly affluence could buy for him; nay, a privilege which no earthly potentate could confer upon him. Wherefore, Christianity, and the church after her, inculcated the doctrine that no one—*no one*—within their pale, could be degraded or impoverished in the eye of all eyes, the eye of God, by any involuntary predicament or condition.

The church, I mean the church catholic, primitive, and apostolic—the church which we believe has been transmitted to us from earliest times, and which we profess our faith in, in the Creeds—*this* church began at once to modify and to repress slavery, to the best of her ability. Doubtless, it was a conflict of ages with human governments, and above all with human purses. It was the purses of London merchants, which forbade the British Ministry to listen to the importunities of South Carolina, when, before the American Revolution, it prayed that no more slaves might be imported into Charleston. It is a battle with filthy lucre, which the church catholic has had to fight,

that the man, whom it would fain hold in life-long bondage, might be, all the while, God's freeman. And yet it has been argued, a thousand times, that, in his Epistle to Philemon, he encouraged a fugitive slave-law. He did no such thing. He fully sustained the doctrine, that no baptized person should be held in bondage. He enjoined upon Philemon (as he had a right to do, Philemon being a professed Christian), to receive Onesimus as "not now a servant, but above a servant, a brother beloved" (see verse 16), or, as the Greek fully authorizes me to render the passage, "as *no longer* a slave, but above a slave, a brother beloved." That is, receive him as your equal and your brother; for, inasmuch as he is a freeman (or *made free*, as the margin has it) of the Lord, his servitude with you, as a Christian, has forever ended!.

in establishing as one of her axioms of Christian law, that the freeman of God should be the freeman of man likewise. But, happily, the axiom *has* been established; and I may now announce to you as a self-evident Christian principle, that no one, be his nation, his rank, or his color what they may, should ever be held in bondage, who has had the name of the Trinity invoked upon him, and the sign of the cross impressed upon his brow. That blessed name, that blessed sign, ought to be a complete protection to any one, be his color or his quality what they may, from the degradation of servitude. That protection was accorded peacefully in Mexico and Russia: England, I am sorry to say it, left out the Christian reason for manumitting her bond-servants. In our own dear land (how much sorrier am I to say so), liberation for the slave has been extorted, by the red right hand of war. But, come by what instrumentality soever, it *has* come at last, with apparent security. And may God Almighty grant, that it never be abused by friend, or wronged by foe!

I cannot stop here, my brethren, to indulge in comments upon the offices and influence of government, upon the condition of those who have been emancipated from thraldom. Time will not permit me; and, moreover, I cannot but think such a topic belongs rather to others. But this I may say, and this I ought to say, as Christ's minister, there is now a future of hope for a down-trodden race, if Christianity may bring to bear upon them, *all* her beneficent and elevating influences and inspirations. I will never despair of the civil, as well as the moral regeneration of any beings, for whom Christ died, so long as Christ's religion may be theirs, in its whole fullness and freedom. Let Christianity then baptize the African as the freeman of man. Let her educate him as such. Let her instruct him as such, how to lead "a godly, righteous and sober life." Let her marry him as such, and give him a home as inviolable as the white man's. Let her offer him a welcome at her goodliest altars. Let her follow him to the grave, with the same commitment which is bestowed upon the highest of human society. And if they who have been esteemed fit to be goods and chattels only, do not reward such treatment, then we may reverse the prophet's petition, and pray for the coming of a day, when the sharp edge of chastisement shall awaken them to sensibility.

But that day, my Christian hopes prompt me to believe, will never come to haunt us with the spectres of ingratitude. Christianity has never failed with the most refractory of human races. It has now but to have its legitimate influence, and we may apply to our united country, the promise of days long gone.

> " Fear not, for I am with thee;
> I will bring thy seed from the East,
> And gather them from the West.
> I will say to the North, ' Give up;'

And to the South, 'Keep not back;'
Bring my sons from far,
And my daughters from the ends of the earth:
Even every one THAT IS CALLED BY MY NAME."*

Now unto him that is able to do exceeding abundantly above all that we ask or think, according to the power that worketh in us, unto Him be glory in the Church by Christ Jesus, throughout all ages, world without end. Amen.†

An Address Delivered in the State Street Methodist Episcopal Church.

BY CHARLTON T. LEWIS, ESQ.

At the close of winter, it is the custom of the Christian part of the nation to observe a day of fasting and humiliation. Many had looked forward, some months ago, with heaviness and anxiety to that day, as it approached. But the nearer it came, the greater was our success in our national struggles; and the whole sky was brightening with triumph and hope, so that the fast lost all its sorrow and became a jubilee. Soon after, the hope was more than realized; the land was filled with joy and exultation; and our late good President, referring all blessings to their source, appointed the twentieth day of April as a day of thanksgiving to God, for his goodness to the na-

* Isaiah, xliii, 5, etc.
† Ephesians, iii, 20, 21.

tion. But just before the appointed day, a sudden and terrible calamity fell upon the world, and most sadly upon our country; and that day became a day of terror, apprehension and unbounded sorrow. Now again, and in memory of that event, we meet for a day of fasting and humiliation. And we find its terror gone; its sorrows lost in a larger joy. Our war, our struggle for national existence, is really ended; the chief plague spot of the civilized world has disappeared; health and peace are brought back to our life as a people. Who can make to-day other than a thanksgiving? Who can suppress the voice of exulting praise to our Father's God?

We are not prophets. We cannot ordain our own emotions for a day. We name hours to come for times of joy or of sorrow; and the great forces of history, which own not us but another as master, reverse our appointments. Our wisest plans are changed to folly; while "our indiscretion ofttimes serves us well, when our deep plots do pall." Shall we not learn from this to look above ourselves to one in whose hand are our ways?

These sudden shocks of feeling are not fortuitous nor worthless. Not in the vast of creation, nor in the elemental forces, shall we look for the scene in which God's plan for history is accomplished; but in humanity. That era of mighty movements which has passed over us, the overwhelming march of events, the tremendous passions waked and lulled in millions, the sublime wrath of the nation followed by a calm, these are forces to develop manhood and build its future. The great value of our records of the past is in their revelation of what is in man. And events should be measured chiefly by their power over the human heart. It is this which makes these last weeks great in world-story. Never before did so short a time reveal on such an imposing scale, the tremendous contrasts of our nature; the infinite possibilities of good and evil which lie in man; the heights and the depths he is capable of.

It is fitting, then, that this call to humiliation comes in the hour of triumph. To-day is a jubilee; aye, this year is one long day of jubilee, wherever man has hopes for freedom. It is the birth-year of a race; half a continent of emancipated manhood dates forever from this time its power to work out a destiny. We have a peace which is peace; a peace fairly won by fighting down the evil. Every household that has lost a hero is lit with joy at the triumph of the cause he died for. Every martyr to liberty in history sees a new garland on his grave, in her future secured. Another of those great struggles of civilization, which determine the world's course for ages, is ended and won. And hark! the cry is, humble yourselves! Fast and pray!

This world is double in all its constitution; as the home of our double humanity. High and low, east and west, right and left, imply one another, and simply repeat themselves through all the relations of infinite space. And as riches imply poverty, as strength exists by contrast with weakness, so good is ever thrown upon a background of evil. Every great revelation of virtue is accompanied with one of crime. Unfathomed depths of .evil lie under all the sun-crowned heights of human nature. And, to-day, we cannot turn our thoughts to our chief, whom God has taken, but we are met at once by the startling sight of the foulest of crimes. When the labors and sufferings of four years for good, culminate in peaceful freedom and the ascent of its first representative to heaven, just then the crime and malignity of four years culminate in one blow, which reveals and exhausts the whole spirit of treason. The names of Lincoln and of Booth stand on the same page of history, and forever the glory of freedom's martyr throws a deeper gloom on the inverted immortality of treason's fiend.

But a few years since, both were obscure. No man in America, if asked for two names, which should be the very emblems, the one of patriotism, the other of murder, to coming ages, would have thought of these. We did not know that we trod the same earth with men of such possibilities. And how little we know, now and always, of others; even of ourselves. Around us and within us, sometimes moving dimly, but mostly asleep, are the forces which, awakened, startle nations and forge history. Each one bears within him that which might become divine manhood, to raise his race to something nobler, or fiendish manhood, to turn its joys to gall. Side by side everywhere they stand and grow, the spirits of love and of murder; the wheat and the tares, both ripening to the harvest. "We walk on powder-mines." Every green field of human life grows over a volcano of human passion.

But, turning from the dark side now, let us look at the man in whose memory we meet. Four years ago, if we had been asked to describe him, one of us might have said, "He is a man of strong practical sense, of fixed principle, firm and resolute, with a wonderful capacity for work, and the ablest debater before the people in this land of speakers. He seems, too, to be patient, tolerant of others' infirmities, and the humblest public man we have ever known." We could have said little more. But events have moved rapidly and greatly, for him as for us; and have developed the capacities of the man, and made them manifest to us. We look back upon his person, now lost, and his career, already transfigured by his departure; and see in him a great gift of God to mankind.

Abraham Lincoln was a man of very keen sympathies for others. Unselfish in his impulses, he labored all his days whether, in a humble life or as a nation's ruler, for the good of those around him. He listened with kindness and close attention to all; he made himself in greatness as accessible as he had been familiar, when himself undistinguished from the throng.

His feelings were strong; so strong that in another man they would be considered a sure index of "a good hater." But he hated only the principles he thought wrong; not the men who held them, nor even the men who hated him. He would not speak a word against a foe. Striving to be the president of the whole people, he exhausted his time and strength in efforts to give to all who claimed it his fatherly care.

With keen native insight, trained in rugged experience, he pierced through the plots around him, and was rarely deceived. His honest sincerity in politics accomplished more than cunning, and he recognized this same sincerity, whenever it appeared, and loved and trusted it.

In spite of his rough early life, his ways were as gentle and tender as a girl's. Compelled to be stern and unyielding in the great outlines of administration, at the painful cost of hardships to individuals, he sought relief for his own mind, in making exceptions of kindness, where the opportunity occurred to him. In war all his aim was a righteous peace; not the grasp of power. And when the tidings reached him of the terrible repulse of Chancellorsville, all thoughts of disappointed hopes and broken policy were lost in his overwhelming sorrow for the wasted life and suffering of men; and the strong man threw off all self-control, and cried like a broken-hearted woman. Few have known, through the struggle, how the sternest and bloodiest of wars was conducted by the gentlest and tenderest of leaders.

The controlling feature of his mind was the sense of justice. He was very slow to work out a moral problem; he must see every step clearly; but then he was fixed. No great measure of his administration was dictated by feeling; all came from calm convictions of right. Holding ever before him, as the compass of his high office, a longing love for his country's welfare, he obeyed its guidance, in preference to personal or political aims, and this welfare he saw only in the free life of the people, making its own future. His faith in the people was invincible, marvellous; in this he surpassed every ruler the world has ever known. When he saw them, as usual, wrong in their first impulse, he awaited, with calm assurance, their final judgment. Never, I repeat, did the people have a man who loved and trusted them so, and richly were this love and trust returned. To learn his glory, go not to the cultured student, or the polished citizen, to the forum or the press: but to the cottage and to the field of labor. Go to the freedmen of the far south; and you will hear "massa Lincoln" named next to God!

Through all his public life, we may trace a steady growth in this man. His views grew steadily broader and firmer. His grasp of power became more confident. He gathered slowly, but most fixedly, to himself the people's love. In nothing is this growth more obvious than in the religious tone of his mind. His later state-papers show a progressing trust in God. And if pure religion consists in doing justice, loving mercy, and walking in genuine humility, we must pronounce him one of the most religious of men. Events placed him high, with little agency and short expectation of his own; and he grew to his circumstances, gathered them into himself, rose in mind and heart to the greatness which each rapidly coming crisis called for. There were times, chiefly in his earlier career, when his language, as well as his form and manners, excited the merriment of critics; but his fame could afford this, for his words by which he spoke to all ages, were deeds. Yet his brief address at Gettysburg stands perhaps unrivalled in modern oratory, and would alone rank him with immortal names in literature.

But why dwell on the sides and phases of character shown us by him whose nature was well delineated, centuries before his birth? Shakespeare makes Wolsey in his disgrace sketch to Cromwell the model ruler and statesman, and every word fits our LINCOLN as if written by a prophetic insight.

"Love thyself last: cherish those hearts that hate thee:
Corruption wins not more than honesty.
Still in thy right hand carry gentle peace,
To silence envious tongues. Be just, and fear not;
Let all the ends, thou aim'st at, be thy country's,
Thy God's, and truth's; then if thou fall'st, O Cromwell,
Thou fall'st a blessed martyr."

Such was Abraham Lincoln on the fourteenth day of April. He then stood on a pinnacle of historic glory, not attained by any other in this generation. It was the anniversary of the first fall of our flag before treason; and after conducting for four years the operations of the largest armies in the world, until his foes were crushed, he had ordered that day to be signalized by restoring the old flag. The same old faithful hands that pulled it down should raise it; and every battery that fired upon it should salute it. This was done; an emblem of war ended, of peace, union and government restored, in the heart of the south. I think that all ages to come, looking back on that triumph, will agree that the first name in the world on that day was ABRAHAM LINCOLN, President of the United States.

We live, indeed, in an age of great rulers, who seem greater, because succeeding an age of little ones. A higher glory sits on the thrones of Europe than for ages past. Even the English court has renewed something of its ancient splendor, by the influence of the purity and refinement of its head, as "mother, wife and queen." France has been at once plundered and made greater by Napoleon, who, after wading "through slaughter to a throne" has based his empire on wisdom and progress. Victor Emanuel has revived the long-faded glories of Italy. Francis Joseph has emancipated himself from the traditional counsels and policy of his house, and strives nobly to give constitutional government and financial life to his empire. And, greatest of all, Alexander of Russia, in the character of emancipator of a continent, appears as an advancer of civilization, and a hope of mankind. Not forgetting these names, but remembering them all, and their greatness, I hesitate not to set one name above them, and to declare that on the fourteenth of April last, the first name in the world was ABRAHAM LINCOLN, President of the United States.

Is Napoleon the architect of his own power? Lincoln won his way, from deeper obscurity, by purer methods, to a nobler throne. Has Victor Emanuel destroyed a hellish tyranny in Naples? Lincoln has abolished more completely one far more odious. Has Alexander freed millions of serfs? Lincoln gave freedom from equal bondage to a better race, and upon ground more fruitful in all that sustains and promises civilization, than Russia's most fertile fields. His administration has sustained its finances through crises more terrible than even Austria has met. And he crowned all by an exalted and modest walk of private virtue sterner and not less pure than that of England's court. But that which stamps his greatness forever, which sets him above all these rulers, is this: he is the only man in history, who, holding in his hand boundless military power, and the destinies of millions; sustained by exhaustless resources and the devotion of the people; has never been suspected of using or wishing to use them for his personal aggrandizement, for any purpose but his country's good. Only in the bosom of republican civilization could such patriotism grow; only there could it even be understood. He was his country's; he is his country's forever. Richer with his work and the memory of all he was, the Union enters the new phase of her history; and on this memorial day, the genius of the Republic he saved bids his soul ascend to sit evermore side by side with Washington; with "Honor, honor, honor, honor to him; Eternal honor to his name."

Farewell, bright spirit; vesper star in the constellation of freedom's martyrs, the last and the brightest; ascend thy throne of fame, and beam on us and on this land in never-fading glory.

Looking to him, we have nothing to mourn. Earth had nothing higher for him; nothing unattained. Amid the acclaims of a triumphant nation, who made him their symbol of triumph, and the exultant gratitude of a new-born race, to whom his name was all the brightness of the future, to step to heaven; was not this a fitting close to his career? A good man, who maintained goodness inviolate, and who believed, beyond the common lot of statesmen, in God and man, has gone from man to God; in the ripeness of honors, in mature years, and in the hour of victory. It is no loss, but all gain for him. For that humanity he served and died for declares, in its purest and complete embodiment, "He that loseth his life for my sake, the same shall save it."

Why is it then that these outward symbols of mourning seem to have their deepest meaning to-day?

Why were our hearts so long shocked and heavy; a burden of undefined apprehension upon them; the nation, as it were, watching a black shadow, and dimly framing of it imaginations of horrible import? We have more to remember to-day than the death of our friend and father. We have to deal with that which has slain him. Now, as of old, a great crime is felt to be "a great perturbation in nature;" and at the first shock of this greatest of crimes, we felt as if nature's laws were yielding; and we trembled for ourselves and our children.

We were dreaming of the sweetest sounds to mortals; peace after war; pardon for mistaken views and impulsive crime; restoration of brotherhood, and a national jubilee. The head of the nation represented its spirit. He was filled with peace and kindness; his mind reacted from the long strain of sternness and contention, and overflowed with gentleness and pardon. He was busied with devices to make repentance easy and restoration pleasant, for his foes. At this moment, in the Capital, amid throngs of those who would have died to save him, he was struck down by treason. And the nation, startled from its dreams of peace, arose to ask, bewildered, what is this human serpent that stings again its double benefactor, in the very hour of mercy and pardon? What is this spirit, which will not be sated with blood, nor suffer kindness to live? It seems a new revelation of the character of our foe. The treason which strikes at our free government is that which murders the great and good; which breaks open the sick chamber and aims the assassin's dagger at the helpless invalid; which even strikes down mercy herself, in the nurse of the sick, whose sacredness was never violated before even by the fiends of barbarous war. It is not that our ruler falls. Epaminondas, Washington, aye, Jesus himself died; but the cause of each went on. The Republic is rich in manhood, and can survive its noblest. But we did not realize before how earnest and terrible are the times we live in and the forces which fill them. Nothing is asleep to-day; God and his foes are in earnest, and we must be. Let the knell of our murdered chief rouse us to duties and labors not understood before.

I have seen in the south a field of blood where the same spirit was shown. Some twenty acres of flat land, skirted by graves, which had been a race course for the chivalry, were made a prison for the soldiers of the Union. There confined, many of them without clothing of any kind, they were exposed to the fierce blaze of the July sun, and to frosts of winter. Everything that an absence of the requirements of decency, health and comfort could inflict was suffered by them. They were nearly, many of them quite starved to death; many more were wantonly murdered; multitudes died of exposure and disease. They dug pits in which to lie for shade or warmth; trenches to drain a few feet of ground for a bed; and the whole field is scarred and pierced thickly with these from end to end. Even their dead at last were not removed, and no tools could be obtained; so with their own fingers they dug graves for their comrades. And pity itself was made a crime; for I saw women in Charleston who had been lashed with seventy stripes for attempting to give these sufferers a morsel of wholesome food. Why allude to this? To show how crime is linked together; how all evil flows from one foul inspiration; how the spirit that murdered Abraham Lincoln is everywhere the same; the spirit of *treason*. Do you ask, where is his murderer? Dissolved into thin air, a vision, a name. But the people of this land will ever feel, that, wherever from. this day a hand is uplifted against this flag, against the nation, against human freedom, there is the inspiration of treason; there is his murderer. The traitor hitherto may have been misled; the traitor henceforth is the conscious ally of the assassin, and adopts as his own all the foul crimes, which, through this war, have humiliated manhood by shewing its strange possibilities of fiendishness.

Amid all our excitements and apprehensions, we have felt one quieting power; one thing is calm, his great spirit looking down upon us. What, could he speak, would be his bidding? Words surely, fuller than ever of his grand characteristics of patriotism and kindness. And his voice would be lifted loudly against the clamor, now so wide and high, for vengeance. He loved ever justice, acting by the forms of justice, and dwelling in the house of mercy. And he would bid us gather calmness and strength; and in the quiet dignity of an outraged nation, without passion, but like God, slowly and surely to hold an inquisition for blood. He would bid us, as uttering the weightiest words of his whole career, to seize the suspected, to bring them only before the ordinary and regular tribunals of justice; particularly to hear all facts, weigh them well, leaning to merciful doubts; and, when guilt is fully ascertained, execute with sublime delay the sentence of justice, amid the acclamations of the world. He would say, this is the only government on the earth possessed of such magnificent self-restraint as to make this possible. That, if this is done, he is glad to have given his life, that the world may see the perfect organization, the dignity, energy and justice of a great republic, in this most bewildering scene. That if this is done, all is done. The problem of reconstructing society in the south has no difficulties invincible to a people who can do this. And we can do it. Let the people themselves demand, as the right of their calm dignity and noble wrath, that this be done. Let them hold back every arm that would strike down even treason and murder, by summary and irregular methods, and await the slow, great stroke of the divine arm of law.

Such would be the lesson of the highest patriotism, above the storm of passion, in the serene calm of heaven. This nation cannot afford a fevered investigation, an irregular judgment, a sentence by a tribunal not known to the laws. We are rich to-day. This war, so wasteful of material wealth, has left us rich in historic life. Our old reproach among the nations was, the want of a storied past. Four years have given it to us, with long rolls of heroic ancestries, countless shrines for pilgrimage, an infinity of noble memories, worth more than a series of ages of less fruitful life. Have they shewn us depths in humanity? They have revealed heights of heroism, beyond the fairy tales of chivalry. The boy who threw himself across a cask of powder to protect the ship from explosion at Roanoke Island, is one of a thousand immortalities. The chief story of fortitude in the French revolutionary wars, was the famous account given by Barrère of the sinking of La Vengeur, going down with all on board shouting defiance at their guns, and "*Vive la Republique.*" This was false; but the true story of the Cumberland more than replaces it in the heroic annals of man. History is enriched and human hopes enlarged by these records. We are left rich too in patriotism, to inspire and hallow heroic force. A tide of passion and of power has been raised by this crisis which will not recede till this flag waves everywhere over this nation, yet waves not over one who does not love it freely, and better than his life. How we love it to-day! How bright its colors seem! They are reawakened in splendor by the storm. They are the brighter, for the very rainbow which the tears of our grief bend over it. The blood of Abraham Lincoln has crimsoned every stripe, and his bright soul shines out as its central star. Let it enfold his ashes to-day, tenderly as a nation's love, and wave over his last resting place, an eternal emblem of peace.

Yes, we are rich to-day, too rich, too great, for any vindictive passion, any haste in wrath. Never had nation such opportunities for moral greatness as ours. We have won greatness in patriotic fervor, in heroism, as well as in resources: now let us crown all with the greatness of forbearance. The law for murder is fixed by the consent of the world. Let it be executed legally. But the law for treason is a shifting code, written through all history in blood, but not based, as the other, on the moral sense of mankind. Let us show that we can afford what no other nation has ever given, magnanimity to a fallen foe. The effect of such a policy, boldly and thoroughly pursued, upon Europe, on posterity, above all on our own national character, can scarcely be estimated. It would strengthen the principle of self-government more than all our victories in war. For it would show that this is not a triumph only of strength, but of law; of that sublime law which can vindicate and administer itself; which can conquer the spirit of treason in the heart, and make patriots of a community of traitors. Without one feeling of sympathy or regard for the murderers of our prisoners and of our President, but because we regard ourselves and law, we must leave all crime to the regular administration of law, we must pardon all but that which is crime by all human codes; and so do greatly the work of greatness.

It is in this spirit, applying the Christian rule of love to our political action, that we can act wisely in this and in every crisis. Love to God, our country and truth, will inspire and consecrate hatred to every spirit that opposes these, and the halo of God's own smile will be upon the nation, as, in the pure spirit of patriotism, we execute his law upon the second crime of history, done on the anniversary of the first and darkest, the murder of the Saviour of the world. Let it be in this spirit of love that the nation stands to-day before its dead, and, yearning with affectionate hope for the return of its thankless children, yet vows undying hatred to the treason that struck him down. By every holy bond that ties men to a solemn duty, we will drive out that satanic inspiration from the land; we will have a nation purified, regenerate, dedicated in love as a shrine to the God of liberty. Accepting as our leaders those who may be spared us by Him, who, while "he buries his workmen, carries on his work," we will do our work, which is his, and then lie down with our greatest, under the flag he died for.

Discourse Delivered at the Third Street Methodist Episcopal Church.

By Rev. David T. Elliott.

And Samuel died ; and all the Israelites were gathered together, and lamented him, and buried him in his house at Ramah.—1 Samuel, xxv, 1.

A spirit of general mourning and universal sorrow swept over the whole land of Palestine. In every household and hamlet, as well as in town and city, a dark shadow rested upon the people. The occasion, the death of Samuel, called up the most sacred reminiscences and awakened the deepest anxieties. Samuel, under the theocratic system of government with which God had honored this nation, was the only visible representative of their glorious King, and the accredited minister between the people and their Divine Sovereign. And when, in their folly, they desired a visible king, that they might resemble the nations surrounding them, he under God was their stay and confidence during the period of their political revolution. Known and honored for his remarkable piety, purity and integrity, a patriotic, devoted man, set apart to the service of God and his own nation, he had evinced the strongest attachment to the people, and this fact joined to his superior abilities in providing for all the interests of all classes of citizens, had made him the general favorite, unto whom they looked for counsel, and upon whose known integrity they relied, without distrust. And thus it was that all the people felt his death as a personal affliction and mourned it as a public calamity. In view of these facts, this general sorrow — this universal gathering of all the people was a fitting tribute to his eminence and worth, a becoming expression of a nation's appreciation of his sincere devotion and unswerving fidelity to all the trusts committed to his hands. We call your attention to this case at this time, as indicating the proprieties of such an occasion, as well as suitably introducing the subject we are, this day, called together to contemplate.

Peculiar and interesting as were the circumstances of the Jewish nation upon the occasion of Samuel's death, they but in part suggest the peculiar and impressive influences that surround this occasion in our national history. A nation greater than the Jews are overwhelmed in sadness and grief. A loss such as Israel could not feel in the death of their beloved and honored prophet (who was full of years and was called away by the visitation of God), has befallen our beloved country and is felt as irreparable by a great nation. On the evening of the fourteenth of April last, fell by the hand of the assassin, Abraham Lincoln, President of the United States of America. He died a martyr for his country and the glorious principle of universal liberty. We are met to-day to recount his virtues, study his character, and pay our grateful tribute to his eminent abilities and moral worth. In this discourse we propose to consider the causes that developed the spirit that devised and accomplished this sad event, his assassination. Then to look at the history, character and doings of our late chief magistrate, and close with such practical reflections as may seem suitable to the occasion.

In undertaking so much in the compass of a single discourse, you will see that our sketch must be very meagre and imperfect. In looking for the influences that culminated in this terrible affliction, we ask you to go back with us to the earliest period of our national history. In the year 1776 the people of the colonies of North America made a bid for independence. They heroically took their stand upon the rights of man. They published and proclaimed as their honest belief the doctrine of universal equality and inalienable rights, saying "We hold these truths to be self-evident that all men are created equal; that they are endowed by their Creator with certain inalienable rights; that among these are life, liberty, and the pursuit of happiness." Appealing to God as the judge of their sincerity and of the rectitude of their intentions, they asked and received the support and confidence of the people at home, and also the sympathy and assistance of people abroad. Inspired by these sentiments they rose with the struggle, until under God they attained victory and nationality. It was the sublime idea of the equality and rights of man that developed and invigorated manhood into the sublimest proportions ever then witnessed upon earth, that brought forth a nation worthy to be free because it manifested the true spirit of freedom. This declaration was the charter, the watchword, the battle cry and the grand central principle of our fathers through the bloody, trying period of the revolution, until the nations of the earth arose and recognized their claims and gave them independence. But when the end was gained—when the men who had struggled and endured through the dark trial of war to attain their own rights, and had sought God's blessing upon their effort until they had succeeded, standing solemnly pledged to each other to forfeit life, fortune, and sacred honor rather than abandon their principles — when these men met in council to form a constitution and adjust a polity for the government of a free people, they strangely and to my mind unaccountably failed in the most essential particulars. It is lamentably true, that the constitution of the United States does nowhere recognize the existence of the Divine Being. And it is unaccountably true also, that it does recognize slavery. The God whose help our fathers had implored in their trial, was forgotten in their prosperity, and the principle upon which they had appealed to the confidence and intelligence of the world was repudiated in this great instrument made to direct and control a nation's destiny. Yes, they did recognize slavery, under another name I admit, but this simple evasion only makes the fact more glaring.

They recognized it under protest, I confess, but in recognizing it at all, they granted it a right to exist, and in so doing ignored and repudiated practically what they were pledged to maintain, at the cost of life, fortune, and sacred honor.

Here began that course of inconsistencies and evil influences, which, in the progress of events, step by step, insidiously led to the dark and bloody period of treason and rebellion through which we have passed. Year after year the glorious declaration was read, and orators waxed eloquent over its noble sentiments, while year by year slavery grew stronger and entrenched itself more firmly in the legislation of the nation. At first it was simply tolerated, and by wise and patriotic statesmen was deplored. Then it was countenanced by the practice and patronage of men of talents. Soon men stood up in its defence and advocated it upon politic grounds. At length its support became a means of political preferment. Later still, it was advocated as the highest style of civilization. Finally it was canonized as a divine institution and maintained as authorized by holy scripture. Churches were divided at its bidding. Legislative bodies the most grave and important were elected in its support, and the judiciary influenced to act in its defence. What was only tolerated at the first, under protest, grew to be the grand central idea with many of the people, until American citizens were mobbed and martyred upon the suspicion that they opposed slavery.

Slave-holders grew more and more arrogant and unscrupulous. While wealth poured in upon them without their effort; while they were tolerated in the greatest sensual gratification, and the unprincipled assigned them the proudest social position; while presidents, senators, representatives and judges were elected in their interest, it is not remarkable that they came to demand that all men should receive their doctrines and the whole national domain be given to them as the theatre of this institution. All who disagreed with them in sentiment were stigmatized as "abolitionists," "mud-sills," "greasy mechanics." The declaration of independence was openly discarded and the statements therein made, pronounced untrue. Free labor or labor by the white man who claimed citizenship was denounced and dishonored. Every right of the common people was either invaded or threatened, and the assurance was given, that unless all their demands were complied with, the union of the states should be broken up and our government overthrown and destroyed.

During this period, however, there were men who sounded the note of alarm. They exposed the practices and exhibited the spirit of slave-holders, they advocated the doctrines of the declaration, to wit, man's equality and the rights of man. As a result of their labors and the reaction produced by the unscrupulous character and arrogant assumptions of the slaveocracy, the people were at length aroused, their moral sense was awakened, and the agitation led to a more perfect understanding of the question and an appreciation of our relation to it as citizens, and our responsibility as American freemen. An organized opposition to slavery extension was attained, and the issue made by an appeal to the electors of the land upon this question. And though in the first attempt the friends of freedom were defeated, still they exhibited such an inveterate hostility to human bondage and such a determination to utterly refuse granting the demands of slavery, that the system was believed in danger, and its votaries prepared to precipitate an arrangement long contemplated, namely, to break up the nation. Aware that they had succeeded in their purpose to elect a man to the presidency in 1856 who was pledged to act in the intersts of slavery, only by massing all the friends of slavery, rum, profligacy and iniquity generally, with office holders and seekers of place, together with thousands of good and honest people who were misled by calling this aggregation of all corruptions by the popular title of Democracy (to which the party as such had no more right than Satan has to divine honors), they determined to find some justification, if possible, for rebellion. The issue was again made upon slavery extension, and Abraham Lincoln was chosen standard bearer, an avowed enemy of the institution, a man from among the people, of tried principle and of known integrity. They knew that neither flattery nor menace would move him, and being resolved to ruin the country which they could not rule, they decided to make his election a pretext for rebellion. He was elected. A good providence gave the United States a ruler worthy to be entrusted with the great interests of the age, and the hopes of the world. Rebellion was inaugurated. Slavery took the field against liberty. The forces were marshaled, and the most appalling struggle waxed hotter and still hotter.

Times there were when men looked on with bated breath, when every bosom swelled with anxiety, and when every interest of man and the nation seemed to be in immediate peril and to hang upon a single thread. But one noble chief seemed to rise with every trial and to comprehend every emergency. When the fitting occasion arrived, slavery, the parent of all this mischief, was abolished and treason disfranchised. Blow succeeded blow that struck the very heart of rebellion, and made all loyal men believe our President worthy to be called honest still. But with every step in the progress of the war, the spirit of slavery, for it was the animus of the rebellion, seemed more and more malignant and unscrupulous. See this evinced in the cold blooded murder of men who on the battle field ask quarter or lie wounded when the struggle is past. See it in the plan to burn our cities and infect whole communities with the plague. See it in the barbaric cruelty with which they hunt, murder and destroy loyal people at the south, who will not join their fortunes with rebellion. See it in the treatment of prisoners of war, herding them without shelter, clothing or food in most malarious places, making pastime of their sufferings, and without provocation, murdering them for sport. And finally, as a fitting sequel to this most infamous rebellion, see the evidence of this spirit, in the conspiracy to assassinate Abraham Lincoln, Lieutenant General Grant, together with the heads of the departments of state.

Such my brethren was the spirit which produces this sad event, and, at one blow, clothes a continent in mourning and causes the greatest grief to a whole people. Slavery acknowledged, tolerated, defended, advocated, canonized, has begotten and brought forth this harvest of consequences. But in the fall of the rebellion slavery itself has fallen. Now the institution lies stark and pulseless. Let the amendment of the constitution bury the hideous corpse beyond the power of a resurrection. But oh, at what a cost of precious blood and agony have we gained this result! How many are the sorrowing households! Fathers mourn for sons like David for Absalom. Rachel weeps for her children. Widowhood and orphanage are made common. Battle-scarred and mutilated heroes are all around and among us, telling of the cost. What patriot blood, scalding tears, and crushed affections, are the price of victory. But God reigns. It is His doing and it is marvellous in our eyes. Liberty lives. Republican institutions survive. True democracy grows strong in the land. A great, proud and powerful nation remains, purged, redeemed, regenerated I trust, to challenge the admiration of mankind and command the respect of the world. In this history are both the argument and example, demonstrating man's capacity to maintain his rights and sustain democratic government.

Let us now look at the history, character and acts of our lamented chief magistrate. Abraham Lincoln was born in Hardin county, Kentucky, in the year 1810, of poor yet pious parents. His childhood and youth were clouded and embarassed by poverty, ignorance and slavery. He belonged to a class who were without social advantages or power to secure them, being at the same time cordially despised by both planters and slaves, and known as "poor whites," a class to whom slavery made labor a disgrace and knowledge a crime. To him, under these circumstances, the prospect for learning and honor was dark and forbidding. Yet whatever advantages he did enjoy were earnestly improved. He learned to regard slavery as a great political and social evil, as well as a crying sin against God and man. During this period of youth he removed with his parents to the then new and wild lands of Indiana. Here his advantages were but little greater than in Kentucky, while here befel him the greatest trial and misfortune of his early life, in the death of his pious and excellent mother, who, like the mother of Washington, instilled into his mind a vigorous and devoted love of truth and honesty, and thus laid the foundation for the integrity of character that caused him to be known as *honest Abe*.

From such a boyhood and such surroundings came forth the great, good, the honest, true, patriotic and talented Abraham Lincoln. He wrestled with difficulties and overcame them: encountered embarrassments and triumphed over them; rising steadily, not because endowed with any remarkable genius, but by the power of steady application; not as the result of patronage of the great and honorable, but by the force of correct principles, honest purposes, and patient perseverance in earnest labors. His greatness is the reward of work, simply work, as God designed for man. Work brought him from obscurity to distinction, and work enabled him to hold the esteem, the affections and confidence of the wise, patriotic and pure, amid all the trials of his position and the differences of opinion upon the many important events of his administration.

When he entered upon the duties of his office, the whole country was wild with excitement. As his old neighbors bade him adieu, his simple, honest request was "pray for me." He sought the national capital, and even then assassins dogged his steps and lay in wait along his path. When he reached Washington, dismay and consternation filled every bosom — so much so, that those whose curiosity led them to witness his induction into office, were hastily organized into a guard to protect him from assault. Under these circumstances he pronounced his inaugural, which was so calm and manly, as to inspire confidence to that extent that the old battle-scarred and war-worn veteran, Lieutenant General Scott, exclaimed with tears, " We have a country left, thank God, we have a country left!" Dispassionate and calm, he looked upon the surrounding omens of trouble and prepared for the shock of war. He found our arsenals plundered of arms and munitions, our navy scattered upon distant and unimportant missions, our treasury robbed, our small standing army hemmed in by rebel plotters who endeavored (too successfully, in many cases) to lead it into treasonable conspiracies, many men educated at the nation's expense in military and naval schools, joined in fortune with the south, our own people mistaken as to the design and power of rebels, and in many minds a feeling of determined hostility to war under any circumstances, owing in general to the former political affinities and fear that party should suffer. Our national capital was threatened by invasion, and alarm and confusion held carnival at the seat of government. He issued a call for seventy-five thousand men to defend Washington, and this was treated, by not a few, as an unwarrantable assumption of power. The avenues of communication with the city were closed up. Union soldiers were murdered on their way to defend our old flag, and almost every thing seemed unpromising and forbidding. In this connection let me accord all honor to Major General John E. Wool of our own loyal city, who nobly sprung to the rescue, and without waiting for express orders promptly forwarded relief to an embarrassed and suffering garrison.

But in the midst of all these excitements Abraham Lincoln never faltered, nor for one moment showed signs of willingness to give up any material interest of his important trust. He rose with each emergency, grasped every question and calmly looked to the ultimate result. United with his noble corps of intimate advisers, he marshaled and organized an army that astonished the world, created a navy, compared to which all the fleets of other nations were feeble and useless, established a system of finance which commanded the entire confidence of capitalists at home and made a loan from other nations unnecessary, and inspired a generous confidence among the masses of the people that assured him of their unwavering support. Seizing the opportune moment, he sent out his emancipation proclamation that gave personal liberty to millions of loyal people who, under all the pressure of their unfortunate condition, had never been untrue to the dear old flag, thus restoring the dishonored declaration of seventy-six, and by his large, magnanimous and prudent policy, and his fearless, indomitable determination to maintain the integrity and unity of the government, compelled even his enemies to respect his principles.

Amid all his cares, anxieties and duties, he listened to the grievance of the poorest, and redressed the wrong that afflicted the meanest loyal citizen. Unintimidated by menace and unseduced by flattery, he held on his way. Reëlected to his more than royal position by such an honorable and astonishing unanimity as no man had ever witnessed in the past, and as may never occur again, he entered anew upon his work in the same spirit and zeal, while almost universal acclamation accorded him wisdom, greatness and worth. He lived to see his desire largely accomplished, to know that his policy was appreciated and approved, that the wisdom and purity of his administration were admitted, and to see the proudest and most defiant leaders of the rebellion prisoners of war or fugitives in their own land. He lived to know that the power of organized treason was broken and well nigh subdued. He lived to receive and enjoy the very highest honors ever paid to mortal man because they were the spontaneous offerings of a free people, to know that his name stood second to none in American history and would be the pride and glory of the American people, and to have millions of enfranchised men, made so by his act, rise up and call him blessed.

And here, in this meridian of his strength, power,

honor and usefulness, on this summit of earthly grandeur and glory, with the future prosperity, power and greatness of the country, he, under God, had saved, opening before him, HE FELL, he fell by the hand of an assassin, who acted in the interest, and, I have no doubt, in the accomplishment of a deeply laid plan of the slaveholders' rebellion. He fell a martyr to his honored principles and for the liberty he had loved so well. And as he fell he bequeathed to his country all the honors he had so nobly won and blessings such as none had ever conferred before, leaving his name written in the proudest place of the proudest history of the freest people that ever dwelt upon the face of the earth, and graven in the hearts of his countrymen, rich as well as poor, learned as well as ignorant, so that their boast shall be to say, "I voted for Abraham Lincoln, I was his fellow citizen." ABRAHAM LINCOLN! A name that will be pronounced with reverence in all lands, and shall be embalmed in the memories and enshrined in the affections of freedom's sons in all ages! While his illustrious character shall be pointed out as a model of true greatness, and his successful struggle with adversity and embarrassment as the inspiration bestowed upon such as are not favored with patronage nor endowed with genius, while his name shall be transmitted to posterity as another glorious example of sincere devotion to liberty and the elevation and happiness of mankind, he also shall be distinguished and remembered as an honest man and as the Saviour of his country. At his death a nation's tears were the most fitting offering to his virtue, while its anxieties and fears evidence the strong confidence it had reposed in him. Blessings rest upon his desolated and stricken household, and peace be to his ashes as well as all honor to his name.

But God, our country and duty remain, and we are called from these sad reflections to other cares and to hold up other hands. Let us look at this call upon us. Andrew Johnson, his successor in office, is now constitutionally the President of these United States, and as upon him much depends as to the adjustment of difficult and important matters, under the present state of things, I am happy to say that he was chosen to fill the second office in the gift of American citizens because of his capability for important position and duty, because he possessed the true American spirit of devotion to liberty, because of his noble stand against secession and rebellion and because he maintained his position in the true spirit of manly devotion to freedom, and sustained the grand old flag of his country. I this day thank God that he, being a man so tried, we, without any misgivings may confide in his patriotic principles, his superior abilities, and his personal sense of justice and right in these trying times. I rejoice, moreover, that he wisely retains as his constitutional advisers those tried and worthy men whom the people have learned to love and trust without reserve. Let us then pray for Johnson as we have prayed for Lincoln, that Almighty God may bless and guide him in all those matters, upon the proper adjustment of which the future peace and welfare of the country depend, such as determining the status of the freedman and applying the proper punishment to traitors. Differences of opinion will arise no doubt, and various policies be strenuously advocated. We want action that will at once be just, wise, generous and in the spirit of liberty, which will result in the greatest good to the greatest number without wronging any.

And here, though the matter be by some supposed difficult, I would also "show mine opinion." First, we should sincerely implore divine guidance and blessing, and weigh the whole matter seriously and well, and be particularly careful that we do nothing, or deny nothing either upon prejudice or partiality. Is the freed negro a man? Then endow him at once with the rights and privileges and responsibilities of a man, as freely and fully as you would accord the same to any white man in the same circumstances. Do you allow ignorant white men the right to exercise the elective franchise unconditionally? Allow the ignorant black man the same exercise. Do you limit that privilege to those whites that are intelligent and can read? Then restrict the colored man upon the same principle. Do you restrict this right, denying disloyal white men this exercise? Do just so with black men.

What I plead for is simply this, that no invidious distinctions, founded on prejudice against color, shall disgrace our action, or dishonor one loyal fellow creature and fellow soldier simply because he is black. And as I speak particularly of the elective franchise, so, did space allow, would I speak upon every mooted question that may or does arise, touching the status of the disenthralled negro. Let us in this matter prove ourselves possessed of the moral intelligence that nobly rises above all the dishonorable relics of that barbarous system that has constituted our national reproach and vexation in all our past history, and has well nigh accomplished our overthrow and ruin of late. Now since Divine Providence has furnished us the opportunity, let us show ourselves equal to the trust, by a noble, magnanimous recognition and endorsement of all the rights of the freed millions among us.

Another question that I desire to present, still remains. Shall treason go unpunished and rebels stand without rebuke after all the evil they have devised and the mischief they have wrought? Here again differences of opinion exist. Men who in spirit or in fact partook of or sympathized with treason, will naturally plead for leniency and a general pardon. They will remonstrate against cruelty and shedding blood. Why did they not remonstrate when rebels were murdering unarmed men, or starving and abusing prisoners of war? Why did they not shudder at the thought of shedding blood when traitors were inaugurating this most sanguinary and inexcusable of wars? I confess, to my mind, the very argument of such men not only looks suspicious, but breeds distrust. Another class plead for tolerance and pardon to subdued rebels upon a much better principle. Actuated by the most humane sentiments, and sincerely desirous for conciliation and peace, they deprecate the possible execution of the guilty criminal, and I respect their humanity though I am obliged to disagree with them as to the method of kindness. I would be distinctly understood as pleading that nothing be done through revenge or in the spirit or at the dictate of retaliation, but solely to promote the authority, stability and influence of law, and thus advance the best interests of all the people. Treason is a crime and a sin against all the people. It is a violation of law, which is the safeguard of the people. It is a repudiation of the authority and a resistance to the duty of the civil magistrate, who is the guardian of the rights and interests of the people under the law And in such a case of treason as this—when the plot has been laid deep and long and the conspirators, by previous perjury and crime, were prepared utterly to overthrow all government that the people had ordained, and were only defeated and prevented in their wicked designs by the strenuous efforts of the government, and after a struggle of years—to pardon indiscriminately is to destroy the authority and sanctity of law.

Had this rebellion been the result of sudden excitement and, as must have been in such a case, of short continuance, without time for men's passions to cool and without opportunity for the government to show that it did not intend to oppress any man or class of men who complained, it were vastly different. But such is not the case. The leaven of treason has been working for years. The government has by many, as I believe, unwarrantable concessions removed all occasion to rebel, but all in vain, and now for such criminals to seek pardon or for persons of doubtful loyalty to plead for their unconditional forgiveness, to me appears the farthest removed from that brave, chivalrous spirit that, having risked every thing upon the appeal to the sword, only shrinks from the result when it is overcome. What would be the temper of those men had they triumphed, had "they their hand now upon the throat of the nation as they have desired and vainly sought to have? I repeat, while I would do nothing out of retaliation or malice, I insist that we must maintain the authority and sanctity of law, or we shall leave the interests of the loyal and true citizen insecure. Treason is the highest crime against the state. Upon the power, authority and purity of the state depend the peace, safety and rights of the people. Slightly to pass over the most flagrant treason or, indiscriminately to pardon rebels, is to weaken if not destroy the influence, authority and power of the state. And such a course is itself a betrayal of every interest committed by the people to the state.

I do not advocate indiscriminate punishment. This, too, were not only improper, it would be radically unjust, for many, if not most of the rebels, are but the dupes and creatures of the master spirits of the occasion. But I will say that, in my judgment, those men who conceived and adopted this scheme, and plotted to plunder that they might destroy the nation, who have accepted place and power to injure us, and especially those who perjured their souls, more effectually to work our ruin, the officers, the master minds, ought to suffer the just penalty of their great sin. Something must be done for justice, and something that shall forever deter men from pursuing a similar course, or we shall cheapen crime, and unsettle the fundamental principles of society, and destroy the foundations of government. What we may call mercy and magnanimity to the guilty, may be the cause of ruin to the loyal and innocent among us. I pray God to bless Andrew Johnson, and the cabinet, and all the people, and especially the emancipated slaves, and give to all, wisdom to devise and power to execute for his glory, and our prosperity and peace.

Substance of a Discourse Preached in the United Presbyterian Church.

BY REV. HUGH r. MCADAM.

Neither will I be with you any more, except ye destroy the accursed from among you.—Joshua, vii, 12.

The history of this nation, in the present crisis, is in many features, the history of the Jewish nation repeating itself. There are many circumstances in our national experiences, corresponding with theirs. In our success we find a counterpart to their prosperity, in our reverses we discover a likeness to their calamities. In whatever circumstances we may be placed as a nation, we may look into the glass of God's word and see ourselves reflected. In every possible condition, we may find some portion of that word suited to our case, and containing a lesson, a warning, or a promise from which we can draw consolation or derive instruction. For the purpose of obtaining this consolation and instruction we have selected for consideration the portion of sacred history, embracing a record of God's dealings with Joshua and the children of Israel.

We propose to notice the similarity between some points in the history of the Israelites, and some circumstances in connection with our own national experience: also to present some of the lessons of instruction which these events are designed to teach.

The "accursed" was that which God had devoted to destruction. Of the spoils which should be taken from the enemy, God commanded Joshua and the children of Israel to destroy everything save the silver and gold and vessels of brass and iron, which were declared to be consecrated to the Lord. To be guilty of trespass in the "accursed thing" was to appropriate these spoils to some other purpose than that which God had commanded.

As long as the Israelites obeyed the command of God they were victorious, every effort was crowned with success. But when they disobeyed His command, nothing but defeat and disaster awaited them. In obedience to His instructions, they make an assault upon the city of Jericho, and the walls of the city totter and crumble before them. When they make a subsequent assault upon Ai, they meet with overwhelming and serious defeat. This calamity was unexpected. The God of battles who before had fought for them and given them the victory, was now turned against them. In view of this catastrophe, the hearts of the people sunk within them, and they betook themselves to mourning and humiliation. "Wherefore the hearts of the people melted and became as water. And Joshua rent his clothes, and fell to the earth upon his face before the ark of the Lord until the eventide, he and the elders of Israel, and put dust upon their heads." In their emergency they humble themselves before God, and inquire why it is He has thus frowned upon them, why it is He has thus turned to be their enemy, and suffered their adversaries to destroy them. God tells them why it is, they had been guilty of disobeying His command, they had sinned, they had "committed a trespass in the accursed thing," and He would not be with them again, until they should put away the "accursed" from among them. On investigation, they discover that Achan has been guilty of transgression in appropriating a portion of the spoils from Jericho to his own use, instead of giving them into the Lord's treasury. As a punishment for this transgression, they took Achan and all that he had, his possessions and family, and "all Israel stoned him with stones, and burned them with fire after they had stoned them with stones. So the lord turned from the fierceness of his anger." While the "accursed" was among them, God would not bless them. Until they would put away the transgressor, and cast out the guilty from among them God would visit them with judgment. But no sooner had they put away the transgressor, and purified themselves from their guilt, and destroyed the "accursed thing" and the accursed from among them, than God smiled upon them, dispelled the clouds that were frowning over them, and removed his judgments that pressed them so heavily. Then their defeats were converted into victories, their reverses into successes, and their disasters into blessings.

In obedience to the call of the chief executive of the

nation, we are assembled here to day, to bow ourselves reverently and with humility before God, owning our dependence upon Him, confessing our sins, and acknowledging His justice and righteousness in this adverse dispensation of His providence sent upon us. While we were exulting in victory, and rejoicing in the triumph of our arms, while we were with interest and anxiety, looking forward to the speedy restoration of our beloved land to peace and renewed prosperity, our joy is suddenly changed to sorrow, our day of national rejoicing is converted into a night of mourning. Before the period had arrived which had been set apart as the occasion for the public expression of our gratitude and thanksgiving to Almighty God for the success of our cause, it became necessary to revoke the appointment, and to designate a day for the purpose of humiliation and prayer, because of national calamity and bereavement. We are assembled to mourn the loss of the nation in the removal of our chief magistrate. The national head has been taken away. Our beloved president has been stricken down by the hand of an assassin. Those who in their deep depravity, hate and maliciousness murdered him, destroyed the head and wounded the heart of the nation. The country mourns his loss as that of a father and protector, for under God he loved the country and preserved the integrity of the Union.

We pronounce no eulogy over Abraham Lincoln. He has built his own monument, has written his own eulogy on the hearts of his countrymen. Of the many virtues, the amiable disposition, the manly traits of character and the administrative abilities of our lamented President, it is not necessary to speak. The results of his labors will live in the heart and history of the country. His unqualified honesty and integrity, his largeness of heart and amiability have endeared him to the people. Even those who opposed his policy, are constrained to admit and admire his honesty, uprightness and sincerity. He is dead, not from natural causes, but murdered, shot down by the bullet of the fiendish assassin. That the President of the United States, the choice of the people, raised to his high position by their act and authority, should be assassinated is something new in the history of our country, and the tragedy has been reserved for the cultivation and the civil and religious advancement of the latter half of the nineteenth century. The event has humbled us in our own eyes, it has humbled us before the nations of the earth. Let it this day humble us before God, that the sins of this nation have merited and provoked a judgment so terrible. That our country is the abode of such depraved beings as were these conspirators,— beings made in the likeness of men —that it has been the scene of such a tragedy, is an evidence of its awful wickedness. That we have those in the midst of us capable of perpetrating such awful crime, and prepared for such fiendish murder and butchery, should prostrate this nation before the God of vengeance, should lead it to implore his pardon, lest he utterly destroy us from the face of the earth, as he did the wicked nations of old. They sinned in the darkness of heathenism, we in the light of God's word and truth. It was fit and proper for the President to set apart this day as a day of humiliation and prayer. Let us bow before God, and confess that we have committed national sin, that we have provoked this national calamity. Let us bow submissively to his will, and say, "the Lord is just in all the evil he hath sent upon us."

It is our duty to-day to learn the lessons of God's providence, to enquire why it is the Lord is thus afflicting us, to search out "the accursed" from among us and put it away, for He has said that unless we destroy it from among us, He will not be with us any more. It is our duty to bow before God as individuals, and confess our sins in His sight, "that He may turn from His fierce anger, that we perish not;" saying in the language of David, "I acknowledge my transgressions, and my sin is ever before me. Against Thee, Thee only have I sinned, and done this evil in Thy sight; that thou mightest be justified when thou speakest, and clear when thou judgest."

We must accept this calamity as sent of God. He who sits in heaven and rules on earth, has ordered and permitted it, for some good purpose. It is one of the movements of the Almighty, in His great plan of providence, in working out the destiny of this nation.

We shall notice briefly some of the lessons clearly taught in this afflictive dispensation. When the heart of an individual is softened, broken under sorrow, that heart is more easily touched, impressed and influenced, than at other times. So it is with a nation when wounded and bleeding. And God designs to impress certain solemn lessons upon the heart of this nation. By this event He designs to turn us from our sins and draw us more closely to himself. I have frequently seen the statement in our papers and have often heard it remarked, that Lincoln was the idol of the people. I fear the declaration was founded in truth. The people of this country are inclined to hero-worship. There is a tendency in the human heart, to exalt the creature to the throne of the Creator, and render him that homage which is alone due to God. It may be on this account our President has been taken from us. God is a "jealous God," and will not suffer the honor and the glory that are due to himself to be ascribed to any creature. When a people or an individual sets up such an idol, and renders that idol homage, God will punish such idolatry. We were disposed to feel, and say, that our President had proposed and disposed; that he by his wisdom and foresight, had planned our campaigns and directed our forces to victory. We extolled Lincoln's "immortal Emancipation Proclamation;" we said of him, that he had proclaimed "liberty to the captives and the opening of the prison to them that are bound," forgetting God, who was controlling and directing all these results. We looked to his experience and wisdom to conduct the war to a successful and honorable termination, and to guide us to a happy and permanent peace. We expected his wisdom and sagacity to settle the remaining difficult questions of restoration and reconstruction. God is saying to us by this dispensation, that the work is not man's but God's, and is teaching this nation not to trust in an arm of flesh, nor in the wisdom of men, but in Him. He brings to the helm of the ship of state one without executive national experience, through whose instrumentality He will accomplish His work.

I believe that God designed also, by this dispensation, to teach us not to invade the sanctity of the sabbath. He has frequently taught us, in our own bitter experience, that we cannot violate and desecrate His Holy day with impunity. This war has taught us, on many a battle field, that God will not succeed that army, that disregards the claims of the sabbath. This seems to be a lesson of the same import — a judgment sent, because we as a people had been guilty of disregarding the claims of the sabbath. When the news of the victory of our arms over the confederate forces and of the surrender of Lee's army, flashed along our telegraph wires on that sabbath evening, what was the conduct of our citizens? We know what the proceedings were here, and saw from the journals of the country that the same demonstrations were witnessed in other sections of the Union. Notwithstanding it was the holy sabbath when the news reached us, the people became intoxicated with excitement, and, in their uncontrolled enthusiasm, proceeded to such lengths in their rejoicings as ill became the sacredness of the day which God has set apart as a day of rest, to be kept holy unto Himself. Appropriate as such proceedings might have been at another time, they were a shameful desecration of the Lord's day. When I heard these demonstrations and remembered that it was the sabbath, and reflected that God is a God of justice as well as a God of compassion, I trembled for the consequences. I felt that there was yet in store for us, a more dreadful retribution, a more awful judgment. God will not suffer the sins of a people to go unpunished, he will not suffer us in our rejoicings over victory, willfully to profane his day, or violate his law and command.

Another design in this judgment — a lesson plainly taught — is to show the enormity of the crime of slavery, the wicked spirit it excites and fosters in the hearts of its abettors, and God's detestation of the system and the men who have endeavored to uphold and propagate it by the instigation of rebellion. That God brought about this war and directed it so as to destroy the system of slavery, the logic of events has convinced the most sceptical. In this matter, the leadings of this providence are unmistakable. But how does God teach his abhorrence of this system by suffering its greatest antagonist, the champion of human rights and liberty to be cut off? He evinces His detestation, by showing that the spirit that supported and upheld slavery, prompted the assassin to murder Abraham Lincoln.

God designs also, by this event, to measure out the punishment due to traitors, a severer punishment than they would have received had our president been spared. Lincoln was compassionate and merciful, and would doubtless have been disposed to pardon, or to mitigate the punishment of those who have been in rebellion against our government. God is a God of justice. To extend mercy to those who have been guilty of instigating and carrying on this bloody and cruel rebellion, would be to sacrifice the justice of God. The justice of God will not be satisfied if the leaders in this rebellion escape unpunished. He would not be with Joshua and the children of Israel, unless they should mete out justice to the guilty; neither will he be with us until we destroy the accursed from among us. The man who deliberately murders his fellow man, forfeits his life under the law of God, and the law of the country. There is something inherently criminal in murder that cannot be expiated save by the blood of the murderer. "The land cannot be cleansed from blood, but by the blood of him that shed it." So may God have ordained that our land shall not be cleansed from the blood of this war, except by the life and blood of those who instituted and supported this war. Mercy to traitors would be injustice to the nation: it would be cruelty to humanity, and would grant a license for murder and rebellion in all time to come. That justice may be meted out to those who are deserving of punishment, God has placed at our head, a man of sterner nature — one who will be disposed to bring them to condign punishment, and suffer the law to visit the crime of treason with its unmitigated penalty — one who has been made to feel the severity of rebel barbarity, and will be the better qualified to determine, when punishment is commensurate with crime. That is a morbid sentiment, existing in sosiety, which transfers our sympathies from the murdered to the criminal, and demands that mercy be extended to him, and that justice be not vindicated. Such a sentiment our better judgment will not approve, and God in his word, and now by his special providence, seems clearly to condemn it.

In conclusion, let us learn this lesson, that men may pass away, but principle and truth will never decay. The enemies of truth and of free government may murder the defenders of truth and the supporters of free government, but the principles still live. Abraham Lincoln is dead, but, God be praised, the government is not dead! Our country and the Union survive. He was raised up for a special purpose, his work is finished, and he has been taken to his account. He was a martyr to liberty, to truth, and free government. For the defence of these he devoted the energy of his life. Upon the altar of his country he yielded that life a sacrifice. The enemies of our nation may plot its overthrow, they may conspire to hinder the progress of truth, justice, and right, but all their schemes will be rendered futile by the God of heaven, and instead of being weakened by their opposition, the nation will be made stronger. God will raise up other defenders, who will support, maintain, and perpetuate it, until every nation upon the face of the earth will have guaranteed and secured to it, a free government, and every individual of which such government is composed, shall enjoy the right to "life, liberty and the pursuit of happiness."

> "Truth crushed to earth shall rise again:
> The eternal years of God are hers;
> But Error, wounded, writhes with pain,
> And dies among his worshippers."

OTHER SERVICES.

At the First Baptist church, the pastor, Rev. Dr. George C. Baldwin, preached a sermon from these words, "*The just Lord is in the midst thereof,*" taken from the fifth verse of the third chapter of Zephaniah. The subject of his discourse was "God's law of retribution as illustrated in our late national history." "He pictured the barbarities of slavery, and showed how the south, in trying to secure the perpetuation of the peculiar institution, had met with its own downfall. He argued that a measure of punishment should be meted out to rebels, and that retributive justice should be poured forth. Punishment, he claimed, was not designed to reform the guilty, but was in the light of a penalty for misdeeds — else the devils, having been so long punished, would have expiated their sins and been released. He was for the exercise of the strong hand in the south for a long time to come."

The solemn service set forth by Bishop Horatio Potter, was held at St. John's church, the Rev. Dr. Henry C. Potter rector; at Christ church, the Rev. J. N. Mulford, rector; at the Church of the Holy Cross, the Rev. Dr. J. I. Tucker, rector; and at St. Paul's church, where also the Rev. Dr. Thomas W. Coit the rector, preached a sermon for the occasion which appears on some of the previous pages of this work.

At the Jewish synagogues the day was solemnized by appropriate religious observances.

The address of Charlton T. Lewis, Esq., late a professor in the Troy University, which is printed in this volume, was pronounced at the State Street Methodist Episcopal church, the service of worship being conducted by the pastor, the Rev. Dr. Erastus Wentworth. The congregation of the North Second Street Methodist Episcopal church, the Rev. Dr. J. Wesley Carhart, pastor, united with the State Street church on this occasion.

A conference meeting was held at the First Presbyterian church, the Rev. Marvin R. Vincent, pastor. At the Second Presbyterian church an address was delivered by the pastor, the Rev. D. S. Gregory. The Rev. Duncan Kennedy D.D., pastor, of the Second Street Presbyterian church, preached a discourse based on passages taken from the sixtieth and the one hundred and twenty-sixth psalms, in which he reviewed the history of the four years of civil war, from which the nation had just emerged; portrayed the terrible character of the spirit of treason which produced it; and enforced various lessons of instruction and duty, which, by means of this baptism of blood, the providence of God seemed to inculcate. At the Park Presbyterian church, the Rev. D. S. Johnson of Waverly, New York, preached a sermon from the sentence, "*The memory of the just is blessed,*" taken from the seventh verse of the tenth chapter of Proverbs. Among the many reasons which he gave for the blessed remembrance in which the late President is held, were his ability as a statesman, his right deeds always performed at the right time, his integrity which led him to think only of his country and his duty even when he had an army at his command and might have been a dictator, his benevolence, his humility illustrated by his partiality for the poem beginning " Oh! why should the spirit of mortal be proud?" and more especially his constant trust in Divine providence. The speaker said that it was the duty of the Christian church to sustain the government in its great labor of restoring peace and harmony; and that as President Lincoln's success was eminently due to his constantly having the prayers of the churches with him; President Johnson should also be accorded the benefit of the same appeals to the source whence all blessings flow. The services at the United Presbyterian church were conducted by the pastor, the Rev. Hugh P. McAdam, who also preached the sermon, a synopsis of which precedes this account. The Rev. Joseph A. Prime, pastor of the Liberty Street Presbyterian church (colored), read the thirty-seventh psalm and commented on the topics thereby suggested.

At the Roman Catholic churches, namely, St. Peter's church, the Rev. James Keveny, pastor; St. Mary's church, the Rev. Peter Havermans, pastor; and St. Joseph's church, the Rev. Aug. J. Thebaud, pastor, services were held similar to those that obtained on Easter Sunday and on the nineteenth of April during the obsequies of the late President at Washington.

The Rev. Edgar Buckingham, pastor of the Unitarian church, read passages from the Scriptures suited to the character of the day and offered appropriate prayers.

The daily Union prayer meeting under the auspices of the Troy Young Men's Christian Association, was conducted at their rooms by the Rev. Dr. George C. Baldwin, with especial reference to the solemnities of the occasion.

Religious services, similar in their nature to those already described, were held in the other places of worship in the city.

At the regular meeting of the Common Council, appointed to be held on the evening of this day, the following proceedings were had.

COMMON COUNCIL PROCEEDINGS.

REGULAR MEETING.

Wednesday Evening, June 1, 1865.

Members Present — Hon. Uri Gilbert, Mayor; Hon. John Moran, Recorder, and Aldermen Cox, Fales, Fleming, Hay, Hislop, Haight, Harrity, Kemp, McManus, Morris, Norton, Stanton, Stannard, Starbuck.

The minutes of the last meeting were approved as printed.

The Recorder moved, as a mark of respect to the day of National Fasting, Humiliation and Prayer, appointed by the President of the United States, that this board do now adjourn until Friday evening, June 2, 1865, at 8 o'clock.

Carried, and the board adjourned.

JAMES S. THORN, City Clerk.

As on the day of the President's death and the days of the obsequies at Washington and at Albany, so on this day, places of business and of amusement, public offices and the public schools were closed, and men ceased from labor as well as from traffic. The publication of the daily papers was also suspended. The occasion was a final public testimonial of the sorrow of the nation on account of its great and irreparable bereavement. The men of this generation will pass away to be succeeded by a generation, who, as children, wondered at the sad faces and the solemn deportment of their fathers and mothers during this long season of mourning. But to these children will be taught the story of this nation's long and desperate struggle for Union and the rights of man: and when, as men they come to appreciate the noble character of the patriot-President who with hundreds of thousands of patriot-soldiers, died for his country, the wonder of infancy will become the admiration and veneration of manhood for the noblest, gentlest, humblest, purest and dearest name in American history — the name of ABRAHAM LINCOLN.

INDEX.

Abraham Lincoln: a poem, 27, 28; an article, 169–175.
African Methodist Episcopal Zion church, sermon preached in the, 43–47.
Ainsworth, Col. Ira, 247.
Albany, invitation from the common council of, 177; invitation from the Young Men's Association of, 243; obsequies of Abraham Lincoln at, 245–254; Burgesses corps, 251; Institute, 251; Turner Verein, 252.
Alexander of Russia referred to, 287, 288.
Allen, Brig. Gen. Darius, order of, 100, 101; 247.
Almighty Lord, before thy throne: a hymn, 9.
Anecdote of Abraham Lincoln, 204–206.
Anshe Chesed, Jewish Synagogue, 99; service at the, 157–160.
Armsby, Asst. Surgeon James H., 247.
Assassination of President Lincoln, effect of the news of the, on the community, vii–xi; effect of the news of, in Troy, 1, 2, 7–9; articles on the, 2, 3, 20–22, 88–90.
Atlantic Monthly, extract from the, 144, 145.
Baermann, Prof. P. H., citizens' meeting addressed by, 30; resolutions by, 102, 103; notice of speech by, 238.
Baker, Col. A. S., 247.
Baker, Col. B. F., 246.
Baldwin, Rev. George C., D.D., remarks by, 79, 160, 161; notice of sermon of, 329, 330; service conducted by, 332.
Baldwin, George C., jr., 243.

Baltimore, obsequies at, x; referred to, xix.
Banker, T. S., clerk of board of supervisors, 168.
Baptist churches. Service at the First Baptist church, 79, 160, 161, 329, 330. Service at the North Baptist church, 19, 79, 80; discourse at the North Baptist church, 104–116.
Barrère, account given by, 294.
Barringer, W. N., citizens' meeting addressed by, 30; resolutions by, 30, 31.
Barron, John, chief of police, thanks to, 253.
Beach, Col. George, 247.
Beardsley, Maj. W. C., 246.
Beaverwyck club, 251.
Beecher, Henry Ward, his address at Exeter hall referred to, xxiii.
Benson, Benj. D., 243; on committee to draft resolutions, 254.
Bentley, Col. R. C., 246.
Berger, Lieut. Albert E., 248.
Bethust society, 251.
Black Hawk war, Lincoln a captain in the, 119, 140.
Board of supervisors of Rensselaer county, resolutions of the, 166–168.
Booth, J. Wilkes, the assassin of President Lincoln, xxv, 282.
Bradford, speech of member of parliament from, xxxv–xl.
Brintnall, Lieut. Col. Charles E., 249.
Brother band, 251.
Brown, Rev. S. D., sketch of a sermon by, 36–42.
Brown, John, referred to, 47.
Brownell, Edwin, motion of, 4.
Bryant, William C., extract from "The Battle-field," a poem by, 329.

Buckingham, Rev. Edgar, sermons by, 66–78, 229–237; service conducted by, 332.
Buffalo, obsequies at, x.
Bullis, Lieut. Wallace F., 248.
Burdick, Julia Adelaide, an article by, 169–175.
Burlington, N. J., Gen. Grant visits, xxvi, 2.
Burns, Robert, referred to, 68.
Bussey, T. Henry, recording secretary of Troy Young Men's association, 243.
Caesar, Julius, referred to, 72, 264.
Calder, Capt. William F., 248.
Cambridge, university of, viii.
Camp, Nathan H., assistant surgeon, 248.
Capo d'Istria referred to, xii.
Carhart, Rev. J. Wesley, D.D., sermon by, 116–127; 330.
Cary, Lieut. John M., 248.
Cary, Lieut. Sidney T., 248.
Cavour referred to, xv.
Charles I referred to, 72.
Chesterfield, Lord, referred to, xv.
Chicago, obsequies at, x; Republican national convention at, 119.
Christ church, service at, 80, 81, 330.
Church, Quartermaster Henry S., order to, 178; 248.
Church, Col. Walter S., 250; thanks to, 253.
Cicero and Lincoln compared, 260–265.
Citizens' meeting, account of the, 30, 31.
City philanthropic grove, 251.
Clark, E. H. G., a poem by, 168, 169.
Cleveland, obsequies at, x.
Clexton, S. R., citizens' meeting addressed by, 30.
Coit, Rev. Thomas W., D.D., discourse by, 268–279; service conducted by, 330.
Colby, John H., district attorney, 4.
Columbus, obsequies at, x.
Common Council of Albany, invitation from the, 177, 240.
Concordia society, meeting of the, 237, 238.

Common Council of Troy, proceedings of the, 93–96, 240, 241, 333; request of a committee of the, 97, 98; 249, 251.
Conners, Lieut. Patrick, 248.
Cooper, Maj. Gen. John Tayler, information from, 100; 247, 250.
Corday, Charlotte, referred to, 72.
Court, proceedings in the Rensselaer county, 4, 5; in the police, 5, 6.
Court house in Troy, dress parade in front of, 252.
Cox, Alderman William, resolutions by, 30, 31; 93, 240, 333.
Cramer, Lieut. Le Grand, 248.
Cromwell, Oliver, referred to, xv.
Cumberland, sinking of the, 294.
Curran, Lieut. James E., 248; commands battery, 249.
Cusack, Capt. James W., 248.
Cuyler, J. C., note from, 177.
Daniels, Lieut. William A., 248.
Davenport, Charles E., secretary of citizens' meeting, 30, 31.
Davenport, Nelson, resolutions by, 30, 31.
Death of President Lincoln, The: a poem, 92, 93.
Decline of amusements: an article, 255, 256.
De Forrest, Col. J. J., 246.
Dickson, Rev. Alexander, notice of sermons by, 83.
Dirge for Wednesday, April 19, 1865, A, 175, 176; dirge on the death of Abraham Lincoln, A, 258–260.
Doring, Charles, band of, 178, 248, 249.
Dorr, Lieut. Philip, 248.
D'Orsay, Count, referred to, xv.
Drowne, Prof. Charles, chairman of a meeting, 102.
Druids, order of, 251.
Duke, Lieut. John, 248.
Easter Sunday, extract from a sermon preached on, 32–35; reflections on, 80, 81.
Eaton, Capt. Thomas B., secretary of meeting of veteran officers, 244, 245.
Eddy, Charles, chairman of citizens' meeting, 30, 31.
Egolf, Maj. Joseph, chairman of meeting of veteran officers, 244, 245.

INDEX.   337

Elliott, Rev. David T., service conducted by, 19; discourse by, 297-317.
Emancipation society, meeting in London, under the auspices of the, xxxiv.
English abuse of Abraham Lincoln, xiv, xv, xxi, xxii; English praise, xxxiv-xl.
English prayer book, service adapted from, 9-14.
Episcopal churches. Bishop Horatio Potter's letter and order of services, 265-267. Service at Christ Church, 80, 81, 330. Service at the church of the Holy Cross, 81, 330. Service at St. John's church, 9-14, 330; extract from a sermon preached at St. John's church, 32-35. Discourse at St. Paul's church, 268-279; service at St Paul's church, 330.
Evans, George, editoral article by, 2, 3.
Evans, William, president of the Emancipation society in London, xxxiv.
Exeter hall referred to, xxiii.
Fales, Alderman Joseph, 93, 240, 333.
Farrell, Col. M. A., 247.
Fenian brotherhood, 251.
Fenton, Gov. Reuben E., proclamation by, 28, 29.
Fire commissioners of Troy, 249.
Fire department, 252.
First Baptist church, service at the, 79, 160, 161, 329, 330.
First Presbyterian church, service at the, 15-18, 83, 161; sermon in the, 181-222; conference meeting at the, 331.
Fitzgerald, Alderman Michael, 93, 240.
Fleming, Alderman James, 93, 333.
Folger, H. C., 243.
Ford's theatre, assassination at, 2.
Forster, W. E., member of parliament for Bradford, speech of, xxxv-xl.
Francis, John M., article by, 20-22.
Francis Joseph referred to, 287.
Free brother lodge, 251.

Galusha, Henry, motion by, 243.
Garnsey, J. Spencer, 243.
Gerard, Balthazar, referred to, xii.
German brothers association, 251.
German literary society, 251.
Gettysburg, slander concerning Lincoln at, refuted, xxxiv.
Gilbert, Col. B. C., 247.
Gilbert, Hon. Uri, mayor of Troy, messages to the clergy by, 8; remarks of, 93, 94; chairman of a committee, 96, 241; signs a request, 98; announcement by, 99, 242; note to, 176, 177; statement by, 240; proclamation by, 267; 333.
Gilbert, William E., chairman of a committee, 243; on committee to draft resolutions, 254.
God moves in a mysterious way: a hymn, xxxvii, 14, 124.
Good Friday, the day of the assassination, 22, 86, 180, 296.
Gould, Hon. George, notice of remarks of, 102.
Grant, Gen. U. S., leaves Washington for Burlington, N. J., xxvi, 2.
Gregory, Rev. D. S., service conducted by, 19, 166; sermon by, 47-66; address by, 127-135; notice of an address by, 331.
Guard of honor, invitation to the, 241; names of the, 246, 247.
Hagan, William, chairman on resolutions, 30, 31.
Haight, Alderman Isaac N., 240, 333.
Hall, B. H., articles by, 22, 23, 260-265; a poem by, 178-181.
Hardin county, Lincoln born in, 118, 306.
Harmony lodge, 251.
Harrisburg, obsequies at, x; referred to, xix.
Harrison, William H., death of, referred to, 105.
Harrity, Alderman James, 93, 240, 333.
Hartsfeld, Frank, address by, 158, 159; remarks of, 237, 238.
Harugarie, order of, 251.
Hastings, Col. John, 247.
Hastings, Geo. S., private secretary of Gov. Fenton, 29.

Havermans, Rev. Peter, service conducted by, 19, 161, 162, 332; sermon by, 84-86.
Hawley, Lieut. Charles E., 248.
Hawley, J. M., resolutions by, 30, 31.
Hay, Alderman Gordon, 93, 240, 333; on a committee, 241.
Hebrew, prayers translated from the, 159, 160.
Heilbron, Rev. Jonas, notice of address by, 238.
Hendrick, Col. James, 247.
Henry IV of France referred to, xii, 72, 139, 158, 159.
Hibernian provident society, 251.
Hislop, Alderman Thomas T., 93, 240, 333.
Hollister, Martin L., 243.
Holy Cross, Church of the, service at the, 81, 330.
Homer's Iliad, reference to, 223.
Hubbell, F. B., articles by, 24-26, 255, 256.
Hull, Hiram, chairman of board of supervisors, 168.
Hung be the heavens with black: an article, 31, 32.
Hunter, W., announcement by, as acting secretary of state, 87, 88; signs the President's proclamations, 240, 257.
Hymn, 9, 14.
Indiana, Lincoln removes to, 119, 140.
Indianapolis, obsequies at, x.
In memoriam A. L.: a poem, 178-181.
Iron moulders' union, 251.
Ives, Capt. Edward A., 248.
Jewish citizens, resolutions of respect by, 98, 99; service at the Jewish synagogue by, 157-160, 330.
Johnson, A. G., article by, 88-90.
Johnson, President Andrew, 126; announcement of the obsequies of President Lincoln at Washington by, 87, 88; proclamation by, 238-240, 256, 257.
Johnson, Rev. D. S., notice of a sermon by, 331, 332.
Kemp, Alderman William, motion by, 93; resolutions offered by, 94-96; on a committee, 96, 241; signs a request, 98; 240, 333

Kennedy, Rev. Duncan, D D., service conducted by, 19; address by, 136-151; notice of a discourse by, 331.
Kentucky the birth place of Lincoln, 109, 118.
Keveny, Rev. James, notice of remarks of, 86, 162; service conducted by, 332.
King Henry VIII, extract from Shakspeare's play of, 286.
Kisselburgh, W. E., article by, 90-92.
Ksinsky, A., chairman of a meeting of Jewish citizens, 99.
Landon, Capt. John M., order to, 6, 178; to fire a salute, 101, 248.
La Vengeur, the sinking of, 294.
Le Roy, Lieut. Col. John I., 247.
Lesson from the Gospel of St. Matthew, 13.
Lewis, Charlton T., address by, 279-296; address of, noticed, 330.
Liberian mission referred to, 41.
Liberty street Presbyterian church, sermon in the, 151-157; service in the, 332.
Lichtensteine, B., secretary of a meeting of Jewish citizens, 99.
Lisbon, earthquake at, 273, 274.
London, meeting of sympathy on the death of Lincoln in, xxxiv.
London Spectator, extract from the, 207, 208.
London Star, editorial article on Abraham Lincoln from the, xi-xvi; account of Abraham Lincoln from the, xvii-xxxiv.
Longfellow, Henry W., extract from the writings of, 150.
Louis XVI referred to, 72.
Loyal league, 249.
McAdam, Rev. Hugh P., sermon of, noticed, 166, 332; sermon by, 318-329.
Mac Arthur, C. L., article by, 31, 32.
Macaulay, Lord, eulogium by, 113.
McAuliffe, Capt. Timothy, 248.
McConihe, Col. Isaac, jr., regimental orders of, 6, 7, 101, 177, 178; invitation to, 240; invitation by, 242; order of thanks by, 253; 247.

McConihe, Capt. William, resolutions by, 244.
McLean, Surgeon Le Roy, 247.
McManus, Alderman Thomas, 93, 240, 333; on a committee, 241.
Manly, Maj. John, 247.
Marat referred to, 72.
Marvin, Col. S. E., 247.
Merchant of Venice, citation from the, 274.
Meredith, Rev. R. R., citizens' meeting addressed by, 30; notice of sermon by, 82, 83.
Merritt, Lieut. Henry A., 248.
Methodist churches. Sermon in the African Methodist church, 43–47. Service at the North Second street Methodist Episcopal church, 82; sermon, 116–127; 330. Service at the North Troy Methodist Episcopal church, 82, 83. Sermon in the State street Methodist Episcopal church, 36–42, 223–229; service, 81, 82, 161, 330; address, 279–296. Service at the Third street (South Troy) Methodist Episcopal church, 19; discourse, 297–317.
Middleton's life of Cicero, extracts from, 261–264.
Miller, Gen. Martin, resolutions by, 166–168.
Mirabeau referred to, xv.
Miserere intoned, 19; chanted, 162, 163.
Moore, Adj. Gurdon G., regimental orders signed by, 6, 7, 101, 177, 178; invitation signed by, 242; order of thanks signed by, 253; 248.
Moran, John, recorder, 93; on a committee, 96; signs a request, 98; motion of, 240, 241, 333.
Morris, Alderman Robert, 93, 240, 333; on a committee, 241.
Mourning for Abraham Lincoln, vii–xi.
Muhlenberg, Capt. F. P., 247.
Mulford, Rev. J. N., address by, 80, 81; service conducted by, 330.
Murphy, Alderman Edward, jr., 93.
Myers, Lieut. John, 248.

Napoleon I referred to, xv.
Napoleon III referred to, xii, 287, 288.
Nason, Prof. H. B., resolutions by, 102, 103.
National beravement, The: an article, 90–92.
National calamity and humiliation, The: an article, 24–26.
National guard, orders of the, 6, 7, 177, 178, 253; invitation from the, 242; organization of the twenty-fourth regiment of the, 247, 248.
Neary, Thomas, remarks by, 5, 6.
North Baptist church, service at the, 19, 79, 80; discourse at the, 104–116.
North second street Methodist Episcopal church, service at the, 82; sermon at the, 116–127; 330.
North Troy Methodist Episcopal church, service at the, 82, 83.
Norton, Captain M. L., 247.
Norton, Alderman Thomas, 93, 333; on a committee, 96; signs a request, 98.
O'Brien, Lieut. William, 248.
Obsequies of Abraham Lincoln at Albany, 245–254.
Odd Fellows, Independent order of, 252.
Officers' meeting, 245.
Orsini referred to, xii.
Our duty on this day: an article, 22, 23.
Oxford, university of, viii.
Palm Sunday, union army entered Richmond on, 86.
Palmerston, Lord, referred to, xv.
Park Presbyterian church, service at the, 83; notice of a sermon at the, 331, 332.
Parks, Rev. S., delivers an address, 161.
Payne, Capt. Martin, engineer, 248.
Peak, Col. C. S., 247.
Pease, A. S., a dirge by, 175, 176.
Peel, Sir Robert, referred to, xv.
Perkins, Henry, drum corps of, 178, 249.
Philadelphia, obsequies at, x.
Police court, proceedings in the, 5, 6.

INDEX

Pomeroy, Maj. George, 247.
Potter, Rev. Henry C., D.D., service conducted by, 9–14, 330; extract from a sermon by, 32–35; absence of, 164; chaplain, 247, 248.
Potter, Right Rev. Horatio, D.D., bishop of New York, recommendation of, 29, 30; letter and order of services by, 265–267; 330.
Powder boy at Roanoke island, 294.
Pratt, Maj. H. C., 247.
Pratt, Maj. Gen. T. R., 247.
Prayers, 10–12, 14, 161, 162; translated from the Hebrew, 159, 160.
Prentice, Alderman James R., 93, 240; on a committee, 241.
Prime, Rev. Joseph A., sermon by, 151–157; service conducted by 332.
Proclamation by Governor Fenton, 28, 29; by President Johnson, 238–240, 256, 257; by Mayor Gilbert of Troy, 267.
Pro quacunque tribulatione, prayers, 161, 162.
Presbyterian churches. Service at the First Presbyterian church, 15–18, 83, 161; sermon at the, 181–222; conference meeting at the, 331. Service at the Second Presbyterian church, 19, 166; sermon at the, 47–66; address at the, 127–135; notice of address at the, 331. Service at the Second street Presbyterian church, 19; address at the, 136–151; notice of discourse at the, 331. Service at the United Presbyterian church, 166, 332; sermon at the, 318–329. Service at the Park Presbyterian church, 83; notice of a sermon at the, 331, 332. Sermon at the Liberty street Presbyterian church (colored), 151–157; service at the, 332.
Pullman, Rev. James M., discourse of, referred to, 86, 87.
Quackenbush, Capt. John H., 248.
Rapp, Capt. Christian W., 248.
Ravaillac, referred to, xii, 158, 159.

Rathbone, Brig. Gen. John F., 246; brigade of, 250.
Recommendation of Bishop Horatio Potter, 29, 30.
Rensselaer county board of supervisors, resolutions of the, 166–168; mentioned, 249.
Rensselaer county court, proceedings in the, 4, 5.
Rensselaer polytechnic institute, proceedings at the, 101–103.
Resolutions at citizens' meeting, 30, 31.
Riley, Lieut. Michael, 248.
Roanoke island, powder boy at, 294.
Robertson, Hon. Gilbert, jr., address by, 4, 5.
Robinson, Brev. Maj. Gen. John C., guard of honor detailed by, 246, 247.
Roman catholic churches. Service at St. Joseph's church, 86, 162–164, 332. Service at St. Mary's church, 19, 84–86, 161, 161. 332. Service at St. Peter's church, 86, 162, 332.
Rousseau, William W., 243.
St. Andrew's society, 251.
St. George's society, 251.
St. James's hall, meeting of sympathy on the death of Lincoln in, xxxiv.
St. John's church, service at, 9–14, 330; extract from a sermon preached at, 32–35.
St. Joseph's church, service at, 86, 162–164, 332.
St. Joseph's society, 251.
St. Mary's church, service at, 19, 161, 162, 332; sermon at, 84–86.
St. Matthew, lesson from the gospel of, 13.
St. Nicholas hall, citizens' meeting at, 30, 31.
St. Paul's church, discourse at, 268–279; service at 330.
St. Peter's church, service at, 86, 162, 332.
St. Peter's society, 251.
Salamon, Rev. H. G., abstract of sermon by, 157; notice of address by, 238.
Schiller grove, 251.
Schoonmaker, J. E., 248.

Scott, Capt. I. Seymour, 248.
Scott, Lieut. Gen. Winfield, warns President Lincoln, xix; an exclamation of, 308.
Sears, Alderman Edwin, 93, 240.
Second Presbyterian church, service at the, 19, 166; sermon at the, 47-66; address at the, 127 -135; notice of an address at the, 331.
Second street Presbyterian church, service at the, 19; address at the, 136-151; notice of an address at the, 331.
Seward, Frederick W., referred to, xix, xxvii.
Seward, William H., attempt to assassinate, xi, xii, xxvii, xxxv, 1-3; as a statesman, 26.
Sheldon, Rev. C. P., D.D., service conducted by, 19; remarks by, 79, 80; discourse by, 104-116.
Sic semper tyrannis: a poem, 168, 169.
Sidney, Sir Philip, account of the mourning for, viii.
Smart, Alderman Robert T., 93, 240.
South Troy (Third street) Methodist Episcopal church, service at the, 19; discourse at the, 297 -317.
Spencer county, Lincoln removes to, 119.
Springfield, obsequies at, x; extract from Lincoln's speech at xix, xx.
Stannard, Alderman Henry D., 93, 240, 333.
Stanton, Alderman John, 93, 240, 333.
Starbuck, Alderman Geo. H., 93, 240, 333; on a committee, 96; signs a request, 98; motion by, 241.
State street Methodist Episcopal church, sketch of a sermon at the, 36-42; service at the, 81, 82, 161, 330; sermon at the, 223-229; address at the, 279- 296.
Staude, Henry, notice of address by, 238.
Steenbergh, Maj. George T., 247.
Stoddard, Richard H., extract from a poem by, 204

Stonehouse, Col. J. B., 247.
Strong, Col. Charles, 247.
Stuart, George, referred to, 190.
Sturbridge, centenarian voter at, 68.
Sumner, Charles, referred to, 111.
Swartwout, Brev. Maj. H. A., 247.
Talleyrand, an expression of, xiv; his wiliness, 201.
Taylor, Zachary, death of, referred to, 105.
Tennyson, Alfred, quotation from his poem In Memoriam, 115, 116; extract from his ode on the death of the Duke of Wellington, 222.
Tenth brigade N. Y. S. N. G., order to the, 100, 101.
Thebaud, Rev. Aug. J., notice of remarks by, 86; address by, 163; service conducted by, 332.
Thomas, Rev. Jacob, sermon by, 43-47.
Thomas, Lieut. Minott A., 248.
Thompson, Lieut. Col. Chas. H., 247.
Thompson, Lieut. George S., 248.
Thorn, James S., poem by, 27, 28; city clerk, 96, 241, 333; resolutions by, 254, 255; article by, 257, 258; 243.
Third street Methodist Episcopal church, service at the, 19; discourse at the, 297-317.
Timpane, Capt. Michael, 248.
Tiro preserves Cicero's sayings, 264, 265.
To everything there is a season: an article, 257, 258.
Townsend, Brev. Col. Frederick, 247.
Townsend, Martin I., remarks by, 4; address by, 15-18.
Tracey, John, chairman of a committee, 177.
Troy Daily Press, articles from the, 24-26, 255, 256; dirge from the, 175, 176.
Troy Daily Times, articles from the, 20-23, 90-92, 169-175, 257, 258; poems from the, 27, 28, 92, 93, 168, 169.
Troy Daily Whig, articles from the, 2, 3, 88-90, 260-265; dirge from the, 258-260.

342 INDEX.

Troy News, article from the, 31, 32; poem from the, 178-181.
Troy Young Men's association, meeting of the executive committee of the, 243; resolutions of the, 254, 255; 249, 251.
Troy Young Men's Christian association, prayer meeting of the, 332.
Tucker, Rev. J. I., D.D., reference to Easter sermon by, 81; service conducted by, 330.
Tenth regiment, 250.
Twenty-fifth regiment, 250; thanks to the, 253.
Twenty-fourth regiment, regimental orders to the, 6, 7, 101, 177, 178; invitation from the, 242, 244; field, staff and line officers of the, 247, 248; returns thanks, 253; 250.
Typographical union, 251.
Union league, 251.
Unitarian church, sermons at the, 66-78, 229-237; service at the, 332.
United Presbyterian church, service at the, 166, 332; sermon at the, 318-329.
Universalist church, service at the, 86, 87.
Upham, Capt. Moses A., 248.
Vail, Lieut. Ezra R., 248.
Vanderbilt steamboat, 244, 249, 252.
Van Santvoord, Mrs. E., poem by, 92, 93.
Veteran officers, meeting of, 244, 245.
Victor Emanuel referred to, 287, 288.

Vincent, Rev. Marvin R., service conducted by, 15-18, 331; notice of sermon by, 83; remarks by, 161; sermon by, 181-222.
Warren, Prof. S. Edward, resolutions by, 102, 103.
Washington, obsequies of Abraham Lincoln at the city of, x.
Washington, George, death of, referred to, 104, 105.
Weeks, Capt. George H., 247.
Wellington, Duke of, extract from an ode on the death of the, 222.
Wells, D. A., citizens' meeting addressed by, 30.
Wentworth, Rev. Erastus, D.D., remarks by, 81, 82, 161; sermon by, 223-229; service conducted by, 330.
Wesley, John, referred to, 68.
White, Capt. William E., notice by, 245.
Wickes, Asa W., aid-de-camp, 101.
Willard, Clarence, President of the Troy Young Men's association, 243.
William, Prince of Orange referred to, xii, 41, 42, 139; Lincoln compared to, 200.
William Tell lodge, 251.
Winne, Lieut. Gabriel T., 248.
Wolfe, Lieut. Gurdon G., 248.
Wool, Maj. Gen. John E., address by, 96, 97; his conduct praised, 309.
Young, Josiah L., 246; a dirge by, 258-260.
Young, Col. W. H., 246.
Zion church, sermon in the African Methodist Episcopal, 43-47.

www.ingramcontent.com/pod-product-compliance
Lightning Source LLC
Chambersburg PA
CBHW030349230426
43664CB00007BB/582